The Dunbars of Ackergill and Hempriggs

The story of a Caithness family based
on the Dunbar family papers

James Miller

Whittles Publishing

Published by
Whittles Publishing Ltd.,
Dunbeath,
Caithness, KW6 6EG,
Scotland, UK

www.whittlespublishing.com

© 2022 James Miller

ISBN 978-184995-489-1

The Dunbar Papers are kept by Nucleus: The
Nuclear and Caithness Archives, Wick, Caithness
on behalf of Sir Richard Dunbar Bt and the
Dunbar Family. Access only by permission.

Printed by
Short Run Press Ltd, Exeter, Devon

CONTENTS

INTRODUCTION

No one admiring the long curve of Sinclair's Bay can overlook the Tower of Ackergill. Its bulk in the low, sweeping Caithness landscape declares it to be a place of consequence. For three centuries it was the home of the Dunbar family of Hempriggs and Ackergill. As one of the largest landowners in the county from the late 1600s, the Dunbars played a major role in local affairs for several generations, making the family story a significant part of the history of Caithness itself. When the Tower was sold in 1986, the family papers were placed in the care of the Wick Society and were later transferred to Nucleus: The Nuclear and Caithness Archives, Wick. They comprise an assortment of documents, including letters, legal papers, accounts, bills and maps, an archive spanning some three hundred years and providing a unique insight into the great social and economic developments that have marked the county.

It was both an exciting opportunity and a challenge when Sir Richard Dunbar invited me to write a book based on the papers. The documents comprise such a rich and diverse resource that I grasped early on that in the time available the best I could do was to make an exploratory dip into the archive to sample some of its treasures and to sketch in broad outline the family story against the background of the wider social canvas. The result is this text, imperfect in many ways, sprinkled with loose ends, but still of value, I hope, to everyone interested in Caithness history. Further research will no doubt tackle some of the questions left unanswered and will fill out the story.

In the first part of the text – Origins – I have attempted to summarise the long pedigrees of the families of Dunbar of Hempriggs and Sutherland of Duffus, and describe how they joined through marriage just over three hundred years ago to form the Caithness branch of the Dunbar kindred. Part 2 focuses on various aspects of life in Caithness in the eighteenth century: the importance of the grain trade, the impact of the Jacobite risings, local politics, and the Dunbars' efforts to maintain a lairdly lifestyle. In Part 3, we find modernising trends having an effect: far-reaching changes in agricultural practice, the birth of the great herring fishery and the building of the new harbour at Wick. These trends and others continue to work in Parts 4 and 5 as the nineteenth century passes. Towards the end of the narrative, we find the Dunbars looking beyond Caithness to find careers in the Empire and in the service of the British state.

I would like to record my thanks to Sir Richard for his trust and patience, and express my gratitude to all the members of the Wick Society who made this itinerant writer welcome. The members of the Society did sterling service in sorting and cataloguing the papers and, without their database, the research for this present volume would have been impossible within the time available.

May Johnston is owed a special thank you for her tireless help in searching for documents in the National Archives in Edinburgh. A number of other people, in Caithness and elsewhere, have helped me at various times and I would particularly like to thank Peter Sutton, chaplain at Gordonstoun, for acting as guide on the visit I made to see the first home of Elizabeth Dunbar; Dr Juliet Gayton for some useful comments on the text; and Valerie Amin, Alan Hendry, Allan Cameron, Roy Mackenzie, and Andrew Bruce and his colleagues for help with images and information. None of them is responsible for any errors.

James Miller
February 2021

Note on references

The reference system for the Dunbar Papers when they were kept by the Wick Society ascribes a unique reference number to each document that reflects where it was placed in the stored archive. For example, the document referred to by the number (83.2.4) is the fourth document in the second folder in the 83rd box. In a few instances the number of a particular document has been found to be unclear, sometimes because two documents have been counted as one or because one has been overlooked in the cataloguing process; in such cases the reference is given as the box and folder numbers only. References to other sources, whether books or documents in other archives, are grouped at the end of each part of the text.

Currency equivalence

It is impossible to equate the values of the many sums of money throughout the 250-year span of the Dunbar Papers. This is especially true in the times when

Fig. 1. *The main line of descent of the baronets of Hempriggs, Caithness*

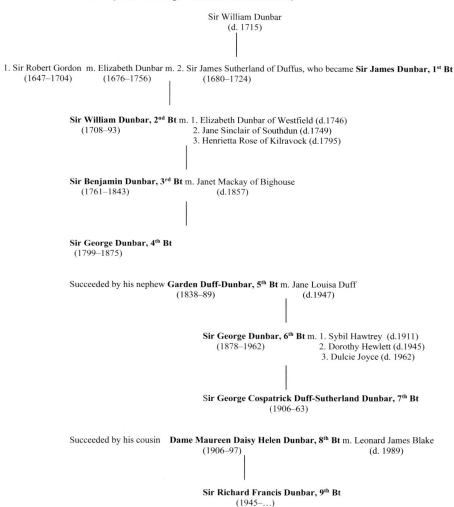

(More detailed family trees for each generation are shown elsewhere)

Sir William Dunbar
(d. 1715)

1. Sir Robert Gordon m. Elizabeth Dunbar m. 2. Sir James Sutherland of Duffus, who became **Sir James Dunbar, 1st Bt**
(1647–1704)   (1676–1756)   (1680–1724)

Sir William Dunbar, 2nd Bt m. 1. Elizabeth Dunbar of Westfield (d.1746)
(1708–93)   2. Jane Sinclair of Southdun (d.1749)
        3. Henrietta Rose of Kilravock (d.1795)

Sir Benjamin Dunbar, 3rd Bt m. Janet Mackay of Bighouse
(1761–1843)   (d.1857)

Sir George Dunbar, 4th Bt
(1799–1875)

Succeeded by his nephew **Garden Duff-Dunbar, 5th Bt** m. Jane Louisa Duff
(1838–89)   (d.1947)

Sir George Dunbar, 6th Bt m. 1. Sybil Hawtrey (d.1911)
(1878–1962)   2. Dorothy Hewlett (d.1945)
        3. Dulcie Joyce (d. 1962)

Sir George Cospatrick Duff-Sutherland Dunbar, 7th Bt
(1906–63)

Succeeded by his cousin **Dame Maureen Daisy Helen Dunbar, 8th Bt** m. Leonard James Blake
(1906–97)   (d. 1989)

Sir Richard Francis Dunbar, 9th Bt
(1945–...)

payments were often paid in kind. Websites such as www.measuringworth.com can indicate relative values of money sums. For those unfamiliar with the pre-decimal British currency, £sd, it should be noted that £1 contained 20 shillings, and each shilling had 12 pence. £1 Scots was equivalent in worth to around one-twelfth of £1 sterling. One guinea was £1 1s, and a merk was 13s 4d, or two-thirds of £1.

Part 1

Origins

1 | The Dunbars

– 'payed & advanced be William Dunbarr of Hemprigs'

The arrival of the Dunbars in Caithness was the culmination of a slow progress up the east coast of Scotland. The surname derives from the fortress of Bar or Barr in East Lothian, now the site of the town of Dunbar, on the lands granted to the family by Malcolm III after they had fled from Northumberland to escape from William the Conqueror.[1] The surname appears to have first been used by Patrick, Earl of Dunbar (1152–1232) who achieved prominence by marrying a daughter of William the Lion and serving as justiciar of Lothian. Alexander Dunbar, the third son of the seventh Earl of Dunbar, had a son – another Patrick – who married Isabella, the daughter of Thomas Randolph, Earl of Moray. Their second son, John, succeeded as Earl of Moray in March 1372. In time the earldom of Moray passed to James Dunbar, who died or was killed around 10 August 1430. Information about this James's first wife is incomplete but what we know tells us that her name was Isobel or Isabella Innes and that she and James were handfasted, pledged to each other by the old custom rather than married by church rite. The couple were second cousins, unable to appear before the marriage altar without special dispensation, and this had not been granted before Isobel died after having a son – indeed she may have died in childbirth. The irregular marriage prevented this boy from inheriting the earldom but in 1450 he was granted in lieu, through his half-sister the Countess of Moray and her husband Archibald Douglas, the lands of Westfield and the sheriffdom of the county. Thus, he became Sir Alexander Dunbar of Westfield, and in 1452 he married Isobel Sutherland, daughter of Alexander Sutherland of Duffus. Their son became Sir James Dunbar of Westfield and sheriff of Moray in his turn (Fig. 2). Westfield lay in the fertile Laigh of Moray on the western edge of what was then a shallow inlet of the sea, the Loch of Spynie. It

Fig. 2. The Dunbar line of descent to Sir William Dunbar of Hempriggs

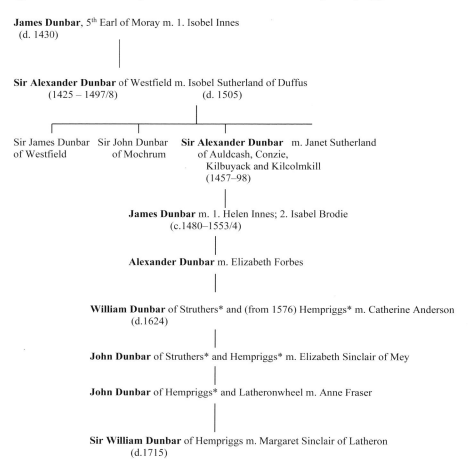

*Hempriggs and Struthers here refer to property in Moray, not in Caithness.

remained a Dunbar possession until it was sold in 1703 when the family ran into financial trouble. Within twenty years, however, they reacquired it and held it until finally in 1769 it was sold to Sir James Grant of Grant. (See page 48.)

The Dunbar kindred prospered in Moray, splitting into a number of families associated with different localities. William, one of the Dunbars of Conzie and Kilbuyack, obtained a charter on 30 March 1576 of an estate lying a few miles from Westfield, on the north side of the parish of Alves and bordering the sea in Burghead Bay, an estate called Hempriggs, presumably because flax was once grown there.[2] On Timothy Pont's map of Morayshire, drawn in about 1590, the house of 'Hemprigs' is clearly marked, as are all the other lairds' houses and castles. William Dunbar's son John married a daughter of the Sinclairs of Mey and was succeeded by his eldest son, also called John, in October 1636. In this instance there was a definite connection between Moray and Caithness but in general we can be certain that the Dunbars, the Sinclairs and the other leading families around the Moray Firth remained well acquainted with each other through travel, trade, common interest and at times hostility. It was perfectly natural for the Dunbars to look northward for opportunity on the other side of the firth but, in their case, trouble at home may have lent urgency to any search for new pasture. Forres was wracked by a feud between factions of the Dunbar kindred at this time. Alexander Dunbar, sheriff of Moray, was shot in the main street in Forres in July 1611 during a fight between the Dunbars of Blery, Kilbuyack and Conzie and the Dunbars of Hempriggs. One source says the sheriff was hit as he happened to ride by.[3] This possibly accidental killing seems to have cooled tempers for a short while, but the bad feelings lingered, and the feud broke out anew. In 1637 a Kilbuyack Dunbar killed two Hempriggs Dunbars. John Dunbar's marriage to Elizabeth Sinclair of Mey would have led to a Dunbar interest in Caithness but a move to the northern county may also have been seen by the Hempriggs family as a way to escape from treacherous neighbours, although there is no hard evidence that such a motive lay behind their decision.

Apart from the documents in the Dunbar Papers, many legal papers relevant to the early years of the family in Caithness exist in some at first glance unlikely places such as among the Breadalbane Muniments in the National Records of Scotland in Edinburgh.[4] As far as is known, no one has delved fully into these bundles of legal documents, some blackened with age, to explore the tangled struggle for ascendancy between the Sinclair and Campbell of Glenorchy families in Caithness in the late seventeenth century, a struggle in which the Dunbars played a major part and from which they emerged as winners of a sort. What follows, therefore, may one day need to be revised in the light of new evidence, and the reader should keep this proviso in mind.

In his monumental work on *Caithness Family History*, John Henderson says that John Dunbar of Hempriggs purchased the lands of Latheronwheel at some point in the mid- to late-seventeenth century but gives no precise date.[5] The designation of Hempriggs in this instance and in other contemporary documents before 1700 refers to Hempriggs in Moray. In July 1653 a precept of poinding was obtained in Caithness Sheriff Court by John Sinclair, bailie of Latheron, against Lady Forse, the widow of James Sutherland of Forse, for non-payment of bonds for 506 merks issued in 1650 and 400 merks issued in 1652. John Dunbar of Hempriggs is recorded as having assigned the latter bond to Sinclair.

Fig. 3. The family of John Dunbar of Hempriggs and Latheronwheel

More detail can be found in Henderson, *Caithness Family History*.

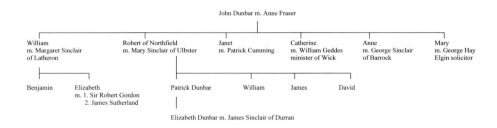

John Dunbar married Anna Fraser, daughter of the commissary of Inverness, in 1624. One of their sons, Robert, married a daughter of Patrick Sinclair of Ulbster in 1675 and later acquired Myreland and Quintfall. One daughter, Catherine, married William Geddes, the minister of Wick, and another, Anne, married George Sinclair of Barrock. The focus of our story falls upon the eldest son, William, who came in time to own the lands of Telstane (which he renamed Hempriggs), Ackergill and much else throughout Caithness. His rise to local prominence was associated with the brief though important intervention in Caithness affairs by the Campbells of Glenorchy.

For a very long time a state of feuding and tit-for-tat raiding existed between the people of lowland Caithness and upland Sutherland. In the winter of 1668–69, all the Sutherland notables – the earl, his son Lord Reay, and others – brought a complaint before the Scottish judiciary against George Sinclair, Earl of Caithness.[6] In the previous March, Sinclair had invaded Strathnaver at the head of a large following – the contemporary documents give the number as a scarcely credible 1,200 men – and had spent a week burning houses, marauding and stealing 900 cattle. George Sinclair's followers listed in the legal records include William Dunbar of Hempriggs. At the same time as the Sutherland complaint, Sinclair and the Caithness men lodged an almost identical counter-complaint against their accusers to the west. Sutherland grievances also referred to the imprisonment and bad usage in Caithness of a William Mackay from Scourie, treatment that resulted in his death; and to the murder by William Sinclair of Dunbeath and accomplices of two other Mackay brothers. William Dunbar's involvement in this affair led to him being locked up in Castle Sinclair for intercommuning with Dunbeath until he was ordered to be released in January 1670 after finding caution for 5,000 merks.[7]

In 1669 the Privy Council commissioned John Campbell of Glenorchy to travel north to sort out the feuding and bring William Sinclair of Dunbeath to justice. Known at this time as Glenorchy or as Iain Glas – Grey John, the 34-year-old Campbell was politically astute and ambitious. Because he was on government business and because the Earl of Caithness's wife, Mary Campbell, was a distant kinswoman (she was the sister of the Earl of Argyll), Glenorchy naturally stayed with them. At this time, George Sinclair was heavily in debt and had been forced to raise loans on the security of his property. In 1662 the earl had borrowed money from Thomas Calderwood, an Edinburgh merchant, and secured the loans on lands in Caithness (91.2.1). Now the earl was being threatened with dispossession by one of his principal creditors, a lawyer called Sir Robert Sinclair of Longformacus, one of the Sinclairs of Roslin. He poured forth his woes to his guest. Glenorchy had an idea: he offered to bail George out of his difficulty – the earl's debts amounted to over a million merks, more than £55,000 sterling, an enormous sum for that period – and in return obtained a conveyance of the earldom lands. In 1676, the hapless George died, in the castle at Thurso where he was living on an annuity of 2,000 merks.[8]

George's marriage to Mary Campbell had been childless. In the absence of a direct heir, Glenorchy immediately moved a claim to the earldom lands and the assumption of the Sinclair name and arms. With the help, it is said, of bribes in the right quarters, he obtained from the crown in June 1677 the titles of Earl of Caithness, Viscount Breadalbane and Lord St Clair of Berriedale and Glenorchy. In April 1678 he married the widowed Mary Campbell and arranged for his elder son Duncan to inherit his lands in the south. He intended his newly gained Caithness estates to go in time to his younger son John. In 1679 Mary bore Glenorchy a third son, Colin.

The assumption of the title to the Caithness earldom was contested by the Sinclairs, in particular by George Sinclair of Keiss who would have been the nearest heir if the Campbells had not intervened in local affairs. In a letter written from Watten on 28 August 1677 a number of the Sinclair lairds threw down the gauntlet by stating that they could not obey the new earl until they had consulted the 'rest of the shire'.[9] The rest of the shire, the other Sinclair lairds and also many of the ordinary people, apparently agreed that Campbell of Glenorchy was not welcome north of the Ord. According to Calder's *History*, David Sinclair of Broynach and William Sinclair of Thura lent a hand to George of Keiss in the pulling down of the earl's castle at Thurso East.[10] Glenorchy's reaction to the unrest in Caithness was to send north an armed force, an incursion that resulted in the battle at Altimarlach, near Wick, on 13 July 1680, in which Glenorchy's Campbell followers were victorious over their Caithness opponents.[11] The antipathy towards the Campbells took on the nature of a campaign of civil disobedience and despoiling of property. Late in 1680 or early in the following year, George Sinclair, whose allies now included some Mackays, laid siege to Glenorchy's men in Castle Sinclair. The Sinclair contingent included John Sinclair of Telstane, probably the father of the man from whom William Dunbar would eventually take over that property.

William appears to have navigated a skilful course through the troubled waters around him. In 1668 he was named as a follower of Earl George Sinclair. One source describes him as having been put to the horn, i.e. declared an outlaw, in 1669 for having killed his brother and supported his brother-in-law William Sinclair of Dunbeath.[12] It has not proved possible to establish any more about this alleged murder, far less that William had a brother other than the afore-mentioned Robert. It is also not known when William married Dunbeath's sister, Margaret. As noted above, in 1669–70 William was incarcerated for his support of Dunbeath, but he was soon bailed and, a few years later, in 1677–78, we find him earning compliments from the Campbell camp for services rendered. Surviving correspondence from the sheriff clerk of Caithness, a man called Harper, to Colin Campbell of Carwhin, Glenorchy's lawyer, in 1677 and 1678, mentions Hempriggs's service.[13] A document in the Dunbar papers (83.2.4) reveals that in 1675–77 William obtained from Glenorchy a wadset of 'the west side of the towne and lands of Keiss [and] The lands of Auckorne & Miln of Keiss' in return for a sum of 11,000 merks. He also served as the representative for Caithness at the Convention of Estates in June 1678.

In the south, Glenorchy had become involved with his brother-in-law, the Earl of Argyll, in a campaign against the Macleans of Duart and in raising independent companies of soldiers, ostensibly to suppress cattle raiding in the west Highlands but seen by many as merely armed instruments of Campbell aggression. In 1681 the government in Scotland ordered the independent companies to be disbanded. Glenorchy lost status and George Sinclair of Keiss, now elected to parliament, was able successfully to challenge the Campbells and press his claim to the title of Earl of Caithness. The Privy Council recognised in August 1681 that Sinclair was the rightful heir and in compensation for his loss Glenorchy was graced with the new title of Earl of Breadalbane and Holland. From this point on, he is known to us as Breadalbane and his second son, John, as Lord Glenorchy.

The Campbells retained possession of extensive estates in Caithness but dislike for them as lairds continued. Letters in the Breadalbane Muniments refer to tenements lying waste in Thurso, loss of livestock, difficulties in collecting the cess (land tax), and other troubles.[14] John Lord Glenorchy took up residence at Ackergill and wrote regularly to his father; for example on 2 March 1682 his letter says that things had grown quiet since Breadalbane had gone south and that he had to send to Inverness for oats to avoid Wick becoming waste, information that suggests that the harvest had been a bad one that year.[15] This letter also says that Glenorchy was paying Hempriggs but does not elaborate on either amount or reason.

In that same year of 1682, William Dunbar took on the lands of Telstane to the south of Wick on a wadset. The entry in the General Register of Sasines is dated 29 May and records the Dunbar acquisition of 'inter alia [the] town of Telstoun with mill and loch thereof Wick Papigoe Noss and Field of Noss manors places of firings and Castle Sinclair half Aikergill Gillock Windles and Penniland Myrlanduorne with half of the salmon fishings upon the Water of Wick etc etc.' (91.2.1). Before William took possession of Telstane, it was tenanted by Alexander Sinclair, who remained in occupation until his death. It is likely that this occurred in 1690 and that Telstane was thereafter, in October of that year, made over to Sir William by Alexander's eldest son, John Sinclair. A legal document of discharge and renunciation survives from 1700 to bear witness to the winding up of the obligations resulting from the transfer. John Sinclair was now most likely also dead as the member of the family featuring in this document is his younger brother, James, described as 'ensign to the regiment of guards commanded by the Earl of Orkney', probably the Royal Scots, whose colonel in 1692 was George Hamilton, created Earl of Orkney in January 1696. William paid James Sinclair 2,000 merks as the surplus from the crops harvested on Telstane in 1690 after the Sinclairs' rent had been taken care of. James Sinclair in return renounced any right or title he may have retained or inherited to the 'lands of Milnstoun milns milne land and pertinents yrof'. This refers to a mill or mills powered by the burn flowing from the loch northward to the Wick River. William renamed Telstane as Hempriggs in memory of the family home across the Moray Firth and had a handsome new house completed there in 1692.

John Lord Glenorchy remained in residence at Ackergill during the mid-1680s, managing the family affairs in Caithness. He was named as his father's main heir in July 1685 and married Lady Frances Cavendish. His older brother Duncan was sidelined, possibly through disability or just because the father considered him to be of insufficient mettle to be his heir. A man called James Stewart was placed in the Mains of Ackergill.[16] At the end of 1686, Breadalbane appointed William Dunbar as his justice and sheriff depute in Caithness, and as bailie – the terms factor and chamberlain are also used – on his estates. This put William in a very powerful position. His duties included the uplifting of all the rents, feu duties and other duties from all the tenants and wadsetters on the extensive acres that belonged to Breadalbane, and officiating as a magistrate in disputes coming before the baron's court. It made the Dunbars wealthy but probably gained them few friends. William confessed as much in a letter a few years later to his cousin, the advocate Robert Fraser: 'I have losed all the Sinclairs for the Earl of Breadalbane, and serving of him has bred me all this trouble, and yet I cannot have the ordinary termes and conditions a Sinclair gets.'[17] That was written in 1703 after Sir William had stood against James Sinclair of Stemster, brother of the laird of Dunbeath, for election to the Scottish Parliament and lost. 'I have done the Earle of Breadalbane service worth all the soume that they have now in prospect out of Caithnes but it has been my misfourtune that my shilling has not the intrinsick value of ane other man's sixpence.' This complaint suggests that the Sinclair lairds who made up the majority in the small county electorate had closed ranks to support one of their own. The election in 1702 was the last before the Treaty of Union was settled in 1707.

The association with Glenorchy gave William the opportunity to enlarge the family landholdings in Caithness. The negotiations are evident in the various drafts of charters in Latin and in Scots in the Breadalbane Muniments and the Dunbar Papers. These date from 1686 and come complete with marginal notes, amendments and spaces for names and dates to be put in, about the selling of the lands of Auldweik, Latheronwheel and other properties to William.[18]

In 1688, the year in which James II was ousted from the throne to make way for William of Orange, Breadalbane was active in national politics, somewhat too active as he kept in touch with the exiled James and displayed an uncommon ability to ride with the government hounds and run with the Jacobite hare. In 1689, for example, he had ambition to come out with an armed force in support of the Jacobite rising by John Graham, 'Bonnie Dundee', but was prevented by gout and by Dundee's death on the braes of Killiecrankie. The extent to which Sir William Dunbar was implicated in Campbell machinations on the national level is unknown and possibly he was entirely innocent of anything smacking as closely of treason as Breadalbane's actions. In Caithness, indeed, domestic matters appear to have been uppermost. In January 1688, we learn from a letter that John Lord Glenorchy was keen to build a new house at Ackergill.[19] Legal transactions involving Dunbar, Sinclair of Dunbeath, Sutherland of Langwell and Breadalbane took place in 1688. Breadalbane's lawyer, Colin Campbell of Carwhin, was at Ackergill in the spring to deal with the family's affairs and in the letters from that sojourn we first come across a term that was soon to become a significant one – the Caithness Bargains.[20] This referred to deals that Carwhin reached with various Caithness lairds over the disposal of land. Carwhin sailed from Caithness for the south at the end of April when Glenorchy was looking forward to the arrival of the timber for his new house.[21] But this was a disappointment – the timber from 'Ballengown' [Balnagown?] was only fit for the lathes for plastering 'and such other broken work about the house', wrote Glenorchy to his father on 26 May. He reported that meal and malt had been shipped from Scrabster and that hawks were being collected for the king, asked for some books to be sent, especially Bloom's Geography, and commented on the extremely harsh weather. The tenants were in a poor way and most of their work horses had perished from the cold.[22] This is a reminder of how severe climatic conditions were at the end of the seventeenth century, with a succession of bitter winters and cool summers, harvest failures and famine so grave that in some places as much as one tenth of the population died. How bad things were in Caithness is not known, so poor are the records, but everyone's life and livelihood must have been affected to some degree. The period was referred to as King William's ill years.

In 1690–91 Sir William Dunbar was serving as one of the Commissioners of Supply for Caithness, a committee of the more prominent landowners that served in many ways as a forerunner to a county council. One of their important duties was to oversee the collection of the cess or land tax to supply the royal coffers, hardly a popular task at any time but probably less so in times of scarcity and hardship. Glenorchy knew this: in a letter to Carwhin in August he was anticipating trouble and feared they had few friends in the county – 'I think we that pay the third of the burden of the shyre should have the ordering the collectione of it...'.[23] In September 1690 many of the Caithness lairds petitioned Glenorchy and Sir William about payments.[24] Early in December 1690 Glenorchy wrote to Carwhin in a pathetic tone to stress how he wished to come south, how his wife was unwell and needed skilful care, far more than the 'kitchin wensh' with her could provide; and how they had already lost a child for lack of medical attention.[25] On that occasion Lady Glenorchy's health improved and after Christmas Glenorchy was writing to Carwhin more cheerfully, including the information that barrels of beef, presumably salted, had been sent from Thurso and that he and his wife intended to come south before Candlemas (2 February).[26]

But this was not to be. Frances, Lady Glenorchy, turned ill again before Candlemas and died in early February, a tragic blow to Glenorchy but also a serious knock to Breadalbane's financial hopes. The Campbell treasury had been seriously drained over the years by Breadalbane's various schemes. Frances's father was still alive – although he too was soon to pass away – and her death deprived any inheritance of Cavendish funds finding its way into Campbell coffers. Now the importance of the Caithness Bargains came to the fore – only by selling lands in the north could Breadalbane meet his debts and secure his position in the south. Breadalbane's wife, who had once been the wife of the Earl of Caithness, at first refused to sign papers to allow the sale of Caithness lands but was then persuaded to do so.

A letter dated in the catalogue of the Breadalbane Muniments as being February 1708 may have been wrongly listed and may also belong to this period.[27] It is addressed to Carwhin in London and in it Glenorchy refers to the news of their poor child's death, having been received at Finlarig, a Breadalbane seat, and complains about the bitter weather and the wind and, because his ship has not arrived, the lack of coal for the fire. Caithness winds can be trying at any time of year but in the cruel winters of the 1690s they must have been especially so. Glenorchy also talks of the sale of the Caithness lands and how he will have to do what he can – the market had been easier seven years before, in his opinion – but 'it is a hen in a rainie day'. Later in the year Glenorchy left Scotland to tour the continent – he was in Berlin in November 1691 and reached Rome in the following summer.

Several documents in the Breadalbane Muniments give details of the Caithness Bargains, the status of the various properties, what they produced in rent and victual, what they were likely to yield to the Breadalbane purse, and so on. One of these, dated 28 July 1692 and approved by Breadalbane himself – his signature is at the foot – summarises the transactions (Appendix 1). The contents of the document hint at hard bargaining between the agents of Breadalbane, who included William Dunbar and Colin Campbell of Carwhin, and the Caithness lairds who gained new property. The largest estate in value – a substantial part of the valley of the Thurso River, including Braal, Gerston, Halkirk, Sibster, Sordale, Hoy and Skinnet – was acquired by Sir George Sinclair of the Ulbster Sinclairs, an early step in the rise to prominence of this particular family. William Dunbar took the occasion to enlarge what he had already acquired and gained sole possession of the salmon fishing rights on the Wick River in 1691 and more properties in and around Wick itself, while continuing to serve Breadalbane as bailie through the early 1690s. In April 1695, Breadalbane instructed William Campbell, his chamberlain, to pay William £100 sterling for his 'pains and expenses in coming south' on the earl's affairs.[28] The extent of the Dunbar acquisitions in Caithness at the end of the seventeenth century is presented in some detail in two charters, one dated in 1700 and the second in 1705. Both are written in the formal Latin phraseology of the Scots legal profession. The first of the two charters, dated at Breadalbane's castle at Taymouth on 4 April 1700, is a much corrected draft in the Breadalbane Muniments, possibly written in Colin Campbell of Carwhin's own hand, and bearing all the marks of having been much pored over to ensure everything was correctly put down.[29] It states how Breadalbane with the consent and advice of his son, John Lord Glenorchy, grants to William Dunbar of Hempriggs various lands in Caithness, including Ackergill, Trailrigs, Reiss, Harland, South and North Kilimster and Wester in the parish of Wick; Dalnaclettan in Strathmore, with various shielings, Achlibster, Olgrinbeg, Tormsdale and Dalnawillan, all in Halkirk parish; and Acharaskill and Shinvall in Latheron parish. By this time William had renounced or given up his wadset on Keiss and also one that he had held on Reisgill. The 1705 Crown Charter of Resignation issued in the name of Queen Anne confirms the grants listed in the 1700 charter and also includes the lands of Auldweik, Kirkfeild, Milntoun, Telstane, Wick and Papigo, Latheronfuilzie [Latheronwheel], Landhallow, Somervall [Smerral?], Knockinnon, Lappan, Noss, Quoystane, Mossedge, Gillock, Winless and Stemsterwick. Among the place names are some no longer in common use such as Laird's Pennyland, Cooksquoy and Beansbarnes [Bain's Barns?] in the vicinity of Wick, Gaulochs Croft in the Latheron area, and shielings called Sleyach, Achnacloich, Badrinacoppock, Dalmaddy and Lochraein in Halkirk parish.[30]

In the manner of charters, there is a formulaic, catch-all listing of the types of property that could be found on any estate – buildings, manors, houses, granaries, gardens, orchards, mills, pastures, huts, doocots, rabbit warrens and so on, some of which suggest a certain optimism with regard to the Caithness environment – but there is also particular mention of Scots and even local features, underlined by a Scots word or two breaking through the Latin. Thus we frequently have 'multuris, hesucken, knaveship sequelis et bannock' in reference to the rights and customs associated with mills; 'thack, flash, wrack, wair' in reference to rights to thatching material, marshy pools, seadrift and seaware; 'sclaitheughs [and] Quarries of frie and roughstane' which needs no translation; and a reference that is indicative of the importance of seabirds in the household economy in the northern counties in the seventeenth century – 'maw's nests' on the cliffs.

The Dunbar charters do not mention sums of money involved in the transfer of property but other documents in the Breadalbane Muniments show how much the sellers stood to gain. One such is called 'A Scheme of the Caithness Bargains' and was drawn up in 1691.[31] It lists lands being disposed of to various people and includes one item to Hemprigs [sic]: 'This additional localitie is the salmond fishing of the Watter of Weik, & a penny 3 fard and octo land off Weik and Papigo the two revenues in the bankhead of auldweik and his owne old ffew dewtie ffor securatie of the teynd …'. With adjustments for teind and feu duties, the transaction earned £1,440 Scots for Breadalbane.

An anonymous document dated 23 July 1700 and probably drawn up by William Dunbar is labelled 'Account betwixt the Ogilvies and me', and gives details of construction work done on an unnamed estate, perhaps Hempriggs (83.3.2). Robert Dunbar and Patrick Falconer are listed as contributing to the costs, along with the writer who appears simply as 'myself'. The Ogilvies were presumably a local family of builders and masons but nothing else is known of them. The account gives costs – 'for hewing the stones and building the smaller mills £28 6s 8d; for building the barn and stables £66 13s 4d … for burning four bolls of lyme £12 12s … beam filling and plastering the loft & building above the gable £5 2s 8d' and so on, to a total bill of £147 4s. The Ogilvies received payment in cash but also in kind, in the form of bolls of oatmeal and beremeal.

Thanks in part to the financial carelessness of the Sinclair earls and in part to their own eye for an opportunity, the Dunbars had become in the space of barely fifty years one of the largest landowners in Caithness, a success celebrated in April 1700 when William was created a baronet in the peerage of Nova Scotia. As a knight and baronet, William became properly styled Sir William, and his wife Lady Dunbar. The system of baronetage of Nova Scotia had originally been created by James VI as a device to fund the settling of the province of that name in Canada – a baronetcy could be purchased by anyone aspiring to the rank – but the connection with land grants in the New World was later cut and it is not known if Sir William had to make any payment for the honour.

The charters also detail the all-important laws governing an entailed estate and define the sequence of inheritance of heirs. In 1700 and again in 1705 Benjamin Dunbar, the firstborn, legitimate son of William and his wife Margaret Sinclair, is named as the first heir. The sequence ensues, each clause beginning with the gloomy Latin *Quibus deficien*, 'to whom failing', and includes what was to prove a crucial provision that in the absence of sons the lands could be inherited by a legitimate female heir, and that whoever inherited had to adopt or retain the name and insignia of Dunbar. The Deed of Entail survives in the Dunbar Papers from 11 October 1707, the date when it was written by David Leitch, servant to the Elgin writer James Craig, and signed at Hempriggs by William Dunbar, his daughter Elizabeth and her husband James, and witnessed by James Oliphant, the minister of the parish, William's own chaplain John Tulloch, and a servant called George Sinclair (79.2.13). This deed contains the information that Benjamin had died. We have no date for this death but we can narrow it down to the first half of 1706. A much eroded wall plaque, now inside the entrance hall of Ackergill Tower, bears the initials BD and JS, the conjoined arms of the Dunbars and the Sinclairs and the date 1706. This undoubtedly refers to the wedding of Benjamin and Janet Sinclair of Ulbster. Benjamin's sister Elizabeth, who became her father's sole heir, married in August 1706.

2 | The Sutherlands of Duffus

– 'The said Mr James Sutherland and
Dam Elizabeth Dunbar were married'

Elizabeth Dunbar was born at Latheronwheel on 14 June 1676. She married Sir Robert Gordon of Gordonstoun, very much her senior, already a widower and a notable figure in his time. Born in 1647 he travelled widely in Europe in his youth and came home to Moray with a passion for chemistry and natural history. His fondness for experiment mystified and frightened the locals, and they whispered that he had made a pact with the Devil, a belief confirmed for a few when he constructed an unusual circular steading close to the house. The steading stands to this day and is part of Gordonstoun School.[32] Sir Robert also invented a water pump, devised a treatment for rabies, is said to have corresponded with Robert Boyle, one of the eminent scientists of his day, and in 1686 was elected a member of the Royal Society. In 1676 he married Margaret Sutherland, the widow of the first Lord Duffus. The couple had one child before Margaret died in 1677. The date of the wedding between Sir Robert and Elizabeth Dunbar appears not to have been recorded in any of the standard reference works but it probably took place around 1692, the year in which Elizabeth reached the age of 16. In September 1704 Sir Robert himself died and in the following year, in his memory, Elizabeth built not far from the house at Gordonstoun a mausoleum to hold her husband's mortal remains. She chose for the site a low ridge sanctified by having once been the location of the medieval parish kirk of Ogston. The mausoleum was graced with funerary urns on the peaks of the gables but was left unroofed, exposing to the elements the tall stone tablet on which were carved the sad details of mortality – 'Sir Robert Gordon ... died 5 of S[eptem]ber 1704 aged 57 years'. The tablet also records the deaths of four of the couple's children beginning with 'William Gordon son to Sr Rt Gordon by D Elizabeth DUNBAR ... died 18 March

1701' and continuing with a daughter Margaret, who died in 1703 at the age of ten, and two more daughters, Katharin and Elizabeth, in 1705. High child mortality was not unusual at the time but still we can only wonder how Elizabeth coped with such massive loss in the space of some three years. She was left with two surviving children, Lucy and young Robert.

In the mansion house of Gordonstoun, probably in the main room on the first floor with its sweeping view of the fertile landscape, on 8 August 1706 Elizabeth married for the second time. She was later to copy the entry relating to the marriage and other family events from an old family Bible (118.3.21). Her new husband is mentioned first – 'Mr James Sutherland now Sir James Dunbar of Hempriggs second son to James Lord Duffus and Lady Margaret Mackenzie daughter to Seaforth was born at Elgin the nynth day of May 1680' – before she herself is described – 'Dam Elizabeth Dunbar only surviving child and representative of Sir William Dunbar of Hempriggs relict of Sir Robert Gordon of Gordonstown … The said Mr James Sutherland and Dam Elizabeth Dunbar were married ....'.

James Sutherland of Duffus belonged to a prominent northern family that could trace its lineage back to the reign of David I, when the king of Scots had advanced into Moray to defeat the incumbent ruling dynasty and draw the province into his own expanding realm. David installed loyal followers, some of whom were Flemings from the Low Countries, in lands in Moray. The most significant member of this group was a knight called Freskin who was granted large parts of the area and began to style himself 'de Moravia'. The heart of the Freskin territory lay to the north of Elgin, declared a royal burgh in 1150. This is the parish of Duffus, a name probably drawn from the Gaelic *dubh uisge*, 'dark water', although *dubh-ais*, 'dark place', has also been suggested as the origin.[33] In the eighteenth century the parish ran along the coast for five miles, from Burghead to the mouth of the Lossie, and extended inland for two to three miles. It is a fertile place, farmland of clay and black earth, underlain by Old Red Sandstone rock instead of the unyielding schists of the barren Highlands to the south. The River Lossie wound down from these hills, swept around Elgin and flowed into the wide, shallow loch of Spynie before finding an outlet to the sea. On a slight ridge at the inmost end of this loch the Freskins built Duffus Castle. Today Loch Spynie has disappeared, drained for agriculture, and the castle is a ruin but when it was built, from 1151 onwards, it must have dominated the landscape with its encircling walls rising to the sky.

From the coast of Moray the Freskins could see on a clear day the distant hills of Caithness and Sutherland, still in Norse hands when they had arrived with David I. It must have seemed the most natural thing in the world to expand their power in that direction, especially as the Scottish royal house also had its eyes on the north. Although mainland Caithness did not officially become part of the

Scottish kingdom until the Treaty of Perth in 1266, the Norse earls who ruled it were already falling under Scottish domination a generation before. The Scottish kings' *nordpolitik* offered opportunities to their supporters and the Freskins did not miss their chance; William de Moravia became the first Earl of Sutherland holding the lands between Strathoykel and the Ord, and Gilbert de Moravia was appointed as the fourth bishop of Caithness and Sutherland with his seat at Dornoch in 1223.

In the early fourteenth century Duffus Castle was in the possession of Sir Reginald le Cheyne, a Norman knight who had married a daughter of the Freskin line. Sir Reginald also held extensive territory in Caithness, including the castles and lands of Auldwick and Berriedale, and it is reputed that he kept a hunting lodge on the shore of Loch More near the Thurso River. He died in about 1350 and, as he had no sons, his estates were divided between his two daughters, Mary and Mariota. Mary married Nicholas Sutherland of Duffus, the second son of the fourth earl of Sutherland. From his elder brother, who became the fifth earl of Sutherland, Nicholas received the barony of Torboll in 1360, an extensive stretch of good land mostly in the valley of the Evelix river to the west of Dornoch. Through his marriage, Nicholas also acquired Auldwick and Berriedale, but the family later lost their Caithness possessions to the incoming Oliphant kindred.[34]

Sir Reginald's daughter Mariota married John, the second son of Edward Keith, and their son Andrew, through his mother, inherited the lands of Ackergill. The castle of Auldwick and the lands of Ackergill, barely four miles apart, therefore came to be occupied by families related through the sisters. Auldwick or Oldwick, sometimes also called the Old Man o' Wick by the seamen who used it as a navigation mark, is a ruin now but the surviving walls are enough to indicate its past strength. It consisted of a rectangular tower or keep rising from an exposed promontory between two geos where the cliffs fall away to the sea. The walls are 7 feet thick at the base and this, combined with the small windows and the door at the level of the first floor, must have made it seem impregnable to an assailant. A ditch cut across the neck of the promontory enhanced the defences. It was already an old place, probably dating back to the twelfth century, when Nicholas and Mary may have stayed there. Though she would have felt safe in Auldwick, Mary may have envied her sister in Ackergill living in a residence less exposed to the searching easterlies. It is not known when the first tower was built at Ackergill. If it was later than 1400, as scholars of castle design maintain, it would not have existed during the lifetimes of John Keith and his spouse, Mariota le Cheyne, although there was in all probability an earlier building on the site.[35] Sir William Keith, John Keith's grand-nephew, was the first in the family to hold the exalted rank of earl marischal; he was born not long after 1425 and died in 1483, and it may have been during his time that the family erected the first keep on the shore of Sinclair's Bay. During the time of the fifth Earl Marischal, George Keith, in 1612 the tower of Ackergill was sold to the Earl of Caithness and, as we have seen, it later passed into the hands of Campbell of Glenorchy and then to the Dunbars.

The Sutherlands of Duffus linked themselves through marriage to other leading families in the north of Scotland. The Duffus title passed through a series of males, all called either Alexander or William, and it is useful to assign them numbers to avoid confusion in describing the parts they played in some of the events of their day. The family tree summarises the line of descent (Fig. 4). Isabella, the daughter and youngest child of Alexander I in our list married Alexander Dunbar of Westfield, a direct forebear of Sir William Dunbar whose daughter Elizabeth reunited the Dunbar and Sutherland lines through her marriage with another Duffus nearly two hundred years later.

The seventeenth century was a time of great unrest in the north as in the rest of Britain. The Sutherlands of Duffus, by luck or judgement, emerged from the turmoil with enhanced status. Alexander III of Duffus was only five years old when he succeeded his father on 11 January 1627, and his uncle James was appointed as his tutor, to guide his education and administer his patrimony until he came of age. Alexander was eventually infeft in his lands in 1643. In the ensuing civil wars, he led the defence of Perth against Cromwell's Parliamentary forces, albeit unsuccessfully. After the death of his first wife, he went abroad for a time but returned in 1660 in the retinue of Charles II and was created a peer, Lord Duffus, for his loyalty. He was to marry four times in his life and he was succeeded by his son James, the second Lord Duffus. James and his wife Margaret, the daughter of the third Earl of Seaforth, had five daughters and three sons. The eldest son, Kenneth, who inherited the title of Lord Duffus, was a captain in the Royal Navy but he fell from favour by supporting the Jacobites during the rising in 1715, an act of political misjudgment for which he was, in the word of the time, 'attainted'. The youngest brother, William of Roscommon, was also attainted, leaving only the middle one, James, to stay on in Moray and marry Elizabeth Dunbar in 1706.

Notes

1. The relationship between the Dunbars and the royal houses of England and Scotland is a complex one that has been explored in detail in *Mighty Subjects: The Dunbar earls in Scotland c.1072–1289* by Elsa Hamilton, 2010.

2. The farms of Upper and Lower Hempriggs lie on the B road between Kinloss and Burghead. This is fertile ground gently sloping towards the north, separated today from the Moray Firth by a belt of coniferous forest.

   On Pont's map of Caithness, the name of Hempriggs does not appear, and the present loch bearing the name is called 'Trumbuster', a word that evolved into the present Thrumster. Pont's map, the first depiction that we know of the county, was possibly drawn in the 1590s. It shows Wick as four rows of buildings on the north side of the river, with a bridge spanning the water to a cluster of buildings on the south side, which appear to bear the name of Newtoun. To the south of Wick Telstane is clearly indicated, with N. Trumbuster and Myltoun between it and Trumbuster Loch

Fig 4. The line of descent of the Sutherlands of Duffus

The diagram includes some links through marriage to other leading north families.

Nicholas Sutherland* of Duffus m. Mary le Cheyne
|
Henry Sutherland of Torboll
\
Alexander Sutherland (I) of Duffus m. Muriel Chisholm of Chisholm
(d.c.1484)
|
William Sutherland of Berriedale
|
William Sutherland of Duffus m. Janet Innes
(d.1514)
|
William Sutherland of Duffus m. Janet Innes
(k.1530)

William Sutherland of Duffus m.Elizabeth Stewart	Elizabeth m. John Sinclair, 3rd Earl
(d. 1543)	of Caithness

Alexander Sutherland (II) of Duffus m.Janet Grant of Freuchie
(d.c.1570)
|
William Sutherland of Duffus m. 1. Margaret Sinclair, daughter of 4th Earl of Caithness
(d.1616)   2. Margaret Mackintosh, daughter of 15th Chief of that Ilk

William Sutherland of Duffus m. Jean Grant of Freuchie
(d.1626)
|
Alexander Sutherland (III) of Duffus m. 1. Jean Sinclair, widow of Master of Berriedale
Created 1st Lord Duffus, 1650   2. Jean Innes
(d.1674)   3. Margaret, daughter of Earl of Moray
                4. Margaret, daughter of Lord Forbes

James Sutherland, 2nd Ld Duffus m. 1. Margaret, daughter of 3rd Earl of Seaforth
(d.1705)

Kenneth, 3rd Ld Duffus**	James Sutherland m. Elizabeth Gordon (nee Dunbar)
(d. 1733)	

Eric, 4th Ld Duffus**
(d.1768)
|
James, 5th Ld Duffus**
(d.1827)

*Nicholas Sutherland was the second son of the fourth Earl of Sutherland.
**Kenneth was attainted as a Jacobite; Eric and James remained titular lords until the peerage honour was restored in 1826. When James died in 1827 without heirs, the title passed to Sir Benjamin Dunbar.

and the burn draining from it to the Wick River. On the seaward side of Telstane lie Sarclet and Old Wick.

3. Robert Douglas, *Annals of the Royal Burgh of Forres*, 1934, p. 39.

4. The online catalogue of the National Records of Scotland has made searching for papers relevant to the Dunbars much easier than it must formerly have been. The references to such documents used in this narrative are given when they occur.

5. John Henderson, *Caithness Family History*, 1884, p. 221.

6. Sir William Fraser, *The Sutherland Book*, 1892, vol. 1, p. 290.

7. Robert Mackay, *History of the House and Clan of Mackay*, 1829, p. 369.

8. A good summary of Glenorchy's life can be found in the *Oxford Dictionary of National Biography*.

9. The letter survives in the National Records of Scotland (NRS), Edinburgh, ref GD112/58/12.

10. James T. Calder, *Sketch of the Civil and Traditional History of Caithness*, 1887, p.185.

11. Various accounts of the battle have been written, for example from a Sinclair point of view in James Calder's History and from a Campbell one in Alastair Campbell's *A History of Clan Campbell* (Edinburgh UP, 2004, vol. 3, pp28–9.). One that was written only a few years after the clash and is arguably more reliable than some of the later accounts is included in 'Answers to the General Queries concerning Caithness' by William Dundas in *Macfarlane's Geographical Collections* (vol. 1, Edinburgh, 1908 (SHS 53), Sir Arthur Mitchell & J.T. Clerk, eds). 'The late George Earle of Caithness, having disponed of his own and Grand Uncles estate with all his Titles of Honour and Jurisdictions to Campbell of Glenurchie, in prejudice of his Grand Uncles Son, who was appearand Heir, Glenurchie did possess himself of all. George [Sinclair] the appearand Heir went into Caithness and by assistance of some friends did repossess his Fathers estate and did some prejudice to the new Earles Houses. Upon which the Earle obtained a party of the Kings forces and what friends he could make to assist the Sheriff of Inverness to repone him to the possession, but he having gathered together about 300 men did enter the countrey without the Sherif, Earle George knowing of his Motion, had gathered two or three hundred Commons together, who having gone to Week, were followed at a distance by E. John. But E. George's men, being far inferiour in number and arms, resolved to return to their Houses quietly, and going without care or order, as from a fair, E. John who waited this opportunity, set upon them about a mile from Week and killed and drowned in the Water of Week above 80, beside many wounded, most part after they had thrown away their Arms and sought Quarter, for which and other crimes there is Process of Treason depending against the said E. John.' The reference to 'process of treason' suggest that the account was written in 1683 as during most of that year until he received a royal pardon in August Campbell stood accused of treason for his actions in Caithness.

12. The reference to William Dunbar being put to the horn for killing his brother occurs in Margaret Young (editor) *The Parliaments of Scotland*, 1992, vol. 1, p. 211.

13. NRS GD112/64/4, items 1 (2 June 1677) and 2 (4 Jan 1678).

14. NRS GD112/58/51.

15. NRS GD112/58/51/32.

16. NRS GD112/58/58/1-2.

17. NRS RH15/13/25.

18. NRS GD 112/58/63.

19. NRS GD112/51/70/30.

20. NRS GD 112/58/72.

21. NRS GD112/39/143/3.

22. NRS GD112/39/143/10.

23. NRS GD112/64/4/ Item 10.

24. NRS GD112/58/77/ Items 7, 13, 14, 18.

25. NRS GD112/39/149/4.

26. NRS GD112/39/149/10.
27. NRS GD 112/39/212/11.
28. NRS GD112/58/98/39.
29. NRS GD112/58/111/1/9.
30. NRS 03390 C2/82.
31. NRS GD112/58/78/29.
32. At Gordonstoun it is known as the 'round square' and houses accommodation, the school library and other premises.
33. Watson, W.J., *The History of the Celtic Place-Names of Scotland,* 1926, p. 499.
34. William Oliphant, the second son of Sir Laurence Oliphant of Aberdalgie – the first Lord Oliphant, married Christian Sutherland of Duffus in 1497 and thereby acquired the Duffus lands in Caithness. The Oliphants later fell on hard times and in 1604 their lands in Caithness were sold to the Earl of Caithness. Of Nicholas Sutherland's stronghold at Berriedale, nothing now remains except a few courses of stone on the narrow finger of land on the south side of the mouth of Berriedale Water.
35. See, for example, John Gifford, *The Buildings of Scotland: Highlands and Islands*, 1992, p. 102.

Part 2

Victual, votes and debt

1 | 'having at least the half of the paroch'

Sir William Dunbar continued to live at Hempriggs while Sir James and Elizabeth took up residence at Ackergill. Henrietta, their first child, was born at Gordonstoun on 2 June 1707 but she survived for only a few months, dying at Ackergill on 14 September; she was laid to rest in the Dunbar aisle in the church in Wick (118.3.21). Elizabeth next gave birth to twins, William and Margaret, in Edinburgh on 2 October 1708; William, carrying his grandfather's name, survived into adulthood but Margaret died at Hempriggs when she was only 8 years old. Two more daughters, Janet (born 22 December 1710) and Charlotte Elizabeth (born 14 March 1712), entered the world in Edinburgh, followed by the three youngest offspring, Elizabeth (born 28 February 1715), Rachel (7 May 1716) and James (6 January 1719), all born at Hempriggs (Fig. 5).

Not many documents survive in the papers from this period but those that do show unsurprisingly that the Dunbars followed the lifestyle of the landed gentry of the period, supervising the working of their estates and taking a role in public affairs. Sir William represented Caithness in 1678 in the Convention of Estates, a substitute parliament called by the king, Charles II, to pass legislation to raise troops and taxes to suppress the dissenting Presbyterians known as the Covenanters. It is also no surprise to know that Sir James had a legal training, often considered an essential attribute of a landowner and a gentleman. He became an advocate on 1 February 1704, and travelled to Edinburgh to take part in the debates in the Scottish Parliament leading to the Treaty of Union in 1707. He voted in favour of union, whereas three other Caithness representatives – the Earl of Caithness (Alexander Sinclair of Murkle), James Sinclair of Stemster and the Wick burgess Robert Frazer – voted against it. A letter has survived among the papers of the

Fig. 5. The family of Sir James Dunbar of Hempriggs, 1st Bt.

More detail can be found in Henderson, *Caithness Family History.*

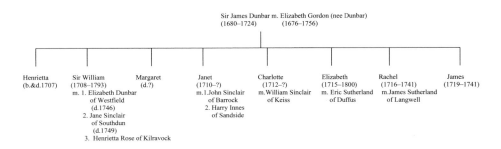

family of Erskine, the earls of Mar and Kellie, from 25 December 1707, in which a brother of the Earl of Mar reports that Sir James Dumbar [sic] of Hempriggs seeks the Earl's direction regarding the next election for the five northern burghs.[1] The Earl's brother was James Erskine, Lord Grange, a leading advocate who was to become notorious in 1732 for having his wife, Rachel Chiesley, kidnapped and exiled to St Kilda and arranging a false funeral for her in Skye (despite her husband's machinations to be rid of her, Rachel survived until 1745). The northern burghs – comprising Tain, Wick, Kirkwall, Dingwall and Dornoch – were represented in the Westminster parliament as a single constituency, the result of the agreement in the Act of Union to reduce the number of Scottish members by squeezing together the representation of various places. Sir James kept well in with the Erskines; on 6 November 1712, he wrote to Lord Grange to say that the designs of his mother-in-law were keeping him at home but he would leave at once should Lord Grange command him.[2]

Sir William Dunbar continued to attend to Breadalbane business. On 7 June 1703 he wrote to Breadalbane to tell him that the bargain with Sir George Sinclair – a member of the Ulbster family and sometimes referred to as being 'of Clyth' – was likely to be concluded.[3] It seems that Sir George was a canny bargainer as negotiations with the Campbells went on for some time and also involved Sir Duncan Toshach of Monzievaird.[4] On 26 July 1705 Sir William informed Breadalbane that he intended to visit him at Taymouth 'if health permits'; but perhaps the journey was too difficult for the Caithness laird as on 20 August we find him still at Ackergill writing to Breadalbane again, this time to tell him that the old girnal at Staxigoe, where the grain from the Campbell lands was stored, had turned 'altogether useless except for the stones': Sir William offered to buy the stones and promised to keep Breadalbane's victual.[5]

One document in the Breadalbane Muniments is a letter dated 26 January 1708 from Sir Duncan Toshach of Monzievaird to Breadalbane with mysterious references to the affair of Sir William and his daughter.[6] It is quite a brief letter and reads: 'My Lord, I have both your Lordships [letters] & by the next shall give a particullar [sic] answer to each, only at present I am to aquent your Lordship, that I was with Sir William and spoke him again, anent the subject I wrote of to your Lordship and his answer was, that himself was bound infirme, and his daughter & he hade discounted the undervaluing all he hade done for her, And albeit he looked on that project, as a thing desireable yet, he did not see how he might accomplish it[.] I understand from others that the [obscure word] and she are like to fall out on other heads, which will make that affaire fall, I shall be more full by the next.' We do not know what lies behind this communication. Elizabeth Dunbar had already married James Sutherland of Duffus six months before this letter, but was there ever any thought by Breadalbane that she may have been a possible wife for Colin, his son from his second marriage to Mary Campbell the widow of the Earl of Caithness? Colin was to die later in 1708, in any case. Sir William Dunbar himself died in 1711. We are unsure of his age but, as his parents married in 1624, he may well have been in his 80s.

A few of the earlier documents in the Dunbar Papers shed some light on the social norms of the period. One such is a petition from Sir William Dunbar to the Reverend Charles Keith, the minister of Wick from September 1701 until his death in June 1705 and the Moderator of the Kirk Session [83.2.16]. The parish kirk in the town remained in a very poor state of repair. Sir William reminded the minister that, although he was the principal heritor and the biggest local landowner 'having at least the half off the Paroch', there was no seating set aside for himself, his family or his tenants in the church. In his petition Sir William 'humblie craves' that the minister and the elders will take this lack into consideration and provide a loft at the east gable extending for 16 feet towards the pulpit and 'in breadth from the south wall to the north wall.' The Kirk Session met on 29 March 1702 and noted that they found the request 'just & reasonable'. Reciprocal obligations were at work here. On 24 May 1709 the leading gentlemen of the parish of Wick met to consider the state of the manse, judged to be 'altogether ruinous', and decided to lay a stent or tax on themselves to build or buy a replacement [44.1.3]. The sums they agreed to pay are an indication of their relative wealth, but the division of the burden down to the last penny also suggests they had a canny eye for business and may well have indulged in some guarded haggling. The document records the amounts each agreed to pay, to be delivered at the two dates of Lammas (1 August, one of four quarter days in the Scots calendar) and Marymas (15 August) to Sinclair of Stirkoke, nominated as the treasurer, as follows:

Sir William Dunbar of Hemprigs	132 merks 4d Scots
Sir James Dunbar of Hemprigs younger	396 merks 1s
Sir James Sinclair of Mey, James Sinclair of Lyth, David Sinclair of South Dunn,	
John Sinclair of Barrock for Myrelandorn	24 merks 6s [each]
James Sinclair of Lyth for the Crooks of How	7s 6d
John Sinclair of Ulbster	63 merks 12s 8d
William Sinclair of Thrumster	63 merks 12s 8d
James Sinclair of Stemster	160 merks 8d
Francis Sinclair of Stirkock	166 merks 10s 8d

Fig. 7. The Sinclair kindred in Caithness

Of the 66 landowners in Caithness in 1751, 37 bore the surname Sinclair.

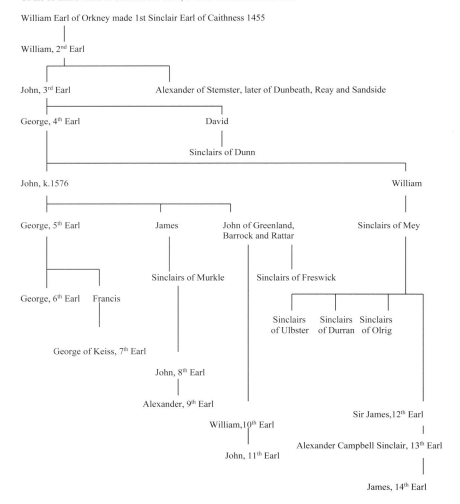

Fig. 8. The Sinclair house of Ulbster

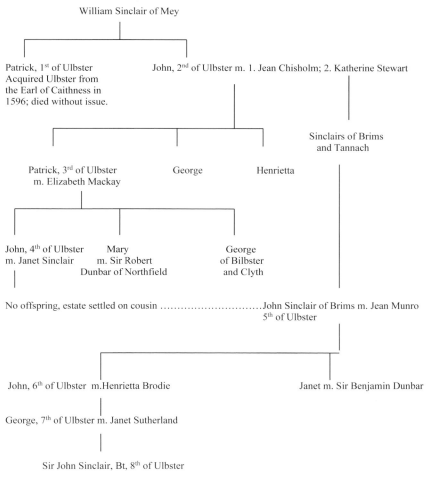

The Dunbar share of the stent, about equal to the sum total of that paid by the others, all Sinclairs, shows how much more extensive were the lands they held by this time (Figs. 7 and 8).

Although William Roy's map of Scotland, the first detailed depiction of the whole country, was not surveyed until the middle of the eighteenth century, the landscape it portrays for Caithness was probably little changed from earlier decades. The map shows a great extent of tilled ground from the environs of Hempriggs House along both sides of the shallow valley stretching to the Wick River, the valley drained by the burn flowing from the Hempriggs loch. Roy calls it the Burn of Charity and assigns the curious name Tylsha, possibly a misprint for Tylsta, a form of Telstane, to the Hempriggs loch. Two major differences between then and now are that then the burns meandered where they are now confined and straightened into ditches and that the fields were then open rigs. Enclosed parks occurred only occasionally in the vicinity of such larger dwellings as Hempriggs House. Most of the country people lived in scattered townships, each one a cluster of cottages and steadings of humble construction. Roy names Brugh [Brough], Ausdale, Barnyards, Milton, Hillside and Charity as some of the farms or townships north of Hempriggs. To the south of the Dunbar house lie Toftcauld [Toftcarl], Yarrows, Thrumster, Borrowston and so on.

2 | *'abounding with Grass and Corn'*

The export of grain, both oats and bere, was the main feature of the agricultural economy in Caithness before the changes in farming practice that took place around 1800. The Reverend John Brand, a member of a commission from the General Assembly of the Church of Scotland sent to see how matters stood in the church in the far north in 1700, recorded his impression of the Caithness landscape. After a frightening crossing of the Pentland Firth, he and his companions passed south by Sinclair's Bay, and found the area 'pleasant and very Fertile, abounding with Grass and Corn'. It was late spring and well before the harvest but the contrast with what the commission had just experienced in Shetland and Orkney may have swayed their judgement. The easy cost of living surprised them. 'Meal is sold at three or four or at most five Merks per Boll,' noted Brand, '… the Gentlemen can live better upon 1,000 Merks than they can do in the South upon 4,000 per annum.' The recent arrival of the Dunbars in the county, strangers among so many Sinclairs, was also noted: 'On the West side of the Bay is the Castle of Hakergil, a strong house at present possessed by a Gentleman who hath a great interest in the Countrey, but is not descended of the Family of Caithness.'[7]

The grain trade has been well explored in *Caithness in the 18th Century* by John E. Donaldson (1938) and in the complementary *The Mey Letters* by John E. Donaldson Jnr (1984), two volumes which contain much detail on the trading of the Sinclairs of Barrogill (now the Castle of Mey). The Dunbars also took part in this business. In the summer of a good year the arable land in Caithness must have been covered by seas of oats and bere, rippling in the breeze. The main ports for trade at this time were Staxigoe and Thurso, whither pack ponies made their way with grain in baskets slung across their backs, and whence ships sailed to British and continental ports. Grain was measured by volume with a scale of units: 4 lippies = 1 peck; 4 pecks = 1 firlot; 4 firlots = 1 boll; 16 bolls = 1 chalder.[8] These units referred to volume rather than weight, and varied in time and place, but a lippie seems to have been just under half a gallon. This would give a boll a volume of approximately 32 gallons. Aeneas Bayne in 1735 gives nine stone for the weight of a boll of oatmeal, and this standard appears to have stayed in use for the century.[9] Merchants in Wick and Thurso, as well as in Edinburgh, bought the Caithness grain for sale and re-export to the west of Scotland and Norway. Brand noted in 1700 that Caithness sent out 16,000 bolls each year (1,072 metric tonnes); Aeneas Bayne agreed with this – 'in any good year … 16,000 bolls'; and Thomas Pennant in 1768 stated that the export stood at 40,000 bolls (2,680 metric tonnes)[10], the latter probably a reference to very good years, with an average figure being closer to the one quoted in the Old Statistical Account for the parish of Wick, written in 1793 – 25,000 bolls per year (1,675 metric tonnes).[11] This is the export figure, of course, and does not include the amounts kept back for home consumption as meal or ale. There is no doubt that in the eighteenth century Caithness was considered to be good country for grain, so good in fact that the people seem to have escaped some of the harsh famines that scar Highland history.

The Caithness merchants did well on the grain trade and on the export of other raw products – tallow, salt beef, pork, ham, geese, skins, hides, fish, feathers, and so on – and imported basic and luxury commodities for their local clients. Indeed, in the eighteenth century, the Caithness lairds enjoyed a high standard of living, often spending beyond their means on wine and a fondness for fine clothes.

The laird also served as a source of investment capital, often in the form of seed grain, for the tenant. A statement of account between Sir James Dunbar and William Miller, the farmer who held the tack or lease of Ackergill, gives details of the transactions lying behind the agricultural practices of the time, with its focus on the cultivation of bere and oats, and the rearing of cattle [81.2.4, Appendix 2]. Horses and sheep were also kept but do not figure in the accounting. The statement is dated 24 February 1722 and concludes that William Miller was owed by Sir James 299 bolls, 3 firlots, 1 peck and 2 lippies 'of victuall [grain] which victuall consists of two third parts Bear in the Boll measure of Staxigoe and the other third in oatmeal at eight stone and a half per boll', as well as £1,069 1s 10d Scots. The statement is witnessed by Sir Robert Dunbar of Northfield, John Sinclair of Barrock, George Manson of Bridgend and James Campbell, sheriff clerk of Caithness. Using the figures given earlier, we can calculate that Sir James's debt to William Miller comprised 8.4 metric tonnes of oatmeal and 17.9 metric tonnes of bere; these are sizeable quantities, and underline not only the acreage under cultivation on the Dunbar lands but also the importance of Caithness as a grain producer.

The Dunbars and their neighbours seem constantly to be lending funds to each other, an indication of the absence of banks as well as of a general shortage of ready cash in a society that depended on the exchange of goods as often as currency. Many of these obligations are recorded in legal documents, such as one from 1704 in which Sir William Dunbar acknowledges a loan of 4,600 merks 'good and usuall Scots money' from John Sinclair of Stirkoke [83.3.4]. On the other side of the same sheet, Francis Sinclair of Stirkoke, John's son, signs that he has received full payment of the loan, in this instance an example of a debt that bridged the generations. Sir William also took part in the buying and selling of debts, a primitive form of banking and one that could result in several men being linked in a chain of debt and obligation. There is an example, a bond or note in which Robert Calder of Wick sold to Sir William Dunbar, probably for cash, a debt owed to him since 13 October 1699 by two merchants in Elgin [83.3.8].

Sir James Dunbar died in 1724 and was succeeded by his and Elizabeth's eldest son William who had been born in 1708. A few years later, Elizabeth, now the dowager lady of Hempriggs, became embroiled in a dispute over the use of common land in and around Wick. The town's charter, dating from 1589, had given it the title and privileges of a royal burgh and the townspeople had the right to use the moors and pastures in the immediate vicinity for extracting peat, grazing animals and other everyday purposes. The Dunbars sought to exert a major influence on the conduct of public affairs in Wick. The constitution or sett of the royal burgh, as was normal for burghs throughout the country, called for the election of a provost and bailies, two or more, every year at Michaelmas, at the end of September.[12] Sir William was chosen as provost for 1705–06, and Sir James held the office for 1707–08, 1708–09, and 1710–11. As provost he sat in charge of the burgh court, trying petty offenders and overseeing the commercial and social affairs of the town. The records of the period are incomplete but the Counsell Record Book survives for most of the years from 1660 to 1711, and give details of some of the issues Sir James had to deal with. In 1710, for example, the council was much exercised over a spate of house-breaking and thefts. At this time Wick was still a small settlement of buildings clustered along its straggling main street on the north side of the river with a population probably fewer than a thousand.

It appears that a political split arose in 1712. The Convention of the Royal Burghs when it met in July that year noted that two commissioners had been sent from Wick to take part in the debates and vote on Convention decisions.[13] It is probable that one candidate was backed by the Dunbars whereas the other had been chosen in opposition. In the event the Convention rejected both commissioners and set up a committee to settle the differences between the parties. A petition from Wick presented to the Convention was considered at their meeting in the following summer – July 1713 – and it is recorded that Sir James Dunbar was allowed to see this and answer the points made in it. Perhaps the 1712 committee had not managed to do much as, in July 1715, another was appointed to meet at Wick and inquire into 'the nature of the discords of that burgh and endeavour to accommodate the same.' The mills of local governance ground particularly slowly during this period, what with political upheavals and the difficulties of travel over long distances. At last in July 1716 the Convention recorded the details of a petition presented by the Wick commissioner John Calder. This explains that it had been the practice for the list of provost, bailies and councillors elected each year to be approved by the Earl of Caithness. This practice had been passed on to Breadalbane and Lord Glenorchy and, although this is not stated in the Convention record, it had probably fallen somehow or been assumed by the Dunbars – not an entirely popular development. John Calder's petition in 1716 reads in part: '… there has been of late some variety in the method of election in the said burgh, especially in the absence of the Earle of Broadalbane [sic] and the Lord Glenorchy his son … and seeing it is absolutely requisit for the good order and government … that a settled rule for the elections in all time coming should be laid doun …'. What Calder and his party wanted was for the person who held the title to the earldom to choose the magistrates from a shortlist, and the chosen magistrates would then choose the rest of the council. The committee appointed in 1715 reported that they had examined the original royal burgh charter of 1589 and that it was clear that the consent of the Earl of Caithness and his successors was 'indispensibly necessar' and that the shortlist with two candidates for provost and four for the two bailie posts should be made up and presented to the Earl in time for the annual Michaelmas election. The committee also found that the sett recorded in the burgh books in 1711 did not conform to the royal charter. The Convention voted to bring the new system into effect immediately, i.e. for the 1716 election.

This decision was a defeat for the Dunbars and may have led to what happened next. In July 1717 the problems in Wick were once again on the Convention agenda. The petition from the burgh council states that Sir James Dunbar of Hempriggs and his lady, William Sinclair of Freswick 'and others of their commanding and hounding out, knowing the toun to be in a very mean condition … have most unjustly and unwarrantably, contrare to all law, inclosed a considerable part of the touns commonty in a park' depriving the townspeople of grazing for their cattle. Furthermore, 'Sir James and other persons above named will not suffer the petitioners to winn their peets in the commone moss, nor pass the commone highways to it without payment of duties imposed by them at their own hand … nor will the said Sir James and other persons above named suffer the inhabitants to fish in the bay of the sea which is commone to every persone, but poynds their nets and other materials for fishing; all which brings the inhabitants of the burgh under very melancholy and straitning circumstances …'. That was not all – the postmaster, William Mullikin, was constrained to give incoming mail for the burgh to Sir James first.

The Convention appointed the burghs of Dingwall, Fortrose and Inverness to look into the matter and meet Sir James Dunbar and Freswick, reinforcing the seriousness with which it viewed Wick's plight by having the president of the Convention write to the lairds. In the following July – 1718 – the report came back to the Convention that the investigators 'fand it proven that Sir James Dunbar had forced a new magistracy and council upon the toun of Wick in opposition to those legally chosen [by the approved sett] and has committed severall other acts very prejudicial thereto …'. Sir James had refused to meet the representatives from the Convention when they had travelled north but enough had been discovered to spur the Convention into offering to provide the legal assistance needed to allow the impoverished burgh to fight for their rights in court. The papers of the Sinclairs of Freswick in the National Archives contain an instrument of interruption dated in 1737 at the instance of a Wick bailie, Robert Winchester, against Sir William Dunbar of Hempriggs and John Lummis, tacksman of Gillock, for their encroachment on the hill and commonty of Wick.[14] In 1738 and again in 1741, the burgh was protesting to the Convention of Royal Burghs about encroachments on its rights and privileges by both Sir William Dunbar and Francis Sinclair, the brother of the Earl of Caithness.

Along with a few other burghs, including Inverness, Kirkcaldy, Kirkwall and Forfar, Wick complained of a decay of trade in 1723 and appealed for relief from tax; and in the following year the Convention agreed to allow relief to the extent of £2. The representatives who went south to speak for Wick at the Conventions include John Sinclair in 1725, a Colonel Robert Monro in 1726, and Patrick Dunbar on four occasions between 1728 and 1730. During several years the burgh had no representative at the Convention.

In 1726, two years after her husband's death, the dowager Lady Elizabeth Dunbar was still being charged with interfering in the burgh's elections and the townspeople's use of the commonty. The details are preserved in a memorial written in the autumn of 1728 [88.3.7] which reads in part: 'My lady Hempriggs by straitning the Inhabitants in their trade and having design to Compell them to Choose the magistrates and council as she inclines that she may easier wrest from them their privileges – she has already driven them out of their Mosses and Commonty and obliges them to pay yearly for liberty of casting peats in their own mosses and is inclosing all their commonty.'

In 1727, Elizabeth failed to have magistrates of her liking installed in office, provoking her son, Sir William, possibly at her instigation, to challenge the election. Elizabeth then launched an embargo on trade with the townspeople, forbidding her tenants to buy or sell there. The local fishermen were threatened with punishment should they sell their fish in the burgh and later attempt to moor in the creek belonging to the estate. Cattle and sheep were banned from grazing on the stubble of her cornfields after the harvest, and her tenants were told not to keep animals belonging to townspeople. To enforce these and other restrictions, she appointed two officers – 'these two fellows are Spies on all her Tenants while they are in town'. The document hints that violence was used. It is not known who drew up this memorial, as it is called, or what the outcome was, but clearly some legal authority, perhaps the Convention again, had been called in to help the locals fight for their rights.

As time passed, it seems that the Ulbster Sinclairs, especially once they had gained the feudal superiority of Wick from Glenorchy in 1718, threatened to erode the Dunbars' former degree of influence. John Sinclair of Ulbster became the heritable provost of Wick in 1723. According to Foden's history of the town, most of the provosts throughout the eighteenth century were to be Ulbster Sinclairs and the family did invest in the town. Unfortunately the burgh records for the years 1710 to 1741 have been lost, and there is nowhere to turn to find out the town's side to the dispute with Elizabeth. Almost a century later the Dunbars and the Wickers were to be at odds again over the enclosure of common land on the north side of the burgh in the Hill o' Wick case.

4 | *'a good new house lately built'*

After the death of Sir James Dunbar in 1724, the title and lands of the estate passed to his son, William, who was aged only 16 at the time. Five years later, on 6 January 1729, William, now a baronet and entitled to be Sir William, married Elizabeth Dunbar, the only daughter of Alexander Dunbar of Westfield in Moray. According to one source, his younger brother James was killed at Cartagena possibly in April 1741, during the unsuccessful attack by British forces on this Spanish port in what is now Colombia[15]; John Henderson says, however, in *Caithness Family History* that James died in Jamaica in 1742, and if this is true then it may have been from wounds received at Cartagena.[16] William also had several sisters: Janet who married, first John Sinclair of Barrock, and then Harry Innes of Borlum and Sandside; Charlotte, born in 1712, who married Sir William Sinclair of Keiss; Elizabeth who married her cousin Eric, the son of Kenneth, the third Lord Duffus; and Rachel who married James Sutherland of Langwell (Fig. 5).

Charlotte's husband, Sir William Sinclair, was initially baronet of Dunbeath but he relinquished his title in favour of Keiss, where he built in 1755 a new mansion to replace old Keiss Castle perched on the edge of a cliff. This new house, a somewhat plain Georgian building, is now enclosed within the more elaborate baronial structure of the present Keiss Castle remodelled by David Bryce in 1859–62, as indeed was Ackergill Tower by the same architect. Sir William Sinclair was briefly in the army, where he became an expert swordsman. He later became an enthusiastic convert to the Baptist mode of worship and established the first congregation of this denomination in Scotland. Unfortunately he was less adept at managing his finances and in the 1760s had to put his estate on the market.

In the account of Caithness written in 1735 by Aeneas Bayne, the principle heritors for the parish of Wick, i.e. those responsible for contributing to the upkeep of the kirk and the minister, are named as Sir James Sinclair of Mey, Sir James Sinclair of Dunbeath, Sir William Dunbar of Hempriggs, John Sinclair of Ulbster, Donald Sinclair of Olrig, John Sinclair of Stirkoke, John Sinclair of Barrock and Charles Sinclair of Bilbster.[17] Bayne goes on to describe the residences of the gentry: 'Seats here are from Wick about 2 miles north Ackergill, 2 miles south Hemprigs, which are convenient and well adorned Lodgings belonging to Sir William Dunbar.' That Sir William had built a new house at Ackergill next to the tower that had been the stronghold of the Keiths is confirmed by Bayne's words: 'Att Ackergill stands close by the sea as does the house itself, an exceedingly strong Tower of a Square Forme about 6 Stories high with a pleasant Bartizan on the tope with a strong wall about 8 foot thick … It has ane outer wall of 16 foot high with a ditch round it wherein the sea flows and ebbs …'. An entry in *Macfarlane's Geographical Collections* in 1726 states the same thing: at Ackergill was 'a strong house and yet in repair' and 'betwixt that and the sea is a good new house lately built, both now belonging to the family of Hempriggs'.[18] These remarks clarify that there were two houses, one the old Keith property and the other the more recent one built by Glenorchy at the end of the 1680s. In an appendix written probably in the late 1760s for Thomas Pennant's *A Tour in Scotland* 1769, the minister of Reay, the Revd Alexander Pope, noted that Sir William Dunbar had 'now rendered a most beautifull and convenient seat' at Ackergill; 'In the old tower is the largest vault in the North of Scotland, beautified with elegant light and plaistering … so that it is now the grandest room in all this part of the country'.[19] Across the bay from Ackergill, Sir William could see the old castle of Keiss on the cliff edge and close by the residence of Sir William Sinclair and his sister Charlotte. To the south, on the other side of the Wick River, lived three Sinclair lairds – Donald (of Olrig) at Thuster, John of Stirkoke and Charles of Bilbster. The Ulbster Sinclairs had their territory beyond Hempriggs in the very south of the parish, and in the north-west the Sinclairs of Barrock had their seat at Lyth.

Many of the surviving letters from the eighteenth century refer to the grain trade and associated business. The Inverness merchant and bailie, John Steuart, bought grain regularly from the Caithness lairds and sold it on to the south of Scotland, the Netherlands, London and at least once to Italy; he also shipped meal from Caithness to the west coast and the Hebrides, where army garrisons formed an important customer.[20] Among the Dunbar Papers, for example, we find on 9 August 1744 the merchant James Murray writing from Fraserburgh to Alexander Sinclair of Lyth, who had succeeded his father in 1743, to say that he had just arrived from Bergen where he had been delayed five weeks by privateers [2.4.49]. Privateers, pirates licensed by governments to raid the shipping of their enemies, were common in the northern seas at this time. Some of the attacks were recorded in the London news-sheet *Lloyd's List* where we read that in June 1741 the *Susanna*, a privateer from Calais, well armed with twenty guns, had captured the *Helen and Margaret* bound from Norway to Inverness: 'They stript the Crew and ransom'd the Vessel; which was their seventh Prize'.[21] Murray's ship had waited in Bergen for good reason but now he was impatient and told Alexander Sinclair to get the grain he had bought from the laird ready for shipment. He ended his letter with a scribbled reminder: 'May Cause Dress the Bear in a Right waye'. It must have taken a long time for Murray's letter to have reached Lyth, for on 12 October we find him writing again to Alexander Sinclair to reassure the laird and protest about the difficulties merchants have to contend with. He had sent 'Dain's Ship' to Staxigoe for Sinclair's cargo but she had returned without it; and a second ship was still waiting for a fair wind for the crossing of the Moray Firth: '… you know that I sent Dains Ship to Staxego in purpos to Receive your Victwell [victual] I bought but Contraer to my Expectation She returned hier from that with the Cargoe of Salt on board & Imedatly on hir Return I frieghted on [another] Ship for that purpos & She haid still layn hier waitteng a fair wind & with the first opportunaty she will be at Staxigo' [2.4.48]. These letters leave the reader with the impression that Murray, harassed though he was by weather and business, was a bluff, plain-spoken man.

The merchants and the lairds depended on each other but the reluctance or inability of the latter to attend to their debts in a timely way was an occupational hazard for the former. In November 1744 we find the Wick merchant, George Petrie, threatening legal action against Sir William Dunbar for a debt of £252 Scots [88.1.10]. The letter also states that Sir William owed £136 18s Scots to John Oliphant in Wick, probably another merchant. The failure to pay on time resulted in a threat of horning and poinding, that is public denunciation and confiscation of goods and livestock, or in the words of the time: 'denounce him as our rebel and put him yrto [thereto] and ordain all his moveable goods and gear to be escheat and inbrought to our use for his contempt & disobedience … that ye in our name and authority forsaid fence arrest apprise & compel poind and distrenzie all and sundry corns cattle horse nolt sheep insight plenishing debts sums of money maills farmes profites and duties of lands and all other moveable goods and gear whatever pertaining and belonging to the sd Sir William Dunbar …'. A note on the reverse of the document, in Petrie's hand, confirms that the merchant soon received enough payment from Sir William to satisfy him. James Sinclair of Durran and Alexander Sinclair of Lyth also had obligations to Petrie, as an account in 1744 makes clear [88.1.10]:

Sir William Dunbar of Hempriggs, James Sinclair of Durren and Alex Sinclair of
    Lyth to George Petrie

To their bond bearing interest from Mar 1742 & payable

Mar 1744	£520	17s	10d

To interest of the said bond from Mar 1742 to

The 2d febry 1745 being 2 years & ¼	£58	12s	

To cash paid & Noter Publick for infefting on Durren and Barrocks Lands

	£2	2s	

To cash paid Hugh Campbell for writing		
The sasine on the above infeftment	10s	6d
To paid to Do for registrating the sasine	13s	4d
To postage of the bond to Edinr to be registrate	2s	
To registrating the bond in booths of Co: of Session	6s	1½d
To postage north wt ye Extract	2s	
To postage again south wt ye Extract after		
The term of paymt	2s	
To horning	4s	10d
To surrenid of adjudication four sheets	6s	4d
To postage for the horning & summonds		
Of adjudication	3s	
To postage south wt ye sumd of adjudication		
Horning & sasine ye money being to be paid at court	3s	4d
To a sheet of stampt parchment on which the sasine		
Was writt	3s	6d

Ster	£584	8s	9½d

NB One guinea to be paid to the writer for drawing the discharges

A note on the back of the account written by a different hand suggests that the
participants in these financial transactions pored over their arithmetic. It draws
attention to an error of £2 0s 6d and reduces the sum to £582 8s 3½d. Other notes
claim that Sir William sent Mr Petrie a statement for a sum of £34 0s 4d sterling
in 1744, perhaps as his share of the above account. A final note signed by Petrie to
Sir William and dated 22 December 1744 at Ackergill records the settling of the
transactions and Petrie's satisfaction with the outcome.

At the same time as he was fending off Petrie's legal threats, Sir William was
shipping grain. John Anderson, the merchant, wrote to him on 27 November 1744
to say that he could not come to Ackergill as he was busy at Staxigoe loading and
preparing a ship for departure so as not to miss the tide [4.1.22]. 'If what you have
to lay cannot be delayed Acquaint me,' wrote Anderson, 'Barrock promised to
deliver all the bear that's in this Parish which he thought would be betwixt 130 &

150 bolls of which there is some wanting … [PS] There is 80 bolls from Sibster I am not sure what Barrocks men delivered but you can know.' The 'Barrock' mentioned in the letter is of course Alexander Sinclair of Lyth, referred to by the name of his estate, as was the custom.

Some of the letters shed curious sidelights on life in Caithness at the time, such as one from John Lumsdaine, an Edinburgh lawyer, to Sir William on 23 February 1744, which shows that even the accident of a whale being cast onshore had financial implications [4.1.31]. Sir William held the post of Admiral Depute in charge of the local court dealing with maritime issues; this clearly brought perks – he was 'entitled to the proceeds of the Whale' – and Lumsdaine reminds him to take expenses into account.

5 | *'the misurabell condision of alle Scotland'*

Overland travel from Caithness to Edinburgh took normally eight days in the mid-1700s. Journeys by sea were in many ways easier and there was a steady traffic across the Moray Firth. Despite these connections, the Caithness lairds lived in some isolation from the rest of Scotland and formed what must have been at times a claustrophobic social world. The families married amongst each other, creating a stew of kinship and an atmosphere in which they were prone to keep a close and critical eye on each other's affairs, seldom loath to find complaint or resort to litigation over their dealings in grain. Their correspondence hints at these concerns. For example, Alexander Sinclair of Lyth wrote to Sir William Dunbar on 13 May 1745 to report a visit from one of the servants of Sir William Sinclair of Stemster with a message that Stemster would make him 'easie & Safe', a pledge that did not impress Alexander Sinclair at all, as he went on to wish Sir William Sinclair 'twixt me and the Stake', presumably so that he could shoot him. It is quite likely that Sinclair of Stemster owed money to Sinclair of Lyth [20.5.1].

Handling the sale of Caithness victual in Edinburgh on behalf of Sir William and other lairds was a certain George Dunbar. He may have been a distant relation to Sir William, probably from one of the Moray branches of the vast Dunbar kindred. Several letters from him survive in the Dunbar Papers. These display spelling eccentric even by the standards of the time, for example in one on 23 May 1745, in which George described his problems in selling the Caithness grain: 'I hop of you to seaill and despose of your beair if possibell for bairley failles in preas efrey day heair and meaill allso and the seaim in the nearest countery but you will be shour to write me efrey post what you cain seaill ore what is on hand' [27.4.3].

While the lairdly families gossiped and bickered among themselves, the bulk of the population laboured on the land. An insight into their condition comes from a document drawn up in November 1737 in which a committee of the justices of the peace gathered at Nether Bilbster to decide on the wages to be paid to different workers (88.3.10, Appendix 3). The resulting scale shows that the ploughman was the top agricultural labourer: 'That every Sufficient Ploughman that can semble his own Plough or keep it in good order after it is sembled to his hand Shall have of ffee for the winter half year Eight pounds Scots, an pair of shoes or ten shillings Scots therefore, a Quarter of a Rochhide & Three bolls of Cost, Whereof half in oatmeall at Eight Ston pr Boll, And half in Bear Meall at Nine Stone pr Boll, the said ffee & cost to be in full of all demands.' (£8 Scots was equivalent to 13s 4d sterling, and had considerable purchasing power at that time.) The payment in money, shoes, rochhide (untanned leather) and cost, the term for payment in kind, was graded; after the ploughman came the drover, the barnman, the sparter and harrower (field workers – the sparter spread dung), women, and general servants. Carters were ranked with ploughmen, possibly because they too were skilled with horses. The justices also ruled on basic conditions of service: both servant and master had to give the other six weeks' notice of termination of employment; masters could not withhold wages indefinitely; masters could not abuse their employees; servants could not just up sticks and go away. The system whereby servants engaged for a six-month period or term was already in place. The justices were also concerned with public order and any servant who did not find a new master within three days of leaving a former post could become a figure of suspicion, liable to arrest. This was a society conscious of rank in which everyone had a place and was usually expected to stick to it. The rules were publicised by being posted on the doors of the parish kirks where, it was presumed, everyone would see them.

In the late summer of 1745 the Caithness lairds suddenly found a new distraction from their worries about grain prices and each other. Prince Charles Edward Stuart raised his standard in Glenfinnan to mark the beginning of his attempt to secure the British throne for his father. The resulting civil war had a disastrous effect on the grain trade, although to a large extent Caithness was bypassed by the hostilities and the Dunbars, like most of their neighbours, stayed loyal to the Hanoverian regime and kept their heads down. This was in contrast to what had taken place during the earlier Jacobite rising in 1715. Then, Sir James Dunbar's elder brother Kenneth, an officer in the Royal Navy who had inherited the title of Lord Duffus, had joined the Jacobite force led by the Earl of Mar. John Master of Sinclair kept a memoir of the events in which he presents an unflattering picture of Kenneth's role in the unfolding crisis: '... my Lord Duffus was sent to Scotland some time before, haveing bargained for as much monie as bear his charges doun; for, I suppose, my Lord Mar did not put that compliment on him of paying his debts, which would have been buying his service very dear. This por creature, who had no other qualitie but that of ane insatiable drouth, and who had neither house nor hold, being turned out of his ship, undertook to raise the countie of Southerland against their master, and his own Chief. Caithness he was no less sure of, and did not make the least scruple of a great part of the countie of Murreys [Moray] following him ...'.[22]

In 1715, the Earl of Sutherland had remained loyal to the Hanoverian king but the Earl of Caithness had bided his time to see what would happen, although most of his followers were reported to be pro-Jacobite. One of the Caithness lairds, none other than Elizabeth Dunbar's uncle, her father's brother, Sir Robert Dunbar of Northfield and Bowermadden, had clattered into Wick with a party of horsemen to drink the health of the Pretender at the mercat cross. Demonstrations such as these, however, seem to have been the extent of disaffection in the county, and there was no rising to follow Kenneth, Lord Duffus. The main force of the Jacobites was defeated in November 1715 on the field of Sheriffmuir. Kenneth evaded capture in the ensuing confusion but he was eventually arrested in Hamburg and thrown into the Tower of London until he was released under the Act of Indemnity. Like many Jacobite officers in the Navy, Kenneth went abroad to seek better fortune and found it in Russia, where Peter the Great was expanding his maritime power.[23]

In 1745, the Dunbars remained at Ackergill and waited for news from the south, conveyed in letters such as one from George Dunbar on 7 February 1746, when the Jacobites were in retreat to Inverness, pursued by the Duke of Cumberland's forces [27.2.2]. The letter, which was accompanied by two pounds of snuff for Lady Dunbar, was as chaotically spelt as ever; George managed even to get the address wrong, putting 'Hemperages' for Hempriggs. He passed on the news that the government forces had just reached Perth and that the 'Heailanders' were dispersing, seeing this as a sign that their troubles should be 'sauin [soon] att an end', but also warned Sir William that he should be attending to his debts - 'the Bank is very pressing. God knows but they will call for the wholle ase you have not bein puintwill [been punctual]'. George was hard-pressed himself and, despite a high demand in the west, the grain trade had been severely interrupted. He advised Sir William that he might get a better price for his Moray grain in Inverness than in the south.

The top part of the next letter from George Dunbar to Sir William is missing, but once again he writes in a tone ridden with anxiety about the political situation [27.2.1]. The date is probably April 1746, possibly after news of the battle of Culloden. '... I am in [such?] great conseren about the misurabell condision of alle Scotland in Generell that I cain not think of writing you particularly what has hapned in this places or oney wher for this nine monethes past,' he writes. 'I hope in God the greatest pairt of our troubles and miserey is over and that God may forgive them whae had the hand in bringing ther Cuntrey to rauien [ruin] and misirey.' George's concern over the state of the nation was matched by his worries about his own affairs, and he asks Sir William to send to him and John Luimesdell [Lumsdaine] money to satisfy the creditors as soon as the roads are open and it is safe to travel.

6 | *'noe man will meak me an offer'*

After the defeat of the Jacobites at Culloden in April 1746 and the subsequent occupation of the north by government troops, the Highlands became the focus of efforts to ensure that never again would they nurture a threat to the Hanoverian regime. The estates of lairds who had come out under the Jacobite banner were confiscated, in effect nationalised and handed over to the Commission for Forfeited Estates. As the Caithness lairds had remained loyal to the government, their properties were unaffected by this measure. The forfeited estates became foci for development which later did have influence in Caithness but in the short term the grain trade continued to be at the centre of economic life for the Dunbars and their neighbours.

George Dunbar kept up a lengthy correspondence with Sir William Dunbar on his efforts to find a market in Edinburgh for victual from Hempriggs and Ackergill. The price for grain fluctuated from year to year in accordance with supply and demand, and it seems that in mid-century good harvests were the norm. There were notable exceptions to this particularly in the years 1740, 1756, 1778 and 1782–83, when bad weather brought dearth to parts of the country[24], but by and large prices stayed moderate[25]. Possibly Caithness victual could not always match the Lowland product in quality because, as his letters show, George Dunbar found it difficult at times to secure a good price and sometimes any price at all and, to complicate matters, was falling into more financial difficulties. On 5 June 1759 he wrote 'I was favoured wt yours the 21 May advising you had 1300 bolles of Vittell to seaill but I dou asshouir you it is not in the power of man to seaill north cuntrey vittell in this pleais att aney prices. I reley belive Ulbster would seaill his att five shillings the bole but noe man will teak it I have spoik to ifrey man in this pleais but to noe purpies'

[6.7.20]. If the information that Ulbster, Sir William's neighbouring laird George Sinclair, father of the famous Sir John Sinclair who succeeded him in 1776, was failing to find a buyer was meant to make the Hemprigas laird feel slightly better, George probably had the opposite effect with his next comment where he mentions an enclosed bond for £200 which he had borrowed to pay what he himself owed on land he had rented. Sir Michael Stewart, the owner of this land, was threatening legal action against George, who sounds quite desperate in the letter – 'God forbide this shall be the last tiem efer I shall engadge wt you on that head'. Clearly much depended on the sale of the Caithness grain.

Almost a year later, in May 1760, George was finding the market for grain in Edinburgh still to be slow and Sir William's creditors to be impatient [6.7.26]. A merchant called Chalmers had offered to buy the Dunbar victual at 4s 6d the boll, and George did not think he could haggle upward to 5s. He appealed to Sir William to let him know what to do. 'Sir Michael Stewart is pressing for his last years Inst. with threats,' continued the unhappy George. 'I wish you would write him, there is severall others dunning me out of my life & God knows I have no money of yours in my hands to answer their demands.' To calm his fears he asked for Sir William's reassurance that no business was outstanding between the Dunbars and a Mr Budge. This was William Budge, probably a member of the Toftingall Budge family who was working in Edinburgh as a lawyer, merchant or agent.

Two weeks later, George had to impart the melancholy news that he had failed to find a buyer – 'it is not in my pouir to find a mercht for your vittell att any prices I have offered it att five shillings and noe man will meak me an offer. Ulbester has offered his att four shillings and sixpences and cannot find a mercht for my speireties is sounk when I think on your condision I shall dou alle in my pouir to meak you but dipend on it if you com to Edr without fondes [funds] you and I will be douned out of our life' [6.7.25]. By December 1761, George was more optimistic – 'There is no prices offering as yet for your Country victuall, however, its generally thought that there will be greater demands for it than there has been for these two years past. Youl write me what quantity you can sell this year' [6.7.22].

Throughout this time Sir William was fending off several creditors. One was the Edinburgh lawyer, John Lumsdaine, who wrote on 20 September 1752 [4.1.30]. Lumsdaine had bought some land and begged Sir William to let him have the money pledged in a bond – 'above two thousand pounds Scots' – so that he could meet the payment to fall due on the coming Martinmas. Despite the debt, Lumsdaine and Sir William were still on terms friendly enough for the lawyer to add a postscript that his son Jock and his new wife, and a few other mutual acquaintances, all sent their compliments to the Dunbars. John Lumsdaine and George Dunbar met to discuss the Dunbars' affairs, although George did not fully trust him, as he confessed in a letter to Sir William on 17 December 1761 [6.7.23]. The main point of this missive, though, was to tell Sir William that he, George, had been busy trying to resolve difficulties with the bank. These are not specified but they may well have been concerned with Sir William's debts.

In January 1762, George wrote to say he and Lumsdaine would do their best to sell Sir William's grain but did not sound optimistic [6.7.27]. Sir William also had a dispute with the Sheriff in Caithness, one in which George said he had the unanimous support of the House of Lords. When the matter with the Sheriff was resolved in February, George sent his congratulations and also said that he and Mr Budge had met the merchant George Chalmers [6.7.28]. The latter had been unwilling to buy grain at the prices George had insisted on – £5 Scots (7s 3d sterling) a boll for oatmeal, £4 (6s 6d sterling) for bere – but Budge had advised George to hold out in the short term and not lower his demand. More alarmingly, George intimates in a postscript a sense of impending illness – 'PS I have had strong threatning pains of my old aquaintance this winter and it is proper matters were settled'.

Though the Caithness lairds on the whole displayed a casual attitude to debts, Sir William may have been growing embarrassed and, if so, would have been depending on the sale of the grain to relieve his obligations. Some of the debts were long-standing: the Commissioners of Supply, the committee of lairds responsible for tax collection and in some ways a forerunner to the modern local authority, recorded in July 1752 how Lady Hempriggs still had not paid all the cess for 1727 (88.3.3). The Commissioners met at Watten and decided to order 'all proper Execution therefore by Quartering [sending troops to stay on her premises] Poinding or otherwayse.' Lady Hempriggs died on 11 March 1756 in her eightieth year, possibly still with unpaid obligations.

At last, in March 1762, George Dunbar found a buyer, apparently beating Sinclair of Ulbster to the deal: George Chalmers bought 1,200 bolls, half oatmeal, half bere, and sent a vessel north to Staxigoe to receive it and bring it south before 1 September; the price he agreed was £4 (6s 6d sterling) per boll, half to be paid at Lammas (1 August) and the remainder at Martinmas (11 November) [6.7.29].

Unfortunately, a shadow now fell across what was otherwise good news. Sir William began to be troubled by a discrepancy in his dealings with George Dunbar. He shied away from confrontation and wrote to William Budge, to express his concern and seek some help on 6 March 1763: '... You have not yet wrote me your opinion plainly of Geo Dunbars £300, nor advised me what I shall do about it. Its much against my inclination to have any question about our accounts But this is so material an article that it would certainly be ridiculous to sustain it without proper evidence, pray take the discretest way possible, to speak to him of it' [19.2.2]. On the reverse of the sheet Sir William enclosed a copy of another letter dated 20 March 1763, seemingly presenting further evidence of George's deceit or carelessness.

7 | *'Denounce him our Rebell'*

Sir William's first wife, Elizabeth Dunbar of Westfield, died on 3 June 1746 and on 21 March 1747 he married Jane Sinclair of South Dunn. Jane did not live for very long after the marriage – she bore no children before she died on 9 August 1749. Sir William then married for the third time – to Henrietta Rose, the second daughter of the laird of Kilravock – on 21 October 1749. Henrietta bore Sir William a son on 28 April 1761, the son who was eventually to succeed him as Sir Benjamin Dunbar of Hempriggs.

On 26 February 1762, Sir William's daughter, Janet, married a distant kinsman, Thomas Dunbar of Grangehill. Through the match, Thomas became Dunbar of Westfield, the family lands in Morayshire. George Dunbar wrote from Edinburgh to congratulate the couple and wish them 'all manner of happeyness' [6.7.29] but followed this a few days later with a warning to Sir William to think carefully about the settlement to be made for the couple – 'I would have you conseder calmley ore

Fig. 6. The family of Sir William Dunbar of Hempriggs, 2nd Bt.

More detail can be found in Henderson, *Caithness Family History*.

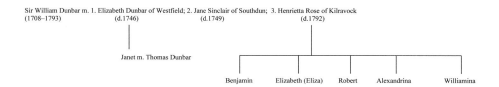

[before] you put a thing out of your oun pouir in your oun tiem [own power in your own time]' [6.7.24], Lear-like advice that was to prove perceptive.

Richard Pococke, a Protestant bishop in Ireland who, fortunately for us, seems to have spent much time travelling and writing, came through Caithness in July 1760, sending letters to his sister to describe everything he thought worth a mention. After a relatively easy crossing of the Firth from Longhope to Rattar, he rode west to Murkle and thence south-east through the heart of Caithness, where the mixture of corn rigs, heath and pasture appeared to him 'very agreeable'. He stayed with Sir Patrick Dunbar and rode on the following day down the valley of the Wick River 'to Acright [Ackergill], Sir William Dunbarr's, situated close to the sea by a fine old castle.'[26] The bishop told his sister nothing about his stay at Ackergill but he says Sir William did ride with him into Wick the next day and accompany him as far as Thrumster where George Sinclair of Ulbster took over as guide. A week later, the hardy bishop reached Forres where he noted that 'A beautiful situation at the West end of the town belongs to Sir William Dunbar; it was the site of an old Castle, on which a Modern house was begun to be built.' This was part of the property that Sir William was shortly to lose.

Late in 1763, Sir William wrote to Dr Joshua Mackenzie, a prosperous Edinburgh physician married to his sister-in-law Margaret Rose of Kilravock. These Mackenzies were descended from the eighth baron of Kintail and the most famous member of the family was to be Joshua's son, the novelist Henry Mackenzie. The reliability of George Dunbar was still much on Sir William's mind [19.2.3]. This time the worry was over a receipt for £100 sterling, a large enough sum to exercise Sir William – '... this is so ugly a story that the enquiry anent it must be gone quickly & discretely about, for it woud be much agst my inclination to charge any man of credit or character, more particularly George Dunbar, with any such gross affair, wherefore if I can come at the truth & can convince him of it Ill take a discharge of that sum and cancell it without more noise'. Sir William suggested to Dr Mackenzie that he use the excuse for inspecting the account books of the merchant George Chalmers without arousing suspicion.

The old acquaintance that returned to haunt George Dunbar in January 1762 remains unknown. It may have been the gout that the merchant William McGhee wrote to Sir William about on 7 May 1764 – 'Mr Dunbar has been above three mounths past confined with the Gout and is stille in such an uncertain way. That altho not in a dangerous way' [19.2.8]. The main purpose of McGhee's letter was to press for payment of a debt of £430 15s.

Bad as they were already, Sir William's financial difficulties grew worse. In September 1761, he and his wife had taken out a bond on a large loan of £2,000 sterling from the Royal Bank of Scotland. At the time, as we have seen, Sir William was having trouble finding a buyer for his grain crop and he may have thought that the bond was a safe way to see him through a financial patch more sticky than usual. The agreement was that Sir William would pay back the bond in annual instalments of £200 and, as surety, he had put up the list of properties comprising the barony of Westfield in Moray, including the castle hill and castle lands of Forres, and the townships and lands of Lingieston, Robertfield, Inschkenneth, Westfield, Inschagarlie and Inschbroch. The barony had been created by charter in July 1745. The Westfield lands had then been conveyed by sasine in 1764 to Thomas Dunbar on the occasion of the latter's marriage to Janet. When the son-in-law discovered that what he thought was his really belonged to the bank, a rift opened between him and his father-in-law.

By 1771 the Royal Bank was pursuing Sir William through the courts. The repayments on the bond had not been kept up since 1766 with the result Sir William owed £748 13s 1d of the principal sum and the interest. He was unable to meet this demand and, whereas friendship could in some cases have been relied upon to ameliorate personal obligations, the Royal Bank was less well disposed towards its debtors. To make matters worse, in 1769 the Westfield lands were conveyed to Sir James Grant of Grant. It is unclear whether this was done by Thomas Dunbar – the author of *A Survey of the Province of Moray* says he did[27] – but if this were the case Sir William after 1769 was no longer in charge of the lands he had put up as surety for his bond in 1761. (In 1773 the estate of Westfield was to be sold by roup, after which it passed into the hands of a London merchant, Joseph Robertson.)

An insistent and ominous demand was drawn up by the Royal Bank on 28 March 1771 according to the law, threatening Sir William with the horn and the poinding of his goods [88.1.5]. After the legal preamble, the document continued, 'Our Will is Herefore And We Charge You Strictly and Command that Incontinent these our Letters seen Ye pass and in our name and Authority Command and Charge the said Sir William Dunbar personally or at his Dwelling place To make payment … [of £748 13s 1d sterling] … Together with the Due and Ordinary Arent of the said remaining Principal sum from [11 January 1766] … and that within six Days next after He be Charged by You thereto under the pain of Rebellion and putting of him to our Horn wherein if he Faill the said Space being past Ye Denounce him our Rebell putt him to our Horn and use the haill remanent orders against him prescribed by law Attour[?] That Ye in our name and Authority foresaid Fence, Arrest, Apprize, Compell, Poind and Distrinzie All and Sundry the said Sir William Dunbar his readiest Goods Gear Corns, Cattles Insight Plenishing Horse Nolt Sheep Maills Farms profites & Duties of his Lands and Heritages Debts and sums of money and all other moveable Goods and Gear whatsoever ….'.

A messenger, Donald Macleod, was despatched north in December 1771 to deliver the legal document to Ackergill. Its arrival was witnessed by John Rosie and Alexander Miller, both described curiously as 'residenters in Thurso' although they must be the same two men who customarily looked after Sir William's affairs in his absence. Sir William had six days to come up with money or be declared a debtor and have all his livestock, goods and rents sequestered. He failed to meet the Bank's deadline and was duly put to the horn. Donald Macleod carried out his duty on 27 December by proceeding to the market cross in Wick and making the necessary public announcement. '… after my crying of three severall oyeses making open proclamation and publick reading of the said letter of inhibition in his majesty's name and authority,' reported Macleod. Everyone was put on notice not to have any dealings with Sir William in case he should try to dispose of any property before the Bank could secure what it was owed.

Sir William had gone from Caithness long before the Royal Bank's messenger had come seeking him. On 21 October 1768 he kept a copy of a letter he wrote to a John McLeland at Wester [19.2.9]. 'Everything has taken a very bad turn since [we] left Caithness, at least my Concerns – except you I think I have none to depend upon …,' wrote Sir William gloomily. His solution to his problems and to meet the need to educate his children was to rent his land to others. He asked McLeland, '… will you try to let all my estate together or in Parcells for a neat Rent payable yearly or half yearly take care of punctual paymentts, of the one half at Edinburgh and the other half at London Might not you, John Rossie [Rosie], Alexr Miller and such substantial people as you would like to bring in partners with you take it amongst your[selves] or would not Willy Innes like to have a lease …'.

Sir William emphasised to McLeland to 'remember to have this always in view that the houses, gardens and parks within dykes at Ackergill are the last to be let; & with them must go one half of custom peats of the whole estate; three days making hay, eight days winning carting & building it; eight full days of lifting [kelp?] from the sea.[?] & as much land plougd by every penney land any season they are call for as woud sow a Boll of Bear And a boll of bears sowing to be Cutt down & put in by every penneyland & killnd & milled if requird besides thatching the houses; so if you will sett the whole other parts of the estate independent of this, there will be no difficulty in making the rent of this'. Sir William wished to retain the option of coming back to his native braes – '[it] woud leave me at liberty to come amongst you some part of my time at least if things turned out more agreeable to me than they are at present'.

McLeland's identity has still to be established but Sir William's proposal of a scheme for renting his lands suggests he may have been a lawyer or tenant trusted to handle estate affairs. Sir William's plea that his beloved Ackergill be let last is touching. In this part of the letter he also mentions some details of rents paid in days of service by the tenants. The letter is also significant in that it contains the earliest mention we have so far found of Alexander Miller of Staxigoe, a man who was destined to become a very important figure in Caithness in the next few decades.

Personal tragedy crowded in on top of the financial problems. Janet, who had married Captain Thomas Dunbar, died in September 1769 at the age of only 27. Relations between Sir William and his son-in-law deteriorated. Sir William was plain about his own efforts to settle matters in a letter he wrote to John Rosie and Alex Miller on 8 February 1770: 'I was at Edinburgh with a view of settling matters with Capt Dunbar but not finding him there I travelled northward resolved to have been at Ackergill but finding at Inverness that he had passed by to Edinburgh I only went to Cromarty to see Lady Kilravock and returned directly to Edinbr where I tryd all methodes of bringing about a settlement but to no purpose; I did my endeavour to bring Mr Nicleson from Inverness to Edinbr believing he would have more influence in bringing the Captain into proper measures than any other; but Mr Nicleson woud not comply' [19.2.4]. It is a measure of the importance Sir William placed on his relationship with Captain Dunbar that, now in his early sixties, he was prepared to undertake hard travelling, probably by sea rather than by horse, in a vain effort to meet him. The Mr Nicleson [Nicolson] referred to was probably an Inverness solicitor.

By 1770 Sir William had been forced to let even Ackergill, except for the house and garden. A Mr Sutherland had taken out a tack on it and Sir William advised Rosie and Miller to deal with him. Perhaps the dispute with Captain Dunbar had unduly stressed Sir William for he tells Rosie and Miller, 'I shall endeavour everything as agreeable to you both as possible, and must still look upon you all as my friends, and honest servants; and I hope there will never be a question amongst any of you but what I will be able to decide to all your satisfactions.'

The tacksman, Sutherland, was to pay Sir William before Martinmas an agreed price for any cattle 'according to their ages' and, in line with this, Sir William asked Rosie and Miller to send promptly 'an exact list' of cattle, horses, implements and crops 'of the Mains'. When it came to the servants at Ackergill, Sir William made special provision for William Petrie and Robert Mackenzie, who were to be allowed the use of the garden and the house in the meantime.

8 | *'what in Caithness may be thought a great deall of money'*

A body of letters to Sir William Dunbar from David Murray of Castlehill survives among the Papers. The Murrays, who were styled of Clairdon as well as of Castlehill, were long established in the west of Caithness, owning or having an interest in properties in, for example, Thurso.[28] In or around the 1750s David acquired the property of Stangergill. With his wife, Margaret Innes of Borlum, he had four children.

In some of the letters, David Murray discusses the financial plight of Sir William Sinclair of Keiss, husband of Sir William Dunbar's sister Charlotte. On 9 March 1761, he wrote with his view of the situation, wording his opinions in a coy, guarded manner that makes tricky the interpretation of his meaning [8.6.12]. It would please him, said Murray, to see the Keiss laird's family relieved of their difficulties and the estate preserved as much as possible intact for the heirs. Sir William Dunbar naturally had an interest in the fortunes of his nieces, nephews and their offspring. According to Henderson's Family History, Sir William and Charlotte had had two sons and one daughter, but David Murray makes clear repeated reference to 'daughters'. There was also a grandson and granddaughter to consider, the children of Sir William's deceased elder son, Alexander.

What would happen to the Keiss estate? Hope rested with what Archibald, Sir William's younger brother, would do. 'If Mr Archibald shall take a concern and purchase the land, those who interest themselves in the mean time, will be soon condemnify'd,' opined David Murray, 'and if he does not I think it's more than probable the land will fall with the present purchaser.' The latter remains unnamed in the correspondence but it could well have been Sinclair of Ulbster. Whoever he was, Murray did not expect too much from him: 'If the gentleman you mention shall involve himself in Sir William Sinclair's affairs and settle them properly, and then dispone them to you or another with his own warrandrice, he'll deceive me greatly on the favourable side,' he said in sarcastic tone. Murray was reluctant to involve himself too strongly on the Dunbar side and told Sir William at Ackergill that he would sooner 'trail one of your harrows, and you us'd to be a pretty severe worker too' than lock horns in a dispute with the unnamed gentleman. Mr Archibald, now cast in the role of a potential saviour, was clearly seen by the Caithness people as having made a pile as a merchant in Jamaica where he still lived. Whether or not Archibald himself owned plantations is unknown, but many members of Highland families were deeply engaged in making money on slave-run plantations in the West Indies.

Sir William Sinclair is best remembered today as the man who introduced the Baptist Church to Scotland. His zeal for this denomination – he preached in his house at Keiss before a church was built, and he composed some sixty hymns[29] – may have puzzled and amused his neighbouring lairds and, whether it was from this evangelical side of him or from some other character trait, they appear to have found him, in David Murray's words, 'not … easy to deal with.' The fact that he had been a noted swordsman in his youth may also have given them pause. Murray went on: 'Tho' I gave you my opinion, I never did nor never will prescribe a measure for Sir William Sinclair of myself, to forward or retard him in any step in his affairs; That falls to those more connected, and who have more skill for it …'.

The next letter surviving in the series is dated in Thurso on 24 May 1767 and addressed to Sir William Dunbar in Edinburgh [8.6.17]. By this time, Charlotte Sinclair had died, and her widowed husband and her family were also residing in the capital or the vicinity. Murray had written to Archibald in Jamaica with the news and now Archibald had answered. 'Inclosed I take the liberty to send you a letter came by late post, under my cover from Mr Archibald Sinclair to Sir William Sinclair's daughters. His letter to me appears to have been wrote immediately upon the receipt of my letter to him, advising him of Lady Sinclair's death: but he says nothing particular to me respecting these young ladies or any of Sir William Sinclairs family; but says he'll write me soon more fully. I thought it best to send you the inclosed in case the ladys are still at Edinr; and if they are not if you shall choose yourself to open the letter to inforce with them anything their uncle may propose, I would think it perhaps necessary; but you can judge for yourself. Youll be so good as to forward it at any rate if they are not at Edinr. If I hear again from their uncle and have anything that is satisfying you shall be first advised of it.'

Two days later, Murray wrote again [8.6.16]. This time it was a short letter and probably penned in haste. The news was out that Sir William Sinclair was intending to sell Keiss but Murray was anxious that no deal should be concluded before definite word had come from the West Indies. 'I wrote his brother [Archibald] that

I believed Keiss would be soon publickly sold, and insisted with his brother that he should purchase it, as his former objection to his making the purchase was now removed Viz! That he never would take his brothers subjects out of his hand while he could keep them; I would think Sir William should not be rash in concluding a bargain about Keiss until ane answer from his brother is got as I think there is great chance if his brother should purchase it, that it may fall in his family...'.

Sir William Sinclair of Keiss was to die on 2 August, only a few months ahead, and at the time of Murray's letter he was probably in poor health, and possibly judged incapable of making decisions that were rational, or at least rational in the eyes of Murray and his friends. In the end, the Keiss estate was bought by the Sinclairs of Ulbster, for £7,000 sterling.[30]

Late in July there was more news from Archibald for Murray to pass on [8.6.15]. Sandy Sinclair, Sir William of Keiss's grandson, who had been out to visit his great-uncle in Jamaica was coming home and bringing with him from Archibald 'Ten hogsheads of our best sugar, and twelve puncheons of our finest rum.' This substantial amount of two valuable commodities was to be sold by Sandy in Glasgow 'to the best account, and when turned into cash, to deliver to you [to Sir William Dunbar] the one half of the neat proceeds, and you are to dispose of the same in such manner as you may think most proper and necessary for the benefit and advantage of Sir William Sinclair's daughters.'

In his letter, Archibald asked Murray to keep him informed about the young women and what he could do for them, but protested that people in Caithness should remember 'tho I may be worth what in Caithness may be thought a great deall of money my present inbromissions are considerable, and I owe likewise a good deall of money: and I have all along thought it my interest and agreeable to my inclination, tho a bachelor, to support such a figure as my fortune could consistently afford: and there are others as well as they, I find myself under obligation to do more or less for, which must be the case with all men who have been engaged in any considerable dealing, where they are not entirely destitute of gratitude: and I have had my friends and support in my time whose very succession I would think it base to overlook. I'll be impatient untill I hear from you how all my friends are.' Archibald was to remain in Jamaica, preferring the salubrious climate and the comfortable lifestyle there to an alternative in Scotland, and died unmarried.

David Murray proposed that the money from the sale of the sugar and the rum brought back by Sandy be kept by his nephew, George Oswald, and spent on necessaries for the daughters. The young women were now in London but Murray was adamant in his letter to Sir William Dunbar that while they remained there 'they will not touch one penny of it ... as money in their hands at London might be dangerous, or at any rate hastily thrown away, which might exasperate their uncle, and prevent his doing anything further for them.' Far better, argued Murray, hoping that Sir William would agree with him, for them to return to Caithness and furnish a room in Keiss, where they could 'have the benefit of the customs and profites of the Mains untill the land is sold and as much money yearly from the fund as you may think proper for their pocket money and cloaths …'. Murray thought £30 or £40 a year would suffice for the latter items in Keiss, or £50 or £60 a year if they moved elsewhere. Similar rules could apply to looking after the grandchildren.

Those of Murray's letters that have been examined make no further reference to the Sinclairs of Keiss, and we are probably safe in assuming that the young ladies and the grandchildren were looked after, perhaps as Murray suggested. Sir William Sinclair's grandson, Alexander, whom we met above as Sandy on his way home from Jamaica with sugar and rum, served in the army, as a lieutenant in the 88th Regiment of Foot, otherwise known as Campbell's Highlanders, which existed for only three years from 1760 to 1763 but saw action in Europe in the Seven Years' War. Alexander became the third baronet of Dunbeath. He returned to the West Indies and it was in the New World, on a voyage from Jamaica to Halifax in 1786, that he died, leaving no heir.

9 | *'one of the best civilized shires in Scotland'*

'This [Caithness] is allowed by all Impartial visitors & writers,' wrote Aeneas Bayne in 1735, 'to be one of the best civilized shires in Scotland, nothing Barbarous or inhumane to be seen even among the vulgar, as for the Gentry they surpass generally some of the northern shires as much in politeness of Behaviour as in nobleness of Spirit and liberall Education…'. The first impression is that Bayne is full of praise for his native braes. A little later in his essay, he observes that the gentlemen make the law their chief study. '…In which they are so great proficients that they can't be satisfyed with a Home Decision,' he continues, 'But must trudge immediately to Edinr to have it decided by the Court of Session, so prevalent is the pride & vanity & turbulent restless humour of this northern shire that time out of memory they have been usefull to the Parliament House at Edinburgh by their law suits.' Now one begins to sense that Bayne may after all be writing in an ironic tone, poking fun at the Caithness landowners.[31]

'The office of Sherriff & Justiciar is heretable and of very great consideration: Justice of peace Courts are also kept …' recorded Bayne. A Commissary Court had jurisdiction over small civil affairs, chiefly to rule in inheritance cases. In Bayne's day, the courts were all held in Thurso, where the clerk and officers of court happened to reside and where the records were kept, but this arrangement was a contentious matter and many would have agreed with Bayne when he said that the courts 'ought to have been holden' in Wick, the royal burgh, where public meetings of the 'gentlemen' and elections of members of parliament took place. According to the terms of the charter of James IV founding the sheriffdom of Caithness in 1503, Wick should have been the seat of the court but it shifted to Thurso at some time during the 1600s and remained there, despite all protests, until 1828.[32]

The heritable office of sheriff had been acquired by the Sinclairs of Ulbster in 1718, when John Sinclair had bought it for £2,000 from Campbell of Glenorchy (who had of course acquired it in 1674 with the takeover of the earl's estates). The heritable nature of the office was abolished in 1748 in the wake of the last Jacobite rising and, although Sinclair of Ulbster retained the title of sheriff, the legal powers associated with it were transferred to part-time judges, designated sheriffs-depute, appointed by the Crown. The sheriff-depute had his own legal practice to run and was usually not compelled to reside within his jurisdiction, where during his absences he could leave much of the work to an assistant called the sheriff-substitute. The first individuals in this new arrangement in Caithness were James Brodie, assisted by sheriff-substitute John Gibsone. Gibsone was the son of Alexander Gibson, minister of the parish of Canisbay from 1713 until his death in 1747. In April 1754 John Sinclair of Freswick became sheriff-depute of Caithness.

Aeneas Bayne also described how in the Westminster parliament Caithness 'has a common member with that of Bute.' Under the terms of the Union in 1707 the number of Scottish MPs was set at forty-five and, as it were, to make the country fit this number of representatives Caithness-shire was combined with Bute in a single constituency and the two places took turns to send a man to London, an arrangement that lasted until the Reform Act of 1832. The first MP for Caithness was James Dunbar of Hempriggs, who returned on 2 November 1710. He was succeeded on 17 February 1715 by Sir Robert Gordon of Gordonstown. The next three MPs were Patrick Dunbar of Bowermadden – from 31 August 1727, Alexander Brodie of Brodie – from 4 June 1741, and Sir Harry Munro of Fowlis – from 22 July 1747. Three of the five MPs in the first half of the eighteenth century were, therefore, men from outside the county but as the lairds around the Moray Firth all knew each other and were often related by marriage or blood this probably mattered little in their eyes. It is also interesting to note at this time that the Sinclairs, later so prominent in parliament, were well represented among those who voted but had still to come to the fore as successful candidates. As representatives and as major landowners, the Dunbars had of course a very close interest in these matters of governance.

Only freeholders who held property from the Crown with a rental value of 40 shillings or more, and men who occupied land rated at £400 Scots (about £35 sterling) or above had the vote. As a result in the whole of Scotland the county electorate numbered only 2,889 men. This system made it relatively easy and tempting to try to influence the outcome of an election by personal persuasion; by stacking the electoral role with one's supporters; and, because the members of the voting roll were determined at a head court held before the sheriff, by making use of the opportunity to challenge who had the right to vote in the first place. The malpractices were well known and widely indulged in – in relation to the election in 1768, a writer in the *Scots Magazine* was moved to enquire 'Does not the highest corruption, prostitution and venality everywhere appear?' – but calls for reform were slow to gain ground.[33]

In her biography of Sir John Sinclair of Ulbster, Rosalind Mitchison argues that in Caithness before 1740 political power lay in the hands of the Dunbars until, in that year, George Sinclair of Ulbster, Sir John's father, took an interest and used his influence as sheriff to get his uncle, Alexander Brodie of Brodie, elected.[34] Brodie served until 1747, and died in 1754, the year of the next election in Caithness. For the general election held in that year, the voters' roll in Caithness had thirty-five names. Sir Patrick Dunbar of Northfield appeared first, with Sir William Dunbar of Hempriggs as number twenty (Appendix 4). The Dunbars' favoured candidate was Captain John Scott of the Royal Scots Regiment, whom they promoted in an effort to wrest some influence back from the Ulbster Sinclairs. Mitchison says that Scott was distant kin to the Dunbars through his mother, and that he was well known as a gambler, reputed to be the richest man in Scotland, and author of a book on the rules of whist. A document in the Dunbar papers dated October 1796 hints at a ploy by which votes could be ensured for the captain [91.4.3]. The estate of Hempriggs had been placed under entail. Sir William's mother, the redoubtable Lady Elizabeth Dunbar who in 1750 was 74 years old, seems to have consented to Sir William parcelling out the valued rental of the estate to afford 'no fewer than eight votes' in the forthcoming election. A temporary arrangement was made whereby the feudal superiority of the estate was assigned to Captain Scott for the sum of the feu duty of £70 Scots. Captain Scott parcelled this into three votes, giving £20's worth each to Sir Robert Gordon of Gordonstown and Peter Hay of Leys, and retaining the third vote for himself. Lady Dunbar's balance of five votes were no doubt assigned to trusted voters in a similar way, possibly explaining why the freeholders' roll in 1754 came to include several names with no obvious Caithness connection. This method of fixing votes was to cause some bother for Sir William's son in the 1790s but in the immediate term it helped to secure its objective and Captain Scott, who appears himself on the voters' roll at number eighteen, was duly returned as the MP for Caithness.

Scott belonged to Balcomie in Fife. At the time of his election as the MP for Caithness he was in his twenty-ninth year. After his years as the county's representative, he became colonel of the 26th Regiment, better known as the Cameronians, and in November 1770 married Lady Mary Hay, the daughter of the Earl of Errol, a union that failed to last – possibly because Mary was only 16 and Scott 45 – and after one year ended in divorce; one account has it that Mary eloped with another man. Scott bought Denmylne Castle in Fife in 1772 and in 1773 married again, this time more successfully, to Margaret Dundas. The couple had three daughters who all made matches of high social standing: Henrietta (born in 1774) married the fourth Duke of Portland[35]; Lucy (born in 1775) married the tenth Earl of Moray; and Joan (born 1776) married George Canning who held government positions as chancellor of the exchequer and as foreign secretary and briefly served as prime minister in 1827.

The next general election did not take place until 1761 when it was Bute's turn to return a representative to Westminster. John Scott weathered the loss of his Caithness seat by being returned unopposed for the constituency of the Tain burghs (a grouping of Tain with Dingwall, Dornoch, Kirkwall and Wick).

Three years before the 1761 election, at the end of March 1758, the Earl of Moray, James Stuart, was in correspondence with Sir William Dunbar to secure the latter's vote in support of the earl's brother, Colonel Francis Stuart of Pittendreich, who had ambition to be an MP. 'The experience of past times prompts me to make this earlie application to you, to beg that favour of your Vote & interest for my brother,' wrote the earl, '… to represent the Shire of Elgin & Forres in Parliament the first vacancy that happens' [4.1.20]. Colonel Stuart was in Ireland at the time with his regiment but the earl said he would pay his respects to Sir William as soon as he could get leave of absence. '…It is natural for me … to apply to the relations of our Family for their assistance to revive its interest in that part of the country where it so long has layne dormant … If upon this occasion you are pleased to honor your Cusin with your Countinance I need not hint to you the advantage it will be to let your friends know in this county as soon as possible the scale into which you have thrown your weight …'.

The earl wrote again to Sir William on 29 August with more campaign news [4.1.18]. He was sure of the vote of George Cumming of Altyre – they had dined together at Dallas a few days earlier – but the earl wished he could 'say as much for Tannackie but I incline to be silent upon that subject until we meet as it is fitter for conversation than paper.' Tannackie, or Tannachy, was the Stuart laird of an estate in the parish of Rathven to the south-west of the present village of Portgordon. The earl felt uncertain of any support from the provost of Elgin, James Robertson of Bishopmill, and possibly did not know him well, as he refers to him as 'Robinson'; and was also concerned that at the head court where the list of freeholders would be determined two claims would be given in for enrolment. In case of objections, it was essential that the earl's friends should attend – 'I make no doubt of your being present,' the earl wrote to Sir William, ending his letter by repeating the need to talk – 'I have something to communicate to you by word of mouth which are by no means fit to be put upon paper as letters sometimes miscarry' – and urging Sir William to come to stay at Darnaway Castle as soon as he could. The Elginshire seat had been in the hands of the Grants for a long time. In 1761, despite the efforts of the Stuarts, nothing changed. Sir James Grant won the seat, succeeding his father Sir Ludovick Grant who had been the MP for the preceding twenty years. In 1768, Sir James was succeeded in turn by Francis Grant.

10 | 'a most exorbitant cruel & ill founded sentence'

The next general election in Caithness took place early in 1768 but before then Sir William Dunbar became embroiled in a dispute with Sinclair of Freswick, sheriff-depute of the county since 1754. According to Henderson, the Dunbars and the Sinclairs of Freswick were on opposite sides of the political fence at this time.[36] The latter family began their rise to prominence in the 1660s when William Sinclair of Rattar acquired the Freswick estate from the Mowats of Buchollie. William was succeeded by three of his sons – James, Robert and David – who all inherited the estate in turn and died childless, with the outcome that in the mid-eighteenth century Freswick reverted to David's nephew, William. This William Sinclair has been accorded by tradition a somewhat unsavoury reputation, possibly because he was a man of ability who rose to challenge some of the leading families, not least the Dunbars. Henderson's family history of Caithness tries to be fair, describing him as 'vindictive and somewhat unscrupulous towards his enemies' but also 'a generous and considerate friend'. William Sinclair was responsible for building in the 1750s the gaunt tower of the House of Freswick, and he also implemented an ambition to expand the family holdings, acquiring wadsets to Dunnet and Greenland, buying lands in Canisbay from the Groat family and, in 1751, purchasing for £3,000 the estate of Dunbeath. The Dunbars and their neighbouring lairds may well have been worried by the growing influence of Freswick and, when Freswick's son, John, an advocate, became sheriff-depute of Caithness in April 1754, the alarm among them must have been boosted to new heights.

The Dunbeath lands abutted the Dunbar lands at Dalnawillan. A dispute arose over the boundary and, more particularly, over allegedly illegal peatcutting by Sinclair tenants on Dunbar ground. In November 1757 William Budge, a lawyer in

Edinburgh, wrote to Sir William Dunbar about two summonses that Sir William had executed on Freswick. The process had been done wrongly, said Budge; the summonses to John Sinclair the sheriff-depute and two of the tenants had been delivered by the leaving of copies of the document in the lockholes of their house doors without either refusal of access or any refusal by servants to take the documents (11.6.2). Litigious lairds revelled in this kind of legal technicality.

Almost a year later, in August 1758, Budge was corresponding with Sir William about where to hold a commission to investigate the boundary claims. Budge was persuaded that Freswick's people would not agree to take the commission hearings at James Sutherland's house and, continued the lawyer, they could not be taken at Dunbeath 'by reason of the Burn' (15.7.11). The objection to holding the hearing at James Sutherland's house was undoubtedly because James Sutherland of Langwell – and it can be no other – was married to Sir William Dunbar's sister, Rachel. His dwelling could hardly be neutral ground. 'The only medium, & which happened att taking the proof betwixt Southdun and Toftingall [not only the Dunbars became involved in boundary disputes] is to order the proof to be taken on the controverted grounds in general,' advised Budge, adding with a comic touch '& in that case you may dwell in Tents like the Antient Patriarchs, or retire to the first house adjacent which necessarily will be Sutherlands.'

In October 1758 Budge received copies of the proof of the case between Dunbar and Freswick with a sketch of the disputed ground, and told Sir William in a letter on the 17th that he could not help observing that if Freswick continued with the proof in the manner he had shown in the report 'it will make a very odd figure here' [15.7.9].

In the end, the case went before the Court of Session in Edinburgh. The law lords found for Sir William, and Freswick had to stump up for expenses and damages.[37] As was often true of such legal disputes, this one rumbled on for a few years. In February 1762, William Budge was still corresponding about the aftermath of the dispute when Freswick's lawyers were contesting the expenses that Sir William had claimed [11.6.27].

Ill feeling from that encounter fed into the next when, four years later, Freswick and Sir William locked horns over a different matter, a more serious business arising from legal proceedings against two men, John MacBeath and William Thompson. The story began on 13 November 1766 when James McKie, officer of excise in Caithness, asked Thompson, skipper of a boat in Dunbeath, and John McBeath, a servant of Freswick, to go with him along the Latheron shore. McKie had three others with him, and two or three guns in the boat, one of which he gave to Thompson to carry. Although the document in which this is recorded, the summons later raised by the sheriff[38], does not give the purpose of this jaunt, we can surmise that McKie was investigating whether or not smuggling may have been taking place and was scouting for signs of the landing of contraband. (A year later, the advocate Charles MacKenzie was to imply publicly that McBeath's smuggling was open knowledge.) The party passed close by the shore at Latheronwheel, a farm belonging to Sir William Dunbar of Hempriggs and at the time held in tack by James Sutherland of Swinzie. Tenants or servants of the latter were up on the braes above the sea and they suspected or pretended to suspect that McKie and company were bent on shooting seals in a cave below, infringing a right that belonged to Sir William and the tacksman. Alexander Miller, one of the Latheronwheel men, threw rocks down into the boat. McKie called to him 'to desist & that their Boat & Lives were in danger from what he was doing, notwithstanding whereof he redoubled his outrage.' McKie and Thompson held up their guns to show they were armed and ready to defend themselves. Miller desisted, and nothing else happened on that occasion.

On the following day, however, John Sutherland in Ladybist [Loedebest] came to Thompson and said he had a warrant from Swinzie as a Justice of the Peace (JP) to summon Thompson to appear before him. No document was shown, according to the summons raised by the sheriff. Thompson was at the beach making ready to go to sea 'with sundry others to bring some goods on shore from a ship which was then on the coast.' McBeath advised Thompson to see Swinzie after they came back ashore rather than break the engagement with the ship. On 18 November, the constable apprehended Thompson and McBeath on Swinzie's orders 'upon pretence of a Warrand', and were brought to Swinzie's house where they were put into a room. After half an hour McBeath sent a message via a servant to Swinzie that he 'had the care of his master's house & would be wanted at home & therefore could wait no longer, & no return being made to the message …[McBeath] went away but had not gone far' before Swinzie followed and called him back. McBeath went back. Swinzie 'then gave reprobius language & flew in a passion That the Complainer [McBeath] did not take of his Bonnett when he spoke to him & acting the part of a Constable himself instead of a judge laid hold of the Complainer by the Breast & dragg'd him to him, but the Complainer knowing no right that he had to do so & that every man is entitled to self defence Grip't on his part the said James Sutherland by the Breast to prevent him doing him a Mischeif, whereupon another Gentleman Came from his house & Interpos'd …'. McBeath was advised to go back to the house which he did 'immediately & peaceably.' Swinzie wrote an account of what he called McBeath's 'obtripious Behaviour' but McBeath refused to sign it. Swinzie then ordered McBeath and Thompson to be put in Wick Tolbooth. They were taken there that night, a distance of 16 Scots miles 'at that severe season of the year' and were in prison at 11 o'clock at night. Freswick happened to be in Wick and saw them arrive. He asked McBeath what was the matter, and promptly granted him a bail bond for £20 sterling. The writer John Russell granted a similar bond for £15 for Thompson.

This overruling of a JP by the sheriff was seen by Swinzie and his colleagues as an act of spite. Sir William Dunbar, Captain James Sutherland of Langwell, David Murray of Castlehill, and Sir William's son-in-law Captain Thomas Dunbar were among the fifteen JPs in the county – all opposed to the sheriff to some degree.[39] They closed ranks in defence of Swinzie, who was elderly and in poor health, and saw the tussle with McBeath and the later bailing of the miscreants by the sheriff as a threat to their position and the peace of the county. Those who saw the matter from the other side felt that the proceedings against the two men had been brought only because one was a tenant and the other a servant of the sheriff. The JPs interrogated the Wick bailies who had released the prisoners on the sheriff's orders: in the JPs' eyes, they were 'certainly highly culpable for so doing but they being ignorant Brewers and retaillers of ale and other liquors seemed to have been influenced & overpersuaded by John Sinclair of Freswick … and it cannot be denied that they the Baillies had reason to think that he was a Better Judge of the Law than they were & would use itt.'

The JPs convened a court in Wick to begin at 10 o'clock on Thursday 27 November and boldly summoned everyone concerned, including the sheriff, to appear. In the usual way, the summons was broadcast throughout the county by being pinned up on kirk doors where everyone who attended worship on the Sabbath, the bulk of the population, would be sure to see it. Warrants were issued for the apprehension of Thompson and McBeath who were to be brought to Wick and kept separately 'in sure and close prison'. The constables were warned by the JPs to do their duty and not be intimidated by the sheriff. Freswick, however, and perhaps unsurprisingly, did not heed the summons.

Judging by the account of this court recorded in the summons against the JPs, admittedly a possibly one-sided report, what transpired that day in Wick was hardly fair on the accused. McBeath in particular was the target of the JPs' wrath. Swinzie had prepared a minute of what allegedly had happened. This was read to Thompson and McBeath. They were asked if the facts were true. They replied that they had given a written warrant to a procutor (a procurator, or solicitor) to speak in their defence and would prefer to be heard by him. The JPs refused to let the procutor, who was Donald McLeod the sheriff-depute's clerk, speak and when McLeod insisted on his right to be heard told him they would be obliged to take him into custody unless he stayed quiet – 'in fact he was soon turned out of the room' despite the protests of Thompson and McBeath that they were now left without counsel and had no documents on which they might prepare a defence. The JPs then had the two men placed in different corners of the room 'to preclude them from even the poorest chance of acting for themselves'.

Swinzie took a prominent role in the proceedings, reading statements and asking witnesses to confirm their truth, and allowing all the witnesses to stay and hear each other's depositions. McBeath refused to answer as to the correctness of Swinzie's minute from the 19th and was told that his obstinacy would aggravate the crime he was accused of, and that the JPs would find it necessary to make an example of him. 'Notwithstanding of all this he persevered in his Obstinacy & muteness ...' reads the summons, before going to report that 'For thrie compleat days did the before mentioned Justices sit upon this Notable affair, their Deliberations terminated in a most exorbitant cruel & ill founded sentence ... McBeath is fined and ammerciated in no less a sum than £30 sterling & ordained to remain in prison ay & untill payment thereoff to John Sutherland Clerk of the Peace, which is neither more nor less than sentence of Imprisonment for Life as it is impossible for any in his situation of life who has not a shilling but his wages to raise and pay such a sum & it is expressly contrary to the Clame of right guarding against the exorbitancy of fines ...'. The sentence further ordained that McBeath was to remain in prison until he find sufficient bail for keeping the peace 'by behaving decently and discreetly to every individual person within the County under penalty of £100 sterling for every such offence he is convicted of.' The summons declared that this was a wanton piece of cruelty on the part of the JPs, as it would be in the power of any of them or any man in the county to levy £100 any time McBeath 'does not lift his bonnett to him in the field ...'. The JPs then ordered McBeath to be detained in prison for one month from the day the fine and the bail were paid. Thompson was given a much lighter sentence, a fine of £5 sterling and prison until it was paid, bail to ensure orderly behaviour and £20 to be fined for every future offence.

The men were kept in prison until 27 December when, by the interposition of the Justice of the Supreme Court after an application by the sheriff to the Court of Session for a Bill of Suspension, they were set at liberty. Freswick called for the JPs to be ordered by the Court of Session to make payments to Thompson and McBeath of £500 sterling or such other sum as the Court should set for damages and reparation for their illegal imprisonment, and a further £300 for expenses.

Sir William and his fellow JPs were now faced with defending their conduct. 'There is no doubt that sentences of the Justices of the Peace except in some revenue matters may be suspended as well as the sentences of any other inferior judge,' explained the advocate Charles MacKenzie, writing from Edinburgh to Sir William on 21 January 1767 [86.2.3], 'The incarcerating [of] Thomson and McBeath after they had found baile [sic] was wrong but I hope it will be made appear that the Justices proceedings arose from no improper motives ...'. The advocate went on to agree that MacBeath had been 'most insolent' and noted that Freswick was in the habit of favouring his own people: 'the Countenance he commonly gave to his own tenants & servants however much in the wrong.' Before moving on to other topics, MacKenzie even hinted that further investigation seemed to be called for: 'If the Justices have committed any irregularity or have gone too great a length on the punishment they proposed to inflict which may prevent the Lords from confirming their sentences yet if the situation of your County with respect to the administration of justice is properly considered & represented in a true light to the Lords I cannot [think] the Lords will give such a judgement as would throw a reflection on the Justices.'

In Sir William's view, Freswick's Bill of Suspension had been 'full of gross falsehood and misrepresentation.' [19.2.22] and perhaps the Lords of the Court of Session had not been able on the eve of the Christmas vacation to give it their proper attention. The passing of the Bill had impressed those who knew nothing of the case to think that the justices had done wrong.

James Sutherland of Swinzie wrote to Sir William on 3 February, including the information that he was putting pen to paper at six o' clock at night. He excused his non-attendance at Ackergill by saying that he had not been quite well for some days with 'a Cough & and a little swimming in my head' and his wife had been confined to bed for ten days [26.3.26]. Apparently there had been a meeting at the Dunbar home about how to proceed in the Freswick affair. A representation to the Court of Session had been drawn up but had not yet been laid before their Lordships. Swinzie thought this was lucky as now it would be presented as a reply to a summons executed by Freswick rather than as a complaint against him. Because of 'Accounts' in the sentences delivered on Thomson and MacBeath, Freswick had charged the justices of the peace with defamation. The justices had opined that there were suspicions of the sheriff 'countenancing disorders in the County'. 'But now as by the Sheriff's Charge you are obliged to defend,' advised Swinzie, 'you can now justly tell out every tenable Article and that can be proven that is contain'd in your Representation …'. Swinzie's ill health was more serious than he probably realised; he was to die before the end of the month.

Sir William proceeded with his dispute and Charles MacKenzie clearly thought he had good grounds for doing so, for in a letter he wrote on 7 February to Sir William he mentioned how the justices had 'several instances' of Freswick's 'misconduct' [86.2.6].

Sir William expressed to Colonel Scott the desire of the justices to be 'quitt of the Sheriff' [19.2.22]. 'I have wrote Lord Advocate on this subject and do expect his regard for publick Order and Decency will prompt him to grant us his Concurrence – and I do positively averr [sic] that no man cane be lookd upon as a good countryman and you in particular [i.e. Scott] cannot be lookd upon as a Friend to this Country or to ye justices of Peace who have been your Friends and support in Parliament and who are now unanimous in this Cause – if you do not at least Remove the Sheriff from us.'

Sir William went to say that their legal advisers had suggested various ways forward, including laying the whole matter before the Lord Advocate, as the senior law officer in Scotland, and presenting a petition to the government or to the king. 'I think myself obliged to tell you that the Sheriff <u>must fall</u> or we must fall,' declared Sir William, '… [we] resolved to bear the expence & not to stop till we get at the King, and we certainly will publish a memorial thro' all Britain if necessary …'.

The legal processes were to go on for some time. A complication arose from the need to appoint a sheriff clerk for Caithness. On 11 February 1767, Charles MacKenzie told Sir William that this was unlikely to be settled until it became known whether J. Gibson, presumably the incumbent in the post of clerk, was likely to recover from illness [86.2.7]. (John Gibson was later to stand as a candidate supported by Freswick in the 1768 general election.) MacKenzie had considered applying for the post himself – it could be a lucrative position – but Colonel Scott was supporting the candidate put forward by Sinclair of Ulbster. By July some of the party opposing Freswick were beginning to feel a chill around their feet: David Murray wrote to Sir William, then in Harrogate, on the 27th that he had told James Sinclair of Durran, one of the JPs, that in a cause such as theirs 'in which we were all equally concerned, it would be very gross and indelicate in any of us to decline to concurring in every measure that you pointed at…' [8.6.15]. 'Fear, or grudging the necessary expence, in any of us, may undoe the whole,' continued Murray.

Sir William's petition on behalf of himself and the other Caithness JPs was rejected in the Court of Session in August 1767. 'We were obliged to give in our Condescendance last night [and] some paragraphs are ordered to be struck out of it,' Charles MacKenzie continued, after breaking the bad news to Sir William. 'I suppose Lord Alemore will on Tuesday next allow a proof as the Court were unanimous in confer you with respect to a proof of the Sheriffs conduct. This case I am afraid will turn out ill.' MacKenzie had written to London to the House of Lords by that night's post to know if an appeal could be entered on the 31st, a legal device 'to evade the proof this vaccance' when the lawyer would face 'many disadvantages', presumably through having to present evidence during a holiday period.

The proof or the hearing of the case did not in fact take place until October in Inverness. On the way back north on the 12th, David Murray paused at Landhallow at Latheron to take the opportunity to bring Sir William up to date with what had happened in the courtroom, emphasising what he was doing by adding as a note at the end of the letter 'I have not yet got home' [8.6.14]. Murray felt confident that if Sir William could bestow on the case his 'weight & a little seasonable attention … it must have a chance of turning the scales, or the Lords will shew themselves as partial as ever they did in any one cause.' In Murray's view, the 'flagrancy' of the sheriff's conduct and the 'propriety' of Sir William's would become increasingly apparent during the proof.

'I was myself sixteen hours under examination,' he wrote, '& they put several questions to me, with the little art they had calculated to get half of the truth, &

that part of it which favoured their purposes, but I attempted at all times as much as I was at liberty from the nature of the questions to lae [sic] out the whole truth.'

Murray gave two instances of how he had performed under this prolonged and, in his view, biased questioning.

'They very judiciously interrogate me "If you [Sir William] pointed at the sherriff as well as MacBeath & Thomson in your minutes & sentence, & what reason did you give me for so doing." I told them "I had no doubt but you pointed at both & that the reasons you gave for so doing were the gross insults offered Swinzie, the extraordinary contempt of the authority of the justices [,] former attempts to lessen the powers of the justices, & your conviction of the great impropriety that Mr Sinclair younger of Freswick, being sherriff of Caithness, & of which conviction you said you cou'd satisfy the world from clear evidence of facts of circumstances.'

'The other question they put me was "Was there any other higher fine or corporal punishment proposed to be put upon MBeath, I told them there was "That I myself from the gross insult he offered Swinzie then in a very valetudinary state of health, & for whom I had a great affection, & his contempt of the justices authority, & my conviction that his circumstances could well bear a higher fine, induced me to propose a fine of £50 Ster which was suppressed by the other justices, & particularly by you & Swinzie; They then enquired who proposed a higher corporal punishment; I told them "It was Capt Dunbar as a military man, that had a high sense of the contempt of authority", but this last part they did not take down; They then enquired, "What cause I had for my belieff of MBeaths circumstances" My answer was "That it proceeded from the information I had, which I never heard contradicted that there was numbers of vessells for many years back that frequented the parish of Lathron coast loaded with wine, brandy, Geneva & tea & that MBeath bought & sold of these goods, & that a clear prooff I was positive would come out of that fact", I likewise weakened if not totally defeat the force of the clamour of the unexamined witnesses being in the court house during the examination of the other witnesses. The sherriff & his lawyer & the Commissioner directed me frequently to dictate my answers myself, which I did, but when they suspected any critical part to proceed from me the Commissioner wou'd insist on dictating my answers, which I wou'd not allow, & upon this they insisted to have a certificate from the Commissioner that I had declined his dictating my oath, & that I was prolix & said many things that appeared to him extranious; which is all byass nonsense & illnature because I wou'd not answer the questions partially to favour them.'

On 26 October Charles MacKenzie wrote to Sir William to tell him that he had until then seen only a part of the sheriff's proof, that in his view the sheriff had failed to prove the JPs had used irregular methods to examine witnesses, and that he hoped that Colonel Scott would be able to prevail with Freswick 'either to make it up or get a submission entered into' [86.2.16]. David Murray was concerned lest Colonel Scott should reach some kind of compromise with the sheriff, an eventuality that would bring upon Sir William and the others 'a stigma, a littleness & lowness … in the character of Caithness justices that will not only stick to you & them but descend to your posterity, & I told John Sutherland that' [8.6.14]. Murray sounded much relieved when he wrote again on 29 October (Sir William was in Pontefract): 'It was the general opinion over all this countery [sic] before Coll Scot appeared, That to make all his friends, the Barrons, in his interest, he might be too anxious and goe too farr in gratifying the Sherriff in a compromise twixt him and the justices…'. After spending time with the colonel, Murray could say 'I am greatly pleased with him as a man of sense and resolution … I heard the Coll lay in all companys publickly that his friends might take any plan most agreeable to themselves in dealing with the Sherriff …'. It was the colonel's opinion, reported Murray that the dispute ought to be submitted to the king's advocate whom he knew would do all in his power to save the justices and that he was to make this proposal to the sheriff (8.6.11). At the end of October Charles MacKenzie had more to say about the case: 'I understand some things which may be of service has come out in our proof viz that Breamore [sic] was sent to the meeting by the Sheriff to be a spy on the Justices & that he brought instructions from him to Donl McLeod & had a meeting with McLeod privately & in these instructions the Sheriff owned his men had done some wrong. It is proved McBeath is a man in good circumstances & concerned in a smuggling made with Hay at the Water of Dunbeath.' [86.2.14].

This must have been good news to Sir William. It may have encouraged him to take up the colonel's idea of approaching the king's advocate, as on 7 December Charles MacKenzie wrote to say that 'The petition to the King which you propose would be proper enough if the whole gentlemen were as earnest in the cause as yourself, but the proceedings before the Court of Session has intimidated them greatly. A sufficient number would scarcely be got to join in it & such an application ought to appear as the Common Voice of the Country. I hope this appeal will hing up the cause for some time & if the Coll does not get matters setled, upon your return to Caithness you must get the whole gentlemen concerned to concur with spirit on whatever measure shall be thought most advisable' [86.2.15].

In the middle of December, James Sinclair of Durran wrote from Tister to Sir William. '…I am truly at a loss what to say on that unlucky [experience?] process with the Sheriff but all your friends are well satysfied [sic] that you have taken a great deal of trouble and done all in your power both to ffree [sic] them of him & it, yea for than was either fit for your health or Interest, Yet I cannot help thinking (had your health permitted you) that if you had returned home in September from Harrogate and taken the direction of the head Court or been in the country when Coll Scott was here, matters would have been so conducted that the Sheriff's process would have been brought to a more speedy & agreeable Conclusion, and you better satisfied with the Conduct of your friends than can be explained to you in a letter' (6.2.7).

Sir William must have been venting his feelings about his neighbours or at least complaining that they could have shown more solidarity with him, as Sinclair went on to provide more excuses for his own actions. 'As to my particular part in the Politicks, you know the obligations I lay under to Coll Scott on account of my eldest son, and the engagements I came under to him in Consequence therof [sic], and since you left the Country he got my son Robert appointed my successor in the Customs, from all which I thought myself in Honour & Gratitude bound to him….'.

The colonel had visited most of the gentlemen 'and engaged [them] in his schemes' before he had called on Sinclair, who had been ill and at home at Tister. 'He came here at 9 at Night & stayed till after brakfast nixt day, in his way to Sandside, and in his return came here with a Croud[?] at 2 o'clock, dyn'd & went away by 4 the same day, as he had appointed a meeting nixt day with all his ffriends that cou'd travell at Wick at which meeting the Letters you mention were brought on foot by what means I never yet heard, not having seen any of the Gentlemen that were there since – and the Coll never mentioned them to me when I saw him. Now Dear Sir upon the whole as matters stand and that your ffriends have engaged themselves, I presume so as in Honour bound to go forward, and as you have fully exonerated yourself to your ffriends in your management of the Sheriffs affir permitt me as a real frind & well wisher to entreat you to act as your ffriends seem resolved to do, and follow your own Interest as doubtless they think they have done, and let that affair take its course.'

'It will give me great joy to see you act with your wonted Spirit at the head of your ffriends in every Controverted Question in the Country,' continued Sinclair, 'much are you missed on every publick occasion … I cannot allow myself to think but that Coll Scott will do his utmost to ffree us of the Sheriffs process….'. Apparently, reported Sinclair, the colonel had told the sheriff that if he did not fall in with his 'measures', he [the colonel] would 'take the part of the Justices against him'.

11 | *'the election here was over yesterday'*

At the approach of the next general election, when it was the turn again of
Caithness to send a member to Parliament, Colonel John Scott, serving as
the member for the Tain burghs, wrote to Sir William from Pall Mall. The letter
is dated 19 April 1766 and covers several topics (143.4.14). Clearly Sir William
had been seeking the colonel's help in securing a place in a regiment for a Captain
James Sutherland who may have been struggling on half-pay. The colonel had
sought to make use of his contacts in government but to no avail: 'I have made
a very unsuccessful effort for poor Jamie Sutherland which vexes me much but I
can't help it,' he protested. Patronage and the exploitation of favours were of course
typical of the political game. The colonel had also been at odds with Ulbster and
had insulted Lady Janet, to whom he had since written a letter of apology. This had
not fully settled the dispute, however, but the colonel did not sound very bothered
by this: 'their declaration of war against me seems to be as ill-timed and has as little
appearance of success as that of the Spaniards at the end of the last war' [this refers
to the Seven Years' War that had ended in 1763]. A substantial part of the colonel's
letter, and probably the principal reason for writing it, was to advance a scheme for
securing votes in the ballot due in two years' time. '... If you have no family scruple
to the scheme I propose,' he explained, 'I wish you would be so good as to allow me
to pass a charter upon the superiority of your estate either in my own name or Capt
Dunbars – I am quite positive both as to the goodness of the votes and that there is
no risk or impropriety whatever in your doing it i.e. first to holding of yourself for
payment of a small feu duty [then] grant a disposition of the property to the heirs
of entail reserving your liferent & your marriage settlements and when that is done
grant a wadsett of the superiority to me or Capt Dunbar on which a new charter

will be propos'd and the precept assigned to four different friends that can attend [the election?] without much trouble.'

Colonel Scott then examined the reactions or opinions of some Caithness lairds. 'I find Barrague [Barrock] will neither hop nor wind … so that his two votes must be cancelled and Sandside cant help me unless David Murray be infeft in Lands holding of the [...obscure word ...] above the valuation of 200 (which I think by any memory they ought to be) and in that case George Cowan [?] may with Sandsides consent dispone the superiority of Borlum (which is £200) to Mr Murray and make up a vote ----- Be so good as to let me know how the matter stands and if Mr Murray will like the operation ------- I see no marks of Freswicks not being [standing?] I wrote to Ratter [Rattar] and got a clear explicit assurance of his vote, I likewise wrote to John Gibsone asking his advice – and I receiv'd a cordial enough answer – I imagine Barrague's behavior is rather the effects of his own humour than of any of his friends – I have receiv'd letters both from Mrs Sinclair and Mr Moody assuring me of Olrigs vote which was rather more than I expected so soon [underlined in the original], Brigend is the only person I have any reason to complain of and I own I am provoked at him (almost to resentment).' At this juncture the writing becomes clumsy as if the colonel's feelings are affecting his penmanship.

At last towards the end of the letter, the colonel deals with what has been taking place in the House of Commons: '… yesterday we had what is call'd the Budget i.e. the supplies sum'd up and the tax voted, we borrowed 1,500,000 at 3 per cent with a lottery on nearly the same terms as last year and for the interest we resolved to bring in a bill to lay an additional duty of sixpence on the windows of all houses exceeding 24 windows in number and 2 pence a window on houses that have 7 or under.' Scott had a low opinion of the window tax: 'I think the tax abominably ill chose both for England and particularly so for Scotland, it will fall intolerably heavy on the middling sort of lairds – I did not care to vote against the ministry in the question of resolution but I don't believe I shall attend to support the bill.'

Colonel Scott travelled north in the summer and, when he returned to Edinburgh towards the end of July, wrote to Sir William, then at Harrogate [143.4.13]. 'I did not find the opposition in Caithness by any means dropt when I came here about ten days ago.' It seems that this opposition (possibly a Sinclair faction with Lady Janet prominent among them) had been making their own arrangements to grant wadsets to stack the roll of freeholders. '...But I suppose they bogled [sic] at the expence joined to the improbability of success, and therefore were ready to listen to an accomodation [sic] upon what I thought very reasonable terms,' explained the colonel. This accommodation was that Colonel Scott was not to oppose the enrolment on the list of voters of two men at Michaelmas 1766 and six more at Michaelmas 1767 'provided they are properly qualified, all the eight declaring themselves previously to be my friends for next parliament.' 'I did not hesitate in agreeing,' wrote the colonel, 'because I was clear I gave up nothing for they coud [sic] certainly force their friends upon the roll before another election and altho I might not have been in real danger they might have put me in hot water for the ensuing election which I wished to avoid.'

Scott also complained about the way the prospects for the Sutherland and Tain burghs seats were being set up. He listed a Mr Wemyss [James Wemyss], the Duke of Atholl, Lord Elgin [Charles Bruce, 5th Earl of Elgin, the father of the man who in time was to acquire the Elgin Marbles], Lord Auchinsleck [sic] [a judge, the father of James Boswell], Sir Adam Ferguson [the leading philosopher and historian and at this time a professor at Edinburgh University], John Mackenzie '& two more whom I forgot' who, Scott had been told, were determined to give Sutherland to Grant [probably Sir James Grant of Grant, 8th Baronet, at the time MP for Elginshire] and the burghs to Colonel Mackay 'without waiting for my approbation or even acquiescence.' From the names in the colonel's list, it would appear that a number of prominent people had an unusual interest in the Sutherland seat. James Wemyss, who was to win it in 1768, was the third son of the Earl of Wemyss and in 1766 the MP for Fife; in 1757 he had married Elizabeth, the daughter of the Earl of Sutherland, and it is therefore hardly surprising to find him standing as an MP for his wife's home county, a role in which in 1784 he was succeeded by his own son William. The Colonel Mackay in Scott's list was probably the Honourable Alexander Mackay who in 1766 held the Sutherland seat and did indeed win the Tain burghs seat in 1768. The colonel would have preferred the Tain burghs seat to go to Seaforth 'from the joint reasons of bearing him good will and thinking him a person of consequence and because he woud [sic] get his own County [Ross-shire] for a second election and give me back the burghs [in 1774].'

Early in September in Balcomie Colonel Scott was thinking about the freeholder's roll in Caithness (Appendix 5). On the 12th he wrote to Sir William in a loose untidy hand possibly indicative of haste: 'I wrote you a week ago calling upon you for your attendance to assist me in my political views in Caithness which hope & trust will have had the effect of bringing you north before this can come to hand but if any unforeseen event should make it impossible for you to come yourself, I beg you will immediately write to all our friends on ye Roll in Caithness that I wish and desire as a particular favour that they will resist the inrollment of Col Campbell, Capt Sinclair, William Sutherland Lybster and Adam Gordon, I shall send to Lord Duffus a copy of objections which I think are certainly solid & good agst three of the five and it is necessary that I shoud see the division of Col Campbells valuation & have Capt Sinclairs titles upon the estate of Rattar explained before they are admitted – agst both of whom there are likewise sufficient temporary objections, Olrig is here and sets out tomorrow with letters from me to that purpose and I trust they will be properly seconded by you which will very much oblige …' [143.4.12].

In November the colonel was still corresponding with Sir William on the same topics. It is clear from the letter he wrote on 26 November [143.4.15] that a satisfactory outcome for Captain Sutherland had still not been secured – 'I rather take amiss your doubting of my doing everything in my power to get him out his present unpleasant situation' – but the colonel was convinced that Sutherland would be granted a lieutenancy during the winter.

The election took place on 11 April 1768. On the following day, David Murray in Wick took to the pen again. 'The election here was over yesterday,' he wrote to Sir William, 'and I believe I am the only one of your friends that did not take a hearty bottle last night, and they perhaps incapable to write you today, & as I suppose youl be a little anxious, I have thought it proper to trouble you with these few lines' [8.6.10]. John Gibson, the sheriff substitute who had stood as a candidate supported by Freswick, had been dissuaded from attending the voting – 'which I allong endeavoured, or it would have grated me to see the Sherriffs friend preferred to yours,' wrote Murray. Colonel Scott had managed the procedure so as 'to supersede the necessity of a second election for Lord Fortrose.'

'Lord Fortrose was brought upon the Roll,' explained Murray, 'then the competition was stated twixt Lord Fortrose & Mr Delziel and carried for Lord Fortrose by the Coll as president has casting vote, so its thought the only complaint agst Lord Fortrose must be att Mr Delziels instance which will be a very tender one.'

Lord Fortrose was Kenneth Mackenzie, chief of the Mackenzie clan. He had been born in 1744, and was to be created Earl of Seaforth in 1771. In 1778 he raised the Seaforth Highlanders and, sailing with them to the East Indies in 1781, died at St Helena on the voyage. By then John Sinclair of Ulbster had superseded him as MP for Caithness.

Murray went on in what became a long letter to inform Sir William that Colonel Scott was bent on reaching a deal of some kind with Freswick. Murray related how he had seen the sheriff and his friends 'fawn much' on the colonel and 'if I could judge of politicians hearts from appearances, I thought their behavior softned him.' The laird of Rattar had overheard the colonel say at the public dinner, possibly on the previous night, that he would 'see Freswick next day to dinner and that he hoped Freswick retained his reason, and if he did it was impossible but they remove all differences.' Murray wanted the sheriff's party to adjust matters without claiming expenses.

On 14 May, Murray wrote to tell Sir William that the sheriff now had 'plenty of work in hand' [8.6.9]. A gang of some sixteen to twenty robbers had been identified: three were now in jail but 'all the rest going att this date openly therow the countrey.' Freswick had gone to Edinburgh. Murray believed that there had not been sufficient evidence to lock up the whole lot at the time the sheriff had gone south. 'I had a man among them (one of the 3 confined),' wrote Murray, 'whom I advised to confess as his conduct would all be proved, and he has detected [identified] the whole.' 'We miss you much for pushing on the execution of the law att this time,' concluded Murray.

The affair between the justices and the sheriff was not yet at an end, and Murray had disappointing news for Sir William on 10 October [8.6.8]. He had attended meetings of the JPs and at the most recent one, at Hempriggs, they had composed a letter to the legal agent in London and to [David?] Lothian, writer in Edinburgh, 'and an amount was made up of the preceding advances for support of the process.' Murray lamented the fact that so few of the JPs were willing to contribute to the costs that it would fall heavily on the rest of them. The amount proposed to be paid to Lothian 'appears … to bear no proportion to the necessary Expence [of the appeal] at London' and ought to remain with Lothian, Murray felt, in case the business returned to the Court of Session. Murray was also beginning to distrust Charles MacKenzie.

Murray had something to say about the crime in Caithness in a letter, written on 7 July from Castlehill [8.6.5]. 'Two fellows Alexr Aug [Oag] and Jas Suthd plainly discovered in Roberys and Intention of Robery goes openly therow the Country and to Kirk and Market; and Campbells Jews have infested the Country much, and the whole of them could have been safely apprehended by the Sheriff, and he left the Country and left us to protect ourselves, and the Sheriff pridence [?] is that he left these fellows for evidences against the others, as if they could not answer if they were secured from doing further harm, and now they have Dissapointed his Design of evidence for the Jews are away …'. These remarks about Campbell's Jews are puzzling: there were few if any Jewish people in the north of Scotland at this time and it may be a careless term of abuse for pedlars or other itinerant people who invited suspicion and prejudice.

In his history of Caithness, James Calder writes about several serious incidences of crime in the late eighteenth century, including about a band of robbers who carried out a series of burglaries throughout the county and murdered one man who had let it be known that he could identify those who had recently broken into a granary at Murkle. This gang, according to Calder, plotted to murder none other than William Sinclair of Freswick, the sheriff's father, but were thwarted by a curious chance that led to their discovery and arrest.[40] The leader of the gang, John Swanson a joiner from Thurso, was whipped through the streets of the town and transported to labour as a slave in the American plantations, a fate he later escaped from to serve in the War of Independence against British rule.

Notes

1. NRS GD 124/15/491/41.
2. NRS GD124/15/1087/1.

3. NRS GD112/39/189/6.

4. See, for example, NRS GD 112/39/197/3. In this document, Sir William states that he has served Breadalbane's interest for 20 years and is too old to change now.

5. NRS GD 112/39/197/21.

6. NRS GD112/39/211/26.

7. John Brand, *Brief Description of Orkney, Zetland, Pightland Firth and Caithness*, 1883, p. 223.

8. Details of weights and measures can be found in *The Concise Scots Dictionary*, 1985.

9. Aeneas Bayne, *A Short Geographical Survey of the County of Caithness*, 1735, unpub MS.

10. Thomas Pennant, *A Tour in Scotland*, 1769.

11. *OSA*, Wick, X, 1793.

12. Morris Pottinger (trans), *Counsell Record Book of Wick, 1660–1711*, North Highland Archive, Wick; also Morris Pottinger, *Parish Life on the Pentland Firth*, White Maa Books, 1997.

13. The details of the business between Wick and the Convention of Royal Burghs can be found in J.D.Marwick (ed), *Extracts from the Records of the Convention of Royal Burghs of Scotland*, vol. 5, 1711–38; and vol. 7, 1738–59, 1866–80.

14. NRS GD 136/47.

15. Dunbars of Hempriggs, Burke's Peerage.

16. John Henderson, *Caithness Family History*, 1884, p. 223.

17. Aeneas Bayne, *A Short Geographical Survey of the County of Caithness*, 1735, unpub MS.

   Judging by his surname and by the praise he bestows on his subject, Caithness was in all likelihood Bayne's native shire. We know nothing about him beyond that he had an MA degree, knew some Latin and may have been familiar with the Macfarlane collections, geographical writings gathered in the Library of the Faculty of Advocates in Edinburgh, which suggests Bayne may have studied law in the capital.

18. The description of Ackergill is by the local minister, Mr Oliphant, in 1726; in Mitchell, A. (ed) *Geographical Collections Relating to Scotland Made by Walter MacFarlane*, 1906, v.1., p. 156.

19. Appendix, Thomas Pennant, *A Tour in Scotland MDCCLXIX*, fac edn, Melven, Perth, 1979, p. 333.

20. John Steuart's correspondence is published in W. Mackay (ed) *The Letter-Book of Bailie John Steuart of Inverness*, 1915 (Scottish History Society).

21. *Lloyd's List*, 10 July 1744.

22. John, Master of Sinclair *Memoirs of the Insurrection in Scotland in 1715*, 1858, p. 69.

23. In the summer of 1722 Kenneth arrived in St Petersburg to be superintendent of the shipyard and naval magazine at an annual salary of a thousand roubles (roughly £500). He married Charlotta Christina, daughter of Eric Sioblade, the governor of Gothenburg in Sweden, and died in March 1734. His son, Eric, born in August 1710, called himself Lord Duffus but probably had no such standing in reality, and married his cousin, Elizabeth, Sir William Dunbar's younger sister. Eric served as an ensign in Disney's Regiment in 1731 and remained loyal to the House of Hanover; in 1745 he lay low at Ackergill and fed intelligence to the Earl of Sutherland. He died at Skibo in 1768. His eldest son, James, had the title of Lord Duffus restored by an Act of Parliament in May 1826, only months before he died in Harley Street. James had no offspring and the title passed to Sir Benjamin Dunbar of Hempriggs.

24. J.E. Handley, *Scottish Farming in the 18th Century*, 1953.

25. A compilation of grain prices mentioned in *The Mey Letters* shows how prices for Caithness victual fluctuated during the middle years of the eighteenth century.

Year	Price per boll (with approximate sterling equivalent)	Page
1739	£3 Scots (5s)	119
1741	£7 10s (12s 6d)	151
1741	£13 1s (£2 15s) This very high price may reflect the bad harvest in 1740.	151

Year	Price per boll (with approximate sterling equivalent)	Page
1742	£4 3s 4d (7s)	163
1742	£6 10s (10s)	169
1743	£4 (6s 8d)	188
1748	£3 16s (6s 6d)	195
1751	£4 (6s 8d)	204
1751	(6s)	205
1754	(6s)	208
1765	(8s)	222
1769	(8s 6d)	225

26. D.W. Kemp (ed), *Tours in Scotland 1747, 1750, 1760*, (Scottish History Society, 1887), p.155.

27. *A Survey of the Province of Moray*, 1888, p. 34.

28. John Henderson, *Caithness Family History*, 1884, p. 196.

29. For more about Sir William Sinclair's role in the birth of the Scottish Baptist church, see *A Rich Inheritance* by Christine Lumsden, Baptist Historical Society, 2013.

30. John Henderson, *Caithness Family History*, 1884, p. 90.

31. Aeneas Bayne, *A Short Geographical Survey of the County of Caithness*, 1735, unpub MS.

32. John Horne (ed) *The County of Caithness*, 1907, p. 427.

33. Information on the background to elections can be found in: William Ferguson 'The electoral system in the Scottish counties before 1832' in: *The Stair Society Miscellany Two*, D. Sellar (ed), Stair Society, Edinburgh, 1984, pp. 261–94.

34. Rosalind Mitchison, *Agricultural Sir John*, 1962, pp. 17–18.

35. Their descendant, the seventh Duke of Portland, owned Langwell estate.

36. John Henderson, *Caithness Family History*, 1884, p. 54.

37. NRS GD 136/83. Papers of the Sinclair family of Freswick. Copies or drafts of decree of molestation and declarator of the marches between Latheronwheel, owned by Sir William Dunbar and tenanted by James Sutherland in Achintoft, and the barony of Dunbeath owned by the Sinclairs of Freswick, and of discharge of expenses and damages. Dated 1762. This document has a remarkably detailed description of the marches between the Dunbar lands at Latheronwheel and the barony of Dunbeath.

38. NRS 02024 GD139-231.

39. The Caithness JPs at the time of the dispute with the sheriff were Sir William Dunbar, Capt James Sutherland of Langwell, David Murray of Castlehill, James Sinclair of Harpsdale, Robert Sutherland younger of Langwell, Capt Thomas Dunbar, James Sinclair younger of Latheron, Donald Williamson younger of Banniskirk, James Sinclair of Durran, Charles Sinclair of Olrick, Swinzie himself, John Gun of Breamore, George Sutherland eldest (bailie of Wick), and Robert Manson Sinclair of Bridgend. They are named in the sheriff's summons, NRS GD 139/231. Unfortunately the Minutes of the Caithness JPs do not survive from before 1843.

40. James T. Calder, *Sketch of the Civil and Traditional History of Caithness*, 1887, pp. 203–4.

Part 3

Soldiering, farming and fishing

1 | 'Alexander Miller now possessor of the Field of Noss'

The relationship between the Dunbars and Alexander Miller of Staxigoe was to be a crucial one for the future of Caithness and of Wick in particular. Miller was a merchant and entrepreneur with a wide range of interests, including fishing and farming, and he played a key role in the economic developments that were soon to transform much of the county. In 1767, in partnership with John Sutherland of Wester and John Anderson of Wick, he fitted out two small sloops to take advantage of the government bounty or subsidy offered to promote herring fishing. This venture went slowly for the first few years, in contrast to what was to come. Miller's father Donald held the tack of Field of Noss, the farm near Staxigoe, until he died in 1762[1] and in 1774 Alexander himself took over the tack on the same property. Alexander died at Field in February 1833 and was buried with his parents in Wick Old churchyard. His age is given then as 93 which would mean he took over Field when he was around 34.

The 1774 tack [80.1.2] follows the conventional wording of the time with some particular provisions, and begins: 'It is Contracted Agreed and Ended betwixt Sir William Dunbar of Hempriggs On the one part and Alexander Miller now possessor of the Field of Noss on the other part, that is to say the said Sir William hath let for the tack duties prostrations and considerations under written and hereby lets to the said Alexander Miller and Catharine Waters his Wife and the Heirs of their body excluding Executors or Assignees whatsoever; … and declaring that as it is meant out of personal freindship [sic] to them, that this tack shall fall when either [one] or other of them or the heirs of their body do not live in the place to occupy it for their own benefit and behoof.'

The boundaries of Field are laid down: 'bounded on the North side by the Lands of East Noss and Quoystain, on the South side by Donald Brims possession and a line within Twenty yards of the new stone Inclosure erected by Wester [probably Sutherland of Wester] and Alexander Miller dividing it from Staxigoe, and on the West side by a line to be drawn dividing Staxigoe from Papigoe continued till it pas the Field.' This notes the enclosing of parks with drystone dykes, a process underway at the time as part of the major developments in agriculture. Sir William reserved for his own use the mineral wealth of Field whatever this might be.

The tack sets out that Miller's lease will run for fourteen years from Whitsunday 1774 and that Miller will pay Sir William £10 sterling [equivalent to £1,000 today] as his annual rent. It goes on to list some stipulations about the cultivation of the ground: '... and as it is hoped [Alexander Miller] will make some enclosures upon these bounds which may be in grass It is hereby stipulated that any field in grass shall not be ploughed up three years before the Issue [expiry] of this tack without the consent of [Sir William Dunbar] ... [Alexander Miller] binds himself and his foresaids that such fields as may be enclosed and under grass shall not be pastured on after the first day of April preceding the issue of this tack, so that the next possessor may have the benefit of good grass at his entry ... [Sir William Dunbar] consents that Alexander Miller shall build a house exceeding the value of the present by Twenty pounds sterling to be paid by Sir William or his successors within two months after the expiry of the [missing word] ... it is agreed that the crop growing shall be cut down and gathered into the Barnyard of these lands by the said Alexander Miller ... and that it shall be kilned and milled and carried to ship or storehouse by the incoming possessor.'

Two years after the tack was agreed for the Field of Noss, Miller extended his holdings by taking a lease on Reiss [80.1.17] and was appointed bailie in Sir William's local or baron court for dealing with petty disputes. The annual rent for Reiss, at £100 sterling to be paid in two instalments, was much more than that for Field, and Miller also had to pay vicarage teinds for Field, Papigoe, Wick and Reiss, a total of £102 15s 11d per year. This was a considerable undertaking. Miller clearly was willing to take high-risk decisions but he was also confident of being able to meet substantial commitments.

Although the 1776 tack makes it clear that two properties at Reiss, those of the blacksmith and the schoolmaster, were to be left in their occupiers' possession, Miller was given 'full power' to accept and evict subtenants as he thought fit, 'and Alexander Miller obliges himself to make the whole possessors of Riess pay their Custom Hens and Egs [sic] unto Sir Williams Family as they are cald for and to cause the Tennants of Riess prepare and bring into Ackergill Twenty two Last [a measure of volume that varied according to the commodity, but always denoted a substantial amount] of Custom Peats, or to bring them to any place of equall distance, And reserving to Sir William power to search for and use or dispose of Lime, Scleate Coall or other Quarries and Mineralls if any be, Allways indemnifying the said Alexander Miller ... for any loss he may sustain by breaking ground and carrying away the same, Alex Miller being always at Liberty to use such for the accomodating [sic] of his Farme Only, and Sir William may use what he please of the Peats in the Links or Sandy Braes as may Alex Miller for the Use of his Farme.'

Miller also acquired a tack of the salmon fishing in the Water of Wick in August 1778, with entry deferred until 1783 when the current tack in the possession of the merchant James Fraser would expire. When Fraser died suddenly in January 1779, Sir William agreed with Miller that they should seek some arrangement with Fraser's heirs over early entry. This did not prove to be as simple as it may have at first appeared. John Anderson, the merchant, whom Sir William described as 'a subtle, cunning fellow', had been involved in business with Fraser and now came forward not only as the manager of the tack on behalf of Fraser's heirs but also as having been a joint tackholder. Miller agreed with Anderson to divide with him the proceeds of the first year's fishing. This, apparently, was not enough to satisfy Anderson who, perhaps, bore a grudge of some kind against Miller, despite their having been partners in the herring venture a dozen years earlier. Perhaps Anderson had had his eye on securing the salmon tack for himself and felt thwarted. Whatever the reasons behind his ire, he began to bully the salmon fishermen: [he] 'Bullied and Blasted and threatend the Fishermen and came to where they were Fishing with the Netts when he first Stripd himself of his Cloths and put himself in a seeming Boxing Posture and Aproached the Men with his Knife upon which the Men run away (they say in fear of his having concealld weapons) and then John Anderson Cutt the Fishing Netts which was lying on the ground and carried away with him some Trouts the Men had catched.' Miller obtained an interdict from the sheriff but Anderson did not desist and threatened one fisherman at his home in front of his wife and children, forcing the fisherman to get a warrant for the merchant's arrest. Anderson found bail and was bound over to keep the peace. Possibly because he still had some sympathy for his former partner, and of course the merchants in Wick were all still each other's neighbours, Miller was 'not willing to drive matters to extremity if he could' and Anderson quietened down. The root of the affair, explained in the summary of the case (90.1.10), lay with 'a poor ignorant country farmer James Fraser in Murrayshire' who claimed to be the other James Fraser's heir and became entangled 'in a litigation to gratify John Anderson's humour'.

2 | *'the dung is now carried off from before the doors'*

Sir William and his third wife, Henrietta, had five children – Benjamin, the eldest, born in 1761, and Elizabeth, Robert, Alexandrina and Williamina. During the long periods when they lived away from Caithness, the parents kept in touch with events at Ackergill through correspondence with Alexander Miller and other locals, and also with their children. A series of letters from Elizabeth, or Eliza as she was styled, survives from 1775 and conveys with much charm a picture of life in the big house and on the estate, mixing farming information with gossip. When Eliza was born is unclear but, at the time of the letters, she must have been in her early teens. She clearly took her responsibility as the in situ head of the family very seriously, and mingles the outrage of a young lady with a clear sense of her own position amid her chatty reporting.

The postal service in Scotland at this time was fairly reliable but expensive. The mail was carried by runners between Wick and Tain, whence a horse post took over the connection to Inverness and the south.[2] A letter sent for over a hundred miles cost 4d, paid by the recipient, a substantial expenditure and equivalent to several hours wage for a day labourer. Within Caithness correspondents probably used private messengers and servants to deliver letters, and some mail would also have been carried by sea as opportunity permitted.

As we have seen, Sir William put great faith in John Rosie and Alexander Miller to look after his interests. John Rosie had a tack on the farm of Reiss before it passed to Miller in 1776 and clearly kept an eye on the Ackergill estate. He may have enjoyed an uneasy relationship with Eliza at times and, for her part, Eliza thought John Rosie was lazy and had a strange way of going about things. On 25 March [1.2.24], she describes to her mother how she sent for him to discuss the business of the farm, in particular, it seems, the start of the sowing, and the mending of dykes. Eliza sounds a little frosty about this interview. 'I said I was to write you tonight and should make you a faithful report,' she tells her mother, 'To which he answered there was no fear of him everything should be done, as Sir Wm should have it.' For his part, John Rosie may have found the young mistress at Ackergill to be overbearing, interfering in things she did not understand. 'In the course of my conversation with John Rosey I took ye liberty though you did not tell me to forbid sheep's being allowed to graze in the parks, for though they are small they are very destructive, as they cut the grass so short, and eat as bare: he promised to take care that none of them should be there for the future and says, you will have the rent of both parks in hay.'

Eliza makes frequent mention of the work on the land as the season progressed. In March, as the winter supply of hay was being used up, she wrote '… the large gilt [haystack] is taken in, it was begun upon, both by the horses and fed cattle the 14 of March. There is only four stacks now in the yard, and none of them very big.' On 25 May, Eliza had more to say about the livestock: 'Mrs Henderson was surprised when you proposed our taking in the lambs, as usual; as you know we have not milk for them having but one cow; and the ewes, though we took them in, would not be able to feed them without some assistance. I shall send Papa's letter to John Rosie but I fear money will be scarce with him to buy all the cattle you propose. However, he will judge of that himself, and give you his own answer.' We do not have the letters from Sir William with his views and instructions but from Eliza's replies we glimpse what they may have been. 'Everything without doors are [sic] going on as you directed,' she wrote on 3 June, 'the dung is now carried off from before the doors', referring, one hopes, to the doors of the steading. Later, in the same letter, she adds, 'John Rosie says the park will just hold sixty head of cattle; no person will put in horses and they are grudging to give so much for black cattle. Indeed there would be no such thing, as keeping the grass, if there was to be horses in the park: we were obliged to put our own into one of the small enclosures' [1.2.22]. Some ten days later, Eliza told her parents that 'John Rosie is writing you about the cattle put into the parks. They begun to come in Monday last. Mrs Henderson took one list of them and John Rosie another. We have got no cows yet nor are likely to get any and cattle are all so high prices that we have not yet got oxen for feeding neither. The peats and all this matters I shall leave to the Governor letter but think it will be proper for me to mention that Mrs Henderson has desired him to speak to George Gun in Achairn to provide us in salt butter as [what] he generally has is good. Another thing I will inform you of John Rosie sent a man through the crees [sheepfolds] and Mrs Henderson sent John Miller along with him to find some weders for us there was none of them good and the people grudged giving them they said they could sell them to more advantage to the herring fishers. Mr

Grant happen to be the [sic] down the country at the time attending an act and commission at Scarmclate and being a day here as he returned home we all thought it best to speak to him and see if he could get us any highland weders he says he will look about for some' [1.2.23]. These remarks show that the tenants on the Dunbar lands were accustomed to graze their animals on the laird's grass, and it is also interesting to note that the tenants who had lambs were unwilling to sell them to Ackergill as they expected to get a higher price for them from the crews of the herring boats. Herring fishing was still in its infancy on the Wick coast at this time but it was already having a seasonal impact on the economy.

Eliza makes several references to Ackergill Tower, for example telling her mother on 25 May that 'as soon as the chimneys are mended, all the inside of the house shall be set to rights'. The housekeeper, Mrs Henderson, was clearly a woman of a thrifty bent as Eliza conveys her request 'to break down the two curtains that used to hang before the press in your closet; she says it would make borders to the three course calico quilts; the middles of them are pretty good'. Mrs Henderson 'has been as careful of us as if we had been her own', wrote Eliza, after suggesting her parents should bring a gift for her.

On 25 May [1.2.25], Eliza protests to her parents about their long absence – 'much do we long to see you again' - before reporting on the progress of housekeeping and the farming year. Coastal sailing vessels kept Wick in regular and, weather permitting, frequent touch with other places along the east coast. Eliza makes mention of this, occasionally noting that sailings or arrivals have been delayed. It is also obvious that the Dunbar household enjoyed a comfortable lifestyle, although shortages of some goods could occur: 'I looked below the cabinet in the alcove for canary seed but could find none; and would be obliged to you if you could send some more, as that sent by John Lieth will not last a year.'

The ship belonging to the merchant John Lieth arrived in Wick or possibly Staxigoe on 26 May 'as likewise a sloop from Murray [Moray] in which was the flour and barly from James Smith & the carts, and the butter churn from Sir Robert Gordon', wrote Eliza, 'the things you sent by John Lieth came all very save. The boys are thanking you for their part of the commissions. They have left the Stilton cheese for me to mention. We are much obliged to you for it but are not to break up on it till you come home.' Lieth's vessel also brought two carts, still quite a rarity in the far north, and Eliza, in referring to them, mentions 'ringwoodies' and 'hems', meaning rigwiddies and hames, parts of a carthorse harness.

With the staff of the house, Eliza also had to look after her younger siblings and the children of the Captain and her half-sister Janet. Her younger brother Robert and sister Williamina appear in the letters as Bob and Minie, Benjamin as Ben, and Captain Dunbar's sons as Sandy and Willy. In an age of high child mortality, their health was always a concern. On 25 May Eliza tells her parents that 'Bob and Minie are this day confined, taking their rubarb and mercury. Mrs Henderson was afraid of not giving the right quantity, that she made the Doctor weigh both the doses the last time he was here' [1.2.25]. The regular administering of medicine was one thing; a potentially more serious development was recorded in the letter of 14 June [1.2.23] when Bob's condition led to the doctor being called. 'Bob was complaining Tuesday of a flying pain throu him,' wrote Eliza, 'Yesterday it fixed to a stitch below his right breast Mr Taylor who is always anxious about him and more so when you are from home sent for the Doctor who came here yesterday. He declared that nothing was the matter with Bob and that the stitch was owing to the clossness of the weather which is scorching hot just now but as it was best to err on the savest side he put a blister [poultice] on the part affected to assure my Dear mam she need not be uneasy in the least for thank God there is nothing the matter with Bob He is as well as ever this day only the blister is not yet taken off I would not have mentioned this at all but to show you we conceal nothing so I hope you will rest satisfied that we are all well when you hear nothing to the contrary. The Doctor has been very attentive and desired that upon the least complaint he should be sent for he came yesterday very readily though he left a patient ill in the smallpox.' The thought that the doctor had come to their son's bedside from visiting a smallpox patient may have given the parents in Edinburgh something to ponder on, and they would have been reassured by the postscript to this letter, written in a different, more cruder, hand than Eliza's, and signed John, perhaps John Rosie himself. 'Dr Madam Miss is so good a correspondant and knows everything so weel that she leaves me nothing to say or I would have wrote oftener – Miss has wrote you about Bob thog he is blisterd I can assure you he is no wors than when you left him but the stitch he took mead Mr Taylor unhapie so we sent for the Doctor he thoght it proper to blister him rather than blood him as he bloods so oft at the Nose it was aplyd at ten last night he slept sownd til four and when he wake the stitch was quiet … the blister has ros viry weel but it is not yet teaken of he is in very good … So I beg you may make yourself easie and be ashurd we wil conceal nothing from you nor would the Doctor if he could observe anything to inform you of.'

Mr Taylor – Joseph Taylor – was working as a tutor for the Dunbar family, and was soon, on 21 April 1779, to be ordained in Watten as the parish minister. He also wrote to Sir William. On 6 November 1775, he reported as usual on the health and education of the Dunbar children: 'Wednesday last, the Classes met & after Breakfast I carried Mr Bob to introduce him to Mr Kennedy Professor of Speech' [19.1.26]. Bob had been anxious for days but also very impatient 'wishing every hour that the time was come' about this foray into the world beyond Ackergill. Kennedy had a school of some kind in the town where Bob – his age is unknown but he was probably about ten years old – was left to continue his education: 'The moment of his leaving me to go under the Charge of Another Person,' wrote Taylor, 'produced a tender & affecting scene on both sides for a little.' Taylor also mentions a Mr Copland, professor of natural philosophy, and a Mr Trail, professor of mathematics, as being in Wick at this time, where presumably they offered their services to those families who could afford the fees. At the end of November, Taylor wrote again [19.1.24]. 'We have all had a touch of the Cold,' he reported, 'Mr Dunbar [the eldest son, Benjamin] has been the worst but never confined by it. Mr Bob held it out for a while quite safe; at last poor little fellow he was seized & has been confined for three, four days. We hope he is on the mend now.' Mrs Henderson the housekeeper had also been unwell, but Dr Brodie had been 'exceedingly attentive.' Sir William had expressed a desire for Benjamin to learn fencing; Taylor promised to try to arrange this, despite the boy having 'handfuls to do' already. 'I cannot imagine you mean that He should this winter apply to Bookkeeping & Mensuration,' protested the Ackergill tutor, 'it is impossible for him to overtake everything at once.' Taylor had reservations about poor little Bob taking up fencing and dancing: 'I'll send him … if you positively order it' but it would be without his assent, as he feared for the lad's health and fencing had 'so many wreathings, twists & contortions.'

The last letter from Mr Taylor is dated 17 February 1779 (19.1.27), just two months before he took up his charge at Watten, and is addressed to Lady Dunbar at Warrington. The young minister was anxious for her, praying as he put it 'with frequent & fervent Ejaculations for a Safe & Prosperous accomplishment of your Rout.' It seems that Lady Dunbar was unwell – he had just received a letter she had written to him from Forres and this had 'sunk him a little' – and he offered her lengthy religious advice and comfort. 'I sympathise with you, I feel for you, but God is good and does nothing in vain … I trust in God the cause of present woe will be removed & our Dear Friend restored to perfect health … Pardon this long & incoherent Rhapsody …'. Lady Dunbar, Sir William's third wife – Henrietta Rose of Kilravock, survived this illness and died eventually in September 1795, outliving her husband by two years.

The letters would not be the proper witness they are without the local news and gossip they contain. One theme running through them relates to some incident in which Eliza had written a letter that had offended Mrs Innes. This lady, Janet, was Eliza's aunt, the sister of Sir William and now the wife of Harry Innes of Sandside and Borlum, and in the narrow social world of the Caithness lairds it may have been quite easy to offend her.[3] Whatever Eliza said had gained the approval of her parents: 'I am glad my dear Papa and you approved of our behaviour to Mrs Innes and hope we shall all conduct ourselves through life in such a manner as will shew the world that [we] have made a proper use of the many opportunities you, through your indulgence, has thrown in our way.' Eliza protests that she had shown her letter to no one except 'Mrs Ferme and the Ladies of Forse who told me they wanted it to shew to Lady Forse; and promised to shew it to nobody else.' The 'Ladies of Forse' had clearly not kept their word. Mrs Innes, says Eliza, 'is railing at us all in a strange manner.' A Miss Belle Sutherland, one of the ladies of Forse perhaps, wrote to Eliza early in June to tell her 'she will not shew my correspondence with Mrs Innes any more; that she would not have shown it all but in any justification, when she hard people giving a false representation of the foolish affair.' 'I hope, my Dear Mama, will not think I showed it to every person, out of vanity, because my behaviour was approven of,' continues Eliza in her letter of 3 June, 'I assure you that was not the case; but, at first, it was also … (?) necessary people should see it as Mrs Innes & her champions had said the way we had told that affair was not true; for she had wrote me, putting the question to me, whether she had behaved in an improper manner, at Ackergill, and I could make her no reply, and likewise that she had wrote to you, and you thought nothing at all of it. This, and a great many more ill natured things was said, which seemed to proceed from mere malice and pique against Mr Taylor. Not only the Ladies and gentlemen but the lowest people had this story; which, I own, provoked me so much that I would have published it at the church doors rather than appeared browbeats by her; but that is needless, for, I believe, all she says, is not taken for gospel.'

Alexander and William, the two sons of the widowed Captain Dunbar, were staying at Ackergill in the spring and summer of 1775. 'I am now come to your enquiries about our Nephews,' wrote Eliza on 14 June, 'I can not pretend to judge as to their scholar craft if it was not for the defect in his mouth Sandy reads English very well. Mr McLeod says he is a pretty good Latin scholar but his two favourite studies are History and Geography. He is very fond of his book and Mr Taylor says he is very sensible and will make a figure his hand of write is pretty good but too much a kin to mine stiff and I hear he is a good accountant. Willy is not such a bookish gentleman as his Brother they are at the same studies but he seems to be like most young men of his years a little giddy thoug he is a fine boy too and his Governor says does very well I saw his write and think it full as good as Sandy's.'

Sandy and Willy were due to return to Westfield in Moray and wanted the Ackergill boys to come with them. Eliza knew that this was a sensitive matter, in view of the dispute between her father and the captain, and chose her words carefully, so carefully that she forgot her punctuation, when she raised the topic in her letter on 14 June: 'If you thought it proper we would willingly spare Ben & Bob for a day or two which is all they would stay it would be a recreation to them and otherwise do good if you approve of it for by what we could learn this visit if it is not return will do no good as it will be said that the shyness between these boys and ours ar all owing to you for that the Capt sent them down to Ackergill and you would not let your sons return the visit However you are best judges in this case and should do as you please Don't be angry at me telling you this you did bid me when you went away acquaint with every thing I wished you should know and I have done so as far as I was able. I hope my Dear Papa and Mama will not think me to presuming and ready to tell my sentiments I am writing them to persons who are both able and willing to put me right when I am wrong I cannot help thinking that what ever reasons you have and I know you have good ones for your quarel with Capt Dunbar yet it would be a pity that children so nearly connected as yours and his first family are should be kept strangers to one another.'

3 │ *'your son has many Embarrassments'*

Debts and obligations followed Sir William for many years. His holdings in Latheron made him responsible for contributing towards the upkeep of the kirk, and in 1776 he and Robert Gun, the parish minister ordained in 1775, agreed at Ackergill on a payment of £100 sterling for repairs to the manse. The wording of the letter summarising the outcome of their conversation hints that this was probably a compromise solution, with the minister reluctant to enter into a dispute over the money. The manse was not in such a state as to necessitate the removal of the roof, it seems, but should it be found later that such a major step would have to be taken Sir William promised to pay a further £20 [19.3.].

The Edinburgh lawyer John Lumsdaine, the son of the John Lumsdaine already mentioned, wrote to Sir William in April 1782 to make a generous proposal [4.1.28]. Although the accounting books held an uncertainty over the date of a payment of £15 due from Sir William to the Lumsdaines, the lawyer promised to settle the matter in Sir William's favour. Lumsdaine senior had clearly held Sir William in high regard and had been willing to overlook the debts owing to him, and his son now was to do the same, although Lumsdaine junior's statement that he was doing this 'out of favour and [a torn page denies us sight of this word] towards you and your family' suggests that his forbearance may have started to run thin.

Sir William was fortunate in his friends. The Edinburgh lawyer, Henry Mackenzie, wrote to him at Auchendinny, a village some seven miles south-west of Edinburgh in the parish of Glencorse, in July 1787 to reassure him over another debt [1.2.1]. The letter was addressed via Mr Cowan's shop, suggesting that Mackenzie was hoping to catch Sir William either as he was passing through the village or at a country retreat. 'As both Mr Davidson and I accomodated [sic] you with the Money in question out of pure Friendship, we will be both extremely willing to give you every Indulgence as to it's Repayment,' wrote Mackenzie, 'I can easily satisfy him of those circumstances which put it out of your power to repay that Money now. I need not say anything on the other hand to you to enforce the Propriety of clearing it as soon as your Affairs allow.'

The rest of the letter discusses the possibility of securing the kirk of Nairn for Mr Taylor through influencing Brodie of Brodie the principal heritor. Mackenzie wisely suggested an approach through Brodie's daughters. The attempt to find Joseph Taylor a place in Nairn came to naught; the *Fasti Ecclesiae Scoticanae*, the record of ministers of the Kirk, states that John Morrison was appointed minister of Nairn in March 1788 with the support of the laird of Brodie. Mr Taylor had to stay in Watten.

Benjamin Dunbar, Sir William's son and heir, was by this time a young man in his late twenties. Unfortunately he, too, had fallen into some financial difficulty, as Henry Mackenzie, who was acting as a lawyer for both father and son, makes clear in a letter to his father written in April 1789 [1.2.2]. 'Dr Sir Willm … It is unprofitable to give a shorter term of payt than Whitsunday, considering that it will be near the end of April before it reached your Son. But I am afraid the Time of Paymt signifies little when there are no Funds out of which to draw the Paytt. Your Son has many Embarrassments, some no doubt of his own bringing on, others which he could not foresee. Of this last sort are [sic] the failure of Alex Miller of the Falls. I understand he is adveysed that he could take some steps to save the greatest Part of his Loss from the Falls if he had the tacks given to them … [?], which are in your Possession. You should certainly comply with his Request, as it is a piece of Justice to him, & which I don't see you can have any reasonable objn against …'. Mackenzie goes on to say that should Sir William object to sending the original tacks to Caithness he should at least see to sending extracts from them. Henry Mackenzie (1745–1831) was famous as a lawyer and as the author of the novel, *The Man of Feeling*. He was a significant public figure, and his son Joshua was appointed Lord Mackenzie, a senator in the College of Justice, in 1822. It has not proved possible to identify the man called Alex Miller of the Falls, or the nature of the scheme in which Benjamin had unwisely invested.

Sir William died in his late eighties in 1793, and Sir Benjamin Dunbar became the laird of the Caithness estates. An inventory of the furniture and contents of Ackergill Tower survives from May 1793 [83.4.3] [Appendix 6]. It may have been drawn up at or after Sir William's death and is a detailed account of the domestic possessions of the family, listed room by room in the Tower and presenting a vivid picture of the daily life and interests of the laird of the time. The rooms are named but unfortunately no plan of the interior of the building is provided.

The main public rooms, named as the little and large drawing rooms and the dining room, contained furniture such as chairs with chintz upholstery, chairs with leather, a sofa, a fire screen and a dining table that could be broken into parts. All the furnishings seem quite in keeping with the fashions of the early and late Georgian periods. For example, chintz fabrics with printed designs of Indian origin or inspiration were fashionable in the eighteenth century, as were many of the other items listed – the japanned [lacquered] coffee pots, and the mahogany wine cooler, tea tables and side board. The little drawing room had a Carron grate, manufactured at the Carron Ironworks which had been established near Falkirk in 1759. The books provided in the drawing room include 'Humes England', presumably *The History of England* by David Hume, in a quarto edition, and 'Smollets England', *A Complete History of England* by Tobias Smollett, published in 1757. There is a case of Hoyles Games. Edmond Hoyle (1671–1769) was the author of books on card games, and the case in the inventory probably included the board and accoutrements for backgammon and other games. The dining room had an eight-day clock, possibly a long case or 'grandfather' clock from Edinburgh. Unfortunately the scenes and subjects in the framed prints and pictures are not described.

Tea was an expensive commodity, kept in a chest in the large drawing room along with a sugar canister. What is surprising to the modern reader is the evidence of the large quantities of wine consumed. The 'inner cellar and box' contained 18 and a half dozen bottles of port, 10 dozen bottles of white wine, four dozen of claret, and 14 and a half dozen empty bottles. This is a reminder that wine was the preferred and popular drink in Scotland in the eighteenth century, the backbone of an important trading connection with France and Portugal.[4] The inventory includes extensive listings of crockery, cutlery and kitchen utensils. In the 1760s, the work of pottery companies such as Wedgwood revolutionised tableware throughout the country and set in motion a big change in households towards a lifestyle that we would begin to recognise. The Dunbars do not appear to have lacked for fashionable silver tableware. The kitchen also seems fully equipped to feed a considerable number of people.

The private rooms – the nursery, the so-called 'coledge' room and others – contain more humble furnishings, presumably assigned there by the capable and thrifty Mrs Henderson and her colleagues as still perfectly serviceable though perhaps old-fashioned. The nursery had three spinning wheels, valued at 18s, and two box beds with presses above. The lettermate room housed the utensils needed for brewing – ale casks, vat and ankers [small barrels] – as well as the wherewithal for laundry, including a 'washing machine', a device that comprised a wooden tub with mechanical paddles for stirring and beating the contents. The charmingly named James Hutton's loft had six ware barrows, for carting seaweed from the beach for fertiliser. James Hutton, a leading figure in the Enlightenment and now regarded as the founder of modern geology, travelled throughout much of Scotland in the mid-1760s and it is possible he came by Wick and Ackergill, but so far this has not been established. One letter in the Dunbar Papers, written in March 1779 by Sir William in apparent haste, mentions a James Hutton and a payment to him of three guineas, but it is not at all certain that this is the same man (26.3.17). A mixture of things was stowed in John Basses' loft – an oven stove, coach harness, casks, a turnip planter, a shovel, old ropes, herring nets, a scythe; while the hall had more chests, casks and barrels, a weather glass, a leather shot bag, powder horn, three old guns, two swords, a double-barrelled gun and candle moulds. The golf clubs, the lantern and the crossbow in the compting house suggest it was being used more as a store than as an office.

4 | *'there are so many recruiting'*

War broke out between Britain and France on the first day of February in 1793 and precipitated a rush to recruit men to the armed forces. To augment the regular army and serve on the domestic front, a number of fencible regiments were raised to form a militia or home defence force, akin to a Home Guard of the Napoleonic period. The first such fencible corps to be embodied was the Royal Manx Corps under the Duke of Atholl but it was soon followed by many others as a fashionable urge to ride as a colonel in the national cause at the head of his own contingent of fighting men broke out among the gentry. Sir John Sinclair of Ulbster raised the two battalions of the Rothesay and Caithness Regiment, and Sir Benjamin Dunbar, not to be outdone, formed the Caithness Legion in 1794.

Details of the uniform designed for the Legion are lacking but, according to James Calder, they wore 'the usual red coat, with white facings and leggins, and a helmet covered with bearskin'.[5] This description does not accord with that in another source where it is stated that the men wore tartan pantaloons or trews, and bonnets, although here the writer may be confusing the Legion with the Rothesay and Caithness battalions.[6] More is known about these, partly because Sir John Sinclair was an excellent publicist and wrote his own account of the unit.[7]

Printed commission certificates for some junior officers survive from the last months of 1794 in the Dunbar Papers [60.4.1-3] with the names of the officers written in – Daniel Banks Gent, Andrew McDonald and William Murray appointed as lieutenants on 15 November. Initially a fencible regiment comprised a colonel, a lieutenant colonel, a major, five captains and eight companies of men, each with a lieutenant, an ensign, three sergeants, four corporals, two drummers and seventy-one privates. Recruitment of officers for the Legion seems to have progressed at a satisfactory pace [Appendix 7] but enlistment of the required number of rank and file proved more problematic, especially with the sudden demand to fill so many units across the country. It could also be expensive, as bounties had to be paid and recruits had to be clothed, accommodated and fed under a government finance system that was not always as speedy in meeting bills as the new colonel might have wished. A large proportion of the Dunbar Papers dealing with the Legion is concerned with money.

Sir Benjamin drew upon his local connections to assist in recruitment. Thus we find in February 1795 Mrs Innes writing from Sandside after an unexpected visit from a James Allan, probably an officer in the Legion, to protest that the 'frosen' [sic] nature of the country was impeding every project. 'All my returns and two or three long letters containing all my likes and dislikes were sent by an Express to Capn Taylor the other day,' she continues, 'if you have not got them yet James Alan [sic] will pick them up on his way down. My returns are all there and what ever may be the Event none more can be looked for from here till Mr Innes comes down … I hope you have received the Men from Town that you heard were shipd when you was here' [60.1.21, 13 Feb 1795]. 'Pray take care that Scotscalder is not shuffleing [sic] and let not his trifleing throw a Slur upon you, only consider how such little people as either me or Capn Taylor can afford to employ our own money in recruiting, you must positively send me £100 as soon as you receive this …'. Mrs Innes remembered at the last minute to write on the back of her letter: 'Pray pacify Sir Robt Sinclair he seems to conceave himself Lieut Col, A letter I had last post from May McDonald at the fort says so.' Presumably there was lively gossip among the ladies over the pretensions of their men. Sir Robert Sinclair, the laird of Scotscalder, to whom Mrs Innes refers, was soon to cause bother to Alexander Miller over the use of fields at Ackergill, as we shall see in Part 8.

Mrs Innes was soon plying her quill again to inform Sir Benjamin that 'to err is human to forgive is devine [sic] May you and me likewise never lose sight of this', a broad hint whose import would soon become clear [60.1.22, undated]. After acknowledging the good account of the Legion that Sir Benjamin had sent her, she went on to tell of a William Stewart who had been 'much thwarted' in his recruiting measures. The purpose of the opening homily becomes plain. This William Stewart had apparently been lured away from joining the Legion to accept a commission in Sir John Sinclair's regiment where his reception had turned out to be less than satisfactory in some way – Mrs Innes is quite vague about what had actually transpired – and he had 'spurnd at the Proposal', as a result of which Mrs Innes was asking Sir Benjamin to show him 'a little lenity … if you please.'

Mrs Innes had recruited some young lads among the tenantry but they had gone to Strathnaver to see their friends. She now gave advice on how they should be treated. 'I have ordered them home directly but God knows if my letter will find them so soon as you wish to have them sent – You must be so obligeing as use a little deception with them – You must know these Highland boys conceave it a great affront to be made drummers and they have a saying among them that a Drummer is next to a Hangman. Now will you oblige me with saying that they are too low [short] at present for the Ranks but as soon as they grow to 5 feet 2 inches you will promote them if they deserve it. This will keep my credit with the Creatures.' She went on to tell Sir Benjamin that they had received their subsistence until 24 March but that they had not spent it, so could be charged for what Sir Benjamin thought they needed before the money went 'idly'. Then there follows an enigmatic piece of information – 'The Chicking breasted Boy is the Straw piper.'

Not long after the above was written, Mrs Innes addressed another letter to Sir Benjamin, dated only as 'Sunday night' [60.1.23] in which she interceded on behalf of a deserter who had been seduced into leaving the ranks by a boy called John Campbell who was, in Mrs Innes's view, 'an arch knave'. 'I well believe everything they say,' she continued, 'he has commited some tricks since his return to the parish that would not disgrace some of your Irish Men.' This boy Campbell – his father had long been an Innes servant – had always been troublesome. 'I think if a party was sent for him and to leave the rest [of the boys] till the Market Day it would humble his pride,' she advised, 'a short visit in the inside of the prison would perhaps do him good and the pay that is due him will do more than clear all charges.' After asking about her husband, from whom no letter had come 'for an age', she added a postscript: 'Don't let me be seen or heard in the Affair of the Boy John Campbell.'

During the spring and summer of 1795 reports were coming steadily to Sir Benjamin on the progress or often the lack of progress of the recruiting parties. On 23 March from Tain Lieutenant John Watson sent in only two names, adding 'it is still impossible to be perfectly correct upon that head as I have people employed at a distance who may have Inlisted [sic] men without my knowledge.' The pair he added to the muster roll were Robert McIntyre, a 34-year-old labourer from Dyke in Moray, and John Munro, a 38-year-old weaver from Tain. Munro had already been a sergeant in the army and asked to have this rank again; clearly he had found earning a living as a weaver a lot less secure than a respectable position in the forces [60.3.4]. Lieutenant Andrew McDonald, sending in a list of nine recruits, possibly from Dornoch, explained the low numbers: '… there are so many recruiting here and the country so much drained that its surprising how many are got …'. The shortage of recruits enabled those who did join the colours to demand a full bounty and sometimes ask for more [60.3.3]. The lists give the names, ages and heights of the men. Some were only teenagers, and young teenagers at that, such as Douglas McGrigor from Redcastle, aged 13, 4 feet 7 inches tall, and Hugh Munro from Nigg, the same age but slightly taller at 4 feet 10 inches – both were marked down by Lieutenant Colonel Innes Munro to be drummers [60.3.6]. Lieutenant Donald

Miller, probably Alexander Miller's son, was recruiting in Caithness in April, where he wrote to Sir Benjamin with the details of eighteen men [60.3.8], and Ensign Peter Innes (as far as we know, no relation to the Sandside family) enrolled two young lads at the same time, a certain Alex McPherson, aged 14, born in Latheron, and a Daniel Thomson, aged 16, born in the parish of Wick [60.3.6].

The Legion recruiters picked up men from the Central Belt, where Lieutenant Daniel Banks was at work in Alloa, and from London where Captain William Innes enrolled a good number. This may be a surprise to those who imagine the Caithness Legion to have been purely a local regiment. Captain Innes arranged for the recruits to be taken north by ship from Gravesend, paying out sums of money that varied for each man depending on the gap between enlistment and departure. The expenses for fourteen men despatched on the *Industry* on 15 February 1795 totalled £10 2s but the amount for each recruit varied from 6s to £1 18s. The contingent included a father and his two sons, by the name of Warren. Perhaps the father, Paul Warren, was a widower and brought his boys along so as to keep the family together. The elder boy, John, was 15 but only 4 feet 10 inches tall – Captain Innes objected to paying the full bounty for him and settled on 10 guineas. John's brother, Henry, 14 and 4 feet 8 inches, received no bounty at all but his father was unwilling to part from him, wrote Captain Innes, so I left him and you [Sir Benjamin] to settle matters. Henry, went on the Captain, seemed 'to be a fine boy and may answer for a Drummer.' This contingent from the streets of the British capital necessitated, between travel, subsistence, bounties and other expenses, a total outlay of £196 8s 6d. Captain Innes pointed to travel and subsistence as 'heavy' items but confessed this was unavoidable as he had failed despite repeated trials to persuade the recruiting agents he names as Barker and Hodges to alter their methods of working. Innes refers to these two characters as 'crimps' and cautions Sir Benjamin against offending them, as word would soon get out among other crimps 'and would finally stop your recruiting in London'. The hiring of crimps to lure or entrap recruits into the army and navy was an unsavoury but common practice, open to all kinds of abuse. In this instance, it seems that Sir Benjamin had agreed with Barker through a Captain Ayton to pay 13 guineas for every recruit above 5 feet in height, adding one shilling for every day 'in town' and the expense of coach hire for travel to the ship [60.4]. A printed form with blank spaces for specific details was used to secure medical treatment for recruits. One specimen [72.2.16] is dated 20 April 1795 and asks St Thomas' Hospital in Southwark, London, to admit Thos Chapman 'afflicted with a sore leg' at a cost of 14d per day. Chapman secured admission on 30 April and was discharged on 12 May, having cost the recruiter the total sum of 4 shillings.

Captain Innes was still in London engaged in recruiting when he wrote to Sir Benjamin on 4 April to tell him that eighteen men were about to be taken north to land at Fort George. The cost of their passage was one guinea per man plus

9d a day for their food, and this amount had to be settled with the ship's captain on their safe arrival. Captain Innes made clear his view on a pipe-dream of Sir Benjamin's to have the men march north: 'Desertion woud [sic] undoubtedly be the consequence…' [60.4]. The captain continued to say that he would take every opportunity to send men to Cromarty where a recruiting officer could be based and the new recruits could be marched 'safe to Wick'. 'In a few days I hope to ship 30 or 40 more…'. On 24 April, Mrs Ann Munro, in the absence of Colonel Munro, presumably her husband, wrote from Cromarty to Sir Benjamin to protest that 'the arrival of a Party of your men has occasioned a great deal of trouble to two of the officers here' [72.2.14]. Presumably these men were recruits shipped north by Innes. 'The Bearer in particular has been very unmanageable & would not go on, without a line to you' complained Mrs Munro, 'in order to represent that he has been unjustly treated in not having received his promis'd bounty.' She concluded with the wish that there will be no more 'of the same kind this way, as it hurts the recruiting.'

Another undated letter but probably in early 1795 from Mrs Innes at Sandside in her usual unpunctuated style made quite clear to Sir Benjamin the competition for recruits [60.1.19]. 'Here is at a compleat stand,' she wrote, 'and I fear Thurso is not likely to produce much good to us every Iron is put in the fire to disappoint you there is not an avinew [sic] leading to the Town in which there is not either a spy for the Rothsay or Orkney fencibles & Mothers for a Standing Corps every soul that can be either by force or Stratigem [sic] got into a House is drunk down and when they wont do they are Inlisted for the Thurso band & from thence taken into Sir John's fencibles.'

'When I observed to Wm Stewart yesterday,' she continued, 'that we had as good a right to Inlist them as Sir John had he told me there was something put in your attestation that the Justice lord told of to stop them entering with you but that they had publickly made known to the Band that anyone belonging to it might Inlist with Sir John's fencibles …'. Stewart had been seeking recruits all over the county, according to Mrs Innes, and when he had offered 15 guineas in Watten, presumably as a bounty, he had been told 'by a Brat not 5 feet 2 that he could get 17 from Sir J [the page is torn, but only John makes sense in the context], why take 15 from him.' Stewart had found four recruits for all his pains. Sir Benjamin's sergeant had been accused of 'fakeing it' when he had offered 17 guineas in Thurso 'for it could not be possible for a Fencible Regiment to give such bounty.' 'Lieutenant Henderson,' reported Mrs Innes, probably referring to one of Sir John's men, 'then sent his party about and laid down 18 guineas on the Drum.' The sergeant was an Englishman – Mrs Innes suggested replacing him.

On 19 May, from the content of a letter written after the one above, Mrs Innes complained to Sir Benjamin about how 'our men' were 'much disconcerted at the contempt shown them by Scotty's party' [60.1.20]. Sir Benjamin had failed to meet the troops at the market – Mrs Innes asked if the bad weather had stopped him – and Scotty had written to her after Sir Benjamin had left the county to order all recruits to headquarters on 20 May. All the recruiting and excitement had deprived Mrs Innes of the labour customarily expected from tenants – 'not one cast of bear [bere] yet sown or the land plough'd for it,' she protested, adding 'It would be total ruin to Sandside to part with the Servts just now therefore I wrote Scotty ... I should not send servants till the last push,' she continued, '... this I hope will not offend you as our men are quick fellows and some of them old soldiers they will take very little drilling compared with awkward clodpoles ...'.

Mrs Innes had more advice for Sir Benjamin. She related how Bighouse (the Mackay laird of the large estate neighbouring Sandside to the west – Sir Benjamin's wife was a Mackay of Bighouse) had told her how he had heard from a Captain Williamson that twenty-five or thirty-five 'of Sir John's boys were cast by Gen Hamilton who said he wd rather an old man that had two years work in him than the finest Boy.' The redoubtable lady of Sandside feared that the rejection of recruits deemed too young would also occur with the Legion: she mentioned two lads whom she had 'never judged fit for anything but drummers' but whom Sir Benjamin had admitted to the ranks, where if they were rejected by the inspecting authority would represent a loss of money. The remainder of the letter is concerned with the current news. There had also been 'a little blood shed at the Market' but the Sandside men had come home in an orderly manner before the fighting had started 'otherwise I dar [sic] say they would have born their share of the Glory.' Sir Benjamin's wife and family had passed Sandside the day before on their way to Bighouse where a christening was about to be celebrated; Mrs Innes thought so many Bighouse children and grandchildren would never again assemble in one body and added that Sir Benjamin's daughter should have been the godmother.

5 | *'the present <u>Ticklish</u> State of the Southern District of Ireland'*

Despite the difficulties with recruitment, Sir Benjamin succeeded in founding his regiment, and late in 1795 the Caithness Legion was posted to County Cork, to join the large military presence that the British government kept throughout Ireland. On 15 December Lieutenant Donald Miller wrote from Staxigoe to Sir Benjamin who at that time was at or expected to arrive at the New Geneva barracks in County Waterford [70.3]. Miller listed the soldiers in his charge. The NCOs comprised three sergeants: James Lunan, who had been sent – we know not from where – to join the regiment four days before, James Dunbar and James Laurie. There were thirty-five privates: among them are a Cormack, a McKay, a Miller, a M'Leod, a Williamson and a Campbell but, otherwise, the surnames are not particularly suggestive of Caithness. The Legion, as has already been suggested by the widespread recruiting effort, held men from many parts of the country (Appendix 8 and 9). Sergeant Laurie and his 'camerades' had sailed from Wick on Wednesday last bound for Leith, and the lieutenant had given him £7 17s 6d to cover subsistence for the voyage. Miller could not resist appending the news that a small sloop from Shetland with a cargo of kelp, fish, butter and oil, also bound for Leith, had been driven ashore at Reiss 'yesterday morning' with the loss of three of her crew of four – 'only one young lad saved' – and totally wrecked.

Ireland at this time was deeply divided between those who maintained loyalty to the British state and the nationalists who saw in the French revolution, which had burst on Europe in 1789, an avenue through which they could gain their own independence. In 1791 the Irish Protestant leader Wolfe Tone formed the Society of United Irishmen in an effort to persuade his Protestant and Catholic fellow countrymen to come together in the national cause. Efforts on the part of

Earl Fitzwilliam, the lord-lieutenant of Ireland, to respond to Irish grievances by, for example, granting Catholic gentry the right to sit in the Irish Parliament were rejected out of hand in London, mainly at the instigation of George III. Fitzwilliam was sacked, leaving the Irish with the firm belief that they could only achieve political progress through armed revolution – and the help of the French. The regime in Paris knew very well that trouble in Ireland would usefully tie down many British troops and that an insurrection there could open up an invasion route. Between 1796 and 1798 the French tried six times to land troops in Ireland. In the event, only two of these were to succeed in putting troops ashore but the Legion, when it was posted there, could not foresee this and could feel only that its experience was unlikely to be an easy one.

Sir Benjamin did not spend a great deal of time with his men, and much of the correspondence in the Papers is concerned with keeping him up to date on administration and expenditure. Ensign Alex Macpherson was in charge of the regiment's purse strings, acting as paymaster from the early days of the unit in Wick in 1795 and continuing in the same role in Ireland. Macpherson's letters are datelined in Bantry and in Bandon, a town some 15 miles south-west of the city of Cork. Bandon was originally founded as a Protestant settlement at a crossing point on the River Bandon, and in 1798 it had a defensive wall extending around the buildings. None other than Sir John Moore, who was later killed fighting Napoleon's forces in Spain, was the governor of the place. It was a pleasant spot with good farming land around it, supporting corn mills and tanneries, and here the Legion was to stay for some time. Bantry, on the shore of the large bay of the same name, lay a good fifty miles further west from Cork. It seems that the Legion shared in the garrisoning of a considerable section of the southern coast.

In an undated letter labelled simply 'Bandon Saturday night', but probably in December 1796, Ensign Macpherson wrote to Sir Benjamin care of Edward Leahy Esq in Dublin. Possibly Sir Benjamin had not stayed with Leahy for the letter bears the annotation Quin Hotel, added in another hand [60.5.10]. 'This I hope will overtake you in Dublin,' wrote Macpherson, 'and as you probably be at the War Office may I take the liberty to remind you to speak to Mr Cooke relative to the Drill money laid out at New Geneva.' This is a reference to the Geneva barracks, near the fishing village of Passage East, a few miles east of the town of Waterford, where British troops were garrisoned and where it was likely the Legion stayed en route to Cork and Bandon. 'The pay of Surgeons Mate Manson and Neville had been disallowed,' wrote Macpherson, 'and without you take the opportunity of looking after it possibly it may be entirely lost which would be a serious loss & at the same time a great hardship …' [60.5.10].

Macpherson comes over in the correspondence as a confident, competent individual, aware he was in a position of responsibility and some power. In January

1798 we find him telling Sir Benjamin, who had apparently become worried over the security of the stream of letters passing to and from the Legion, that he had 'ever been particularly cautious of keeping up that secrecy which must at times exist betwixt you as a master & me as a servant' [60.5.11]. As usual, Sir Benjamin was feeling the financial pinch. 'As to paying of money to officers I shall certainly have your interest in view and be as much on my guard as possible,' Macpherson reassured him, 'but you know they must receive their subsistence; They must receive the baggage money because they lay it out of money paid them for the Mens Subsistence & in future they certainly would require to receive their lodging money also.' The Legion's captains had received only their first half-year's allowance and had been protesting – 'a sufficient clamour and noise,' said Macpherson, when Sir Benjamin's back had been turned. The ensign cautioned that if their dues were to be put to some other use there would be 'some unpleasing tendency'. As it was, he said, he did not have enough money to cover everything – 'when I left Bantry I could only pay 30 guineas per Company in place of about 70 guineas each ought to have received …'.

Macpherson's duties took him on journeys between Scotland and Ireland. In November 1797 he was in Dublin but at the beginning of the following January he was writing to Sir Benjamin from Ayr, en route from Aberdeen back to Ireland, on a matter more personal than army business: he was reminding Sir Benjamin of three acres of land that he had spoken of for his father. Macpherson says that the exact location has not been fixed but suggests a blank sheet be signed for John Cormack back in Caithness to fill up. Then, as if he remembers Sir Benjamin's status, he adds 'unless you would think [im]proper to sign a blank sheet', before stating that it would be convenient to settle the matter as his father is a 'poor man miserably ill accomodated [sic] in a dwelling place.' As if to restore Sir Benjamin's humour, he says he was much gratified to have heard Miss Dunbar perform at the pianoforte the song 'Croppies ly down'. This song, a Protestant loyalist piece attacking the Irish nationalists, nicknamed croppies from their tendency to keep their hair short, was composed in 1798. Clearly the Dunbar family was right up to date with popular culture [60.5.14]. One verse of 'Croppies ly down' runs as follows:

> Should France e'er attempt, by fraud or by guile,
> Her forces to land on Erin's green isle,
> We'll show that they n'er can make free soldiers, slaves,
> They shall only possess our green fields for their graves;
> Our country's applauses our triumphs will crown,
> Whilst with their French brothers the croppies lie down.
> Down, down, croppies lie down.

Ensign Macpherson concluded his letter from Ayr with some news about other regiments. The Lanarkshire Militia had arrived and about one hundred men of the 2nd Battalion of the Breadalbane Fencibles had orders to hold themselves in readiness to march, to make room for the Sutherland Fencibles on their return from Ireland. Regarding the disbandment of the Perthshire Highlanders, Macpherson opined 'better could not happen [to] them.'

In the spring of 1798, Sir Benjamin sought leave to raise a 2nd Battalion for the Legion and on 19 June the all-important communication came from the War Office: 'Sir, I am commanded by the King to acquaint you that His Majesty approves of your offer …' [60.1.4]. The unit was to be raised in three months and to comprise eight battalion companies, and a company each of grenadiers and light infantry. Each company was to have forty-seven men and, in the case of the grenadiers, two pipers instead of the brace of drummers. Five guineas levy money was to be allowed for each recruit approved at the final inspection. None was to be enlisted who was over 35 years of age or shorter than 5 feet 5 inches, although 'well made, growing lads between sixteen and eighteen' could be taken at 5 feet 4 inches. Sir Benjamin could choose his own officers but they had to be 'well affected to His Majesty'. 'In all respects of Pay, Clothing, Arms and accoutrements the Corps is to be on the same footing as His Majesty's Infantry Regiments of the Line,' continued the regulations. The battalion had to serve in any part of Britain, Ireland, Jersey or Guernsey but were not to be reduced except in the county where they were principally raised 'or as near thereto as possible.'

To Sir Benjamin's dislike, there were discrepancies here in what he had understood to be the terms of service. When he had been assured that his offer would be accepted, he had more or less promptly raised around one hundred men without waiting for more formal agreement. Now '…to my astonishment I find in the Letters of Service … important differences …' he was to write at a later date in summary of the transactions [60.1.5; 61.4.8]. The principal matter of contention was the size of the bounty. When the 1st Battalion had been raised 'when men were much easier got', this had stood at 10 guineas (now it had been reduced to 5) and there had been no restrictions on age or size, and service was to be only in Britain and Ireland. A further communication from the War Office amended the terms slightly and confirmed that the 2nd Battalion of 600 men would be raised on terms that allowed a bounty of 8 guineas if service were to be confined to the home territories or 10 guineas 'if extended to Europe generally'.

Just as Sir Benjamin was launching his campaign to be granted the right to raise a second battalion, the Caithness Legion itself saw some action. Typically Sir Benjamin was absent from the scene, in fact back in Ackergill when Captain Robert Kennedy wrote to him from Bantry on 13 April 1798 to tell what had happened [72.2.33]. Kennedy had just received a letter from Sir Benjamin that had been sent on 20 March. 'When I reflect upon the present <u>Ticklish</u> [sic] State of the Southern District of Ireland and upon your Description of your <u>lonely</u> (tho' at the same time Tranquil & Safe) Situation while writing that letter in your family Mansion at 12 at Night I cannot well avoid making a Comparison between your Situation and that of your friend Lord Bantry very much in favour of the land of Cakes,' began Kennedy, underlining for emphasis. Lord Bantry was Richard White, the largest landowner in the neighbourhood; he had led the local resistance to the French attempt in 1796 to land forces in Bantry Bay and had placed his home, then known as Seafield but later renamed Bantry House, at the disposal of the British commander, service for which he was created a baron.

Kennedy related how 'the <u>United-Men</u>', as he calls them, had been active for the last eight to ten days and had cut down woods between Bantry, Skibbereen and Dunmanway. 'We had Parties out after them & caught some, who will be brought to Trial.' The rebels had also started to cut down trees in Lord Bantry's woods at Glengariff and had broken into his house there, stealing some arms. These men had also been pursued and several had been captured and jailed to await the assizes in Cork.

'On Monday night,' continued Kennedy, 'a party of these Banditti attacked the house of a Mr Gilman near Dunmanway who having rec'd some hint of their Intentions had procured a party from Major Innes of a Sergt & 5 men – The Major made his Dispositions (I understand) and gave his Instructions with a Degree of Judgment & Precision that would have done honour to Buonaparte – About 3 o'clock in the morning they arrived, to the Tune of 3 Hundred and surrounded the House, threatning audibly to Rob & Burn it & Murder every Person within it – Tho the night was very Dark the Sergt (our Friend Andrew Cormack, never supposed a <u>Dasher</u> til now) Sallied quietly out of a Barn where he had concealed himself and his little Party (and where they had by the Major's Directions arrived in the course of the Evening in Disguise and by Different Routes) and having Drawn up his Men without Noise let Drive amongst them – the Rascals thinking there was none but the family about the House returned some Shotts but without Effect, and on Finding their Mistake took to their Heells in all Directions, Swearing <u>By Jesus, St Patrick & the Virgin</u> – that their were Soldiers in the House. Andrew had sent the contents of his Piece thro' one fellow's head (whose Carcase they carried to Dunmanway with them) & instantly drove his Bayonet into another, who escaped notwithstanding, in the Dark – Another was taken alive who no Doubt will String for it & several of the Gang were wounded as they were traced by their Blood next day to a Considerable Distance. The man who was killed & the other who was taken are Inhabitants near Drumaleague [Drimoleague, a district a few miles east of Bantry] where we hear 2 or 3 funerals have taken place within these 2 or 3 days "of People who have died Suddenly"'. Kennedy wrote that every night saw some 'fresh instance of Depredation

& Rascality.'[8] The government's response was to quarter troops across the country in an attempt to overawe the rebels into giving up their arms. General Moore had written to each contingent to recommend that in furture skirmishes 'To bring in no prisoners', a severe measure that Kennedy suspected was the result of the assizes in Cork releasing too many of the accused 'in the Teeth of Positive Proof.' In May that year there were insurrections in Dublin, Meath and Kildare, bloody outbreaks of fighting attended by atrocities, but, remaining at its base in Bandon, the Legion seems to have had no involvement in these. They would, however, have heard about the murders of prisoners that took place in County Wexford, some 150 miles away.

Much of the correspondence deals with recruitment. Major-General G. Nugent wrote from Belfast to Sir Benjamin, then in Edinburgh, on 4 June 1798 to say that he would escort the recruits safely to the regiment on their arrival [61.1.4]. Presumably these were men coming over from Scotland to join the Legion. Later in the same month, Ensign Alex Macpherson wrote from Glasgow to Captain George Sinclair at 14 Frederick Street, Edinburgh, to ask him to intercede with Sir Benjamin in favour of Duncan MacNicol 'a relative of mine who prompted by a martial spirit is desirous of holding a commission' in the newly forming 2nd Battalion [60.5.16]. On 14 July Major General Sir Charles Ross inspected the recruits at Bandon: he accepted fifty as suitable for service and rejected twenty-eight. The names that are listed – McBeath, Manson, Doul, Miller, Swanson, Sutherland, Monro etc. - are typical of northern Scotland [61.2.17]. Later musters in 1798 contain, however, many Irish names, showing that recruits also came either from localities in Ireland or from among the many Irish living in England or Scotland [72.6.8]. Some of the attested oaths of recruits survive among the Dunbar papers in various printed versions with filled-in blank spaces; for example this one from later in 1798: 'I James Quinn do make Oath that I am a Protestant and by Trade a Weaver and to the best of my Knowledge and Belief was born in the Parish of Loughgall in the County of Armagh Ireland and I have no Rupture, nor ever was troubled with Fits, and that I am no ways disabled by Lameness or otherwise, but have the perfect Use of my Limbs; and that I voluntarily inlisted [sic] myself at Aberdeen in the County of Aberdeen the 10th Day of Dec 1798 to serve His Majesty King George the Third as a Private Soldier in the 2nd Battn Caithness Legion regiment, commanded by Sir Benjamin Dunbar Bart and that I am not an Apprentice, nor belonging to the Militia, nor to any other Regiment, nor have belonged to His Majesty's Navy or Marines, or Merchant Service, As witness my hand at Aberdeen' [72.4.11]. James Quinn was 16 years old and 5 feet tall. The signing of the oath included the reading to the recruit of the second and sixth sections of the Articles of War, against mutiny and desertion, and also a declaration that the man had been found fit by the surgeon. There is one fully handwritten attestation [72.4.10] – perhaps the officers had run out of printed forms – that omits the declaration about being a Protestant [an oversight?]; the recruit was John Butler, born in Ballymordern in County Cork, a cottoner by trade, and he signed on in Kirkcudbright on 7 September. He was only 15 years old but slightly taller than Quinn at 5 feet 2 inches. It is possible that these lads were joining the Legion as a way to secure a passage back to Ireland. In a list of recruits dated 6 October, Lieutenant Forrest provided some background information, including the following, on the men he had taken in but gave no clue as to individual motivations [72.2.18]:

Name	Occupation	Parish	Age
Jas Frain	Writer	Kelso	22
Wm Muir	Porter	Kirkcudbright	23
John Froth	Coachman	Halifax	27
Jas Downs	Weaver	Newcastle	17
John Rannals	Indeweaver	St James's, Dublin	16
John Smith	Potter	Carbiehill, York	31
Wm Dixon	Labourer	North Berwick	33
Henry McKinnon	Weaver	Carlisle	31
Wm Wellward	Shoemaker	Dunfermline	16
John Burt	Coalier	Dunfermline	16
Wm Sinclair	Coalier	Dunfermline	16

6 | *'about 1500 French have landed'*

The turmoil in 1798 in Ireland climaxed with the landing of a French invasion force of around one thousand men on 22 August on the sparsely populated coast of County Mayo a few miles from the town of Killala. Joined by some five thousand local rebels, the force routed a British army at Castlebar, the county town, five days later. On the same day, on a brig anchored in the harbour at Cork, Alex Macpherson wrote to Sir Benjamin [60.5.17]. Macpherson was of course unaware of what had just taken place in far-away Castlebar but the Legion had been placed on alert. '…On Wednesday last, the regiment marched from Bandon to Cloghnakilty [sic], Ross & Courtmasherry all on the coast side in consequence of accounts being received by the government that some of the French vessels with arms etc had been seen off these places but when I left Cloghnakilty on Saturday last no attempt had been made to throw in any arms in that quarter nor have I heard of any since,' wrote Macpherson, 'but at a place called Killalee [Killala] in the County of North Mayo about 1500 French have landed & rather unfortunately for us scarcely any troops were there to oppose them but the first news I expect to hear is that they are all cut to pieces – One comfort is that the country people are cumming [sic] away from them instead of aiding them as was thought – Yesterday a prize was carried into Cove [Cobh] by the Hazard sloop of war of a French vessel armed en Flute [that is, with reduced armament to make room for cargo] with 350 men on board & several hundred stand of arms.'

The events in Mayo also figure in a letter from Captain Robert Kennedy to Sir Benjamin, who was in Edinburgh all the while. Kennedy's letter [72.2] was written in Clonakilty possibly on 6 September (or is it October? – the early part of the letter is missing): '…by this time the Banditti landed in Mayo are subdued and taken, as the Lord Lieutenant has gone in person against them with what is thought a sufficient force to stop their doing further mischief – General Lake at first met with a check [at Castlebar] in which it was mostly falsely reported that Fraser's Fencibles had misbehaved, and [the page has a hole at this point] happy to hear that they have been most publicly & honourably whitewashed by Lord Farnham & the Chancellor in the House of Lords from all Imputation of Blame.' On the night of 26–27 August the French had advanced over rough hill country to the west of Lough Conn and had encountered a contingent of Fraser's Fencibles sent out on reconnaissance; the Fencibles, only fifty men under Major James Fraser of Belladrum, had then withdrawn to join the main army. In the French assault militia in the first line of troops had given way, throwing the second line where Fraser's were stationed into confusion. In the ensuing rout Fraser's had recovered sufficiently to make a stand at a bridge crossing but it had not been anything like enough to affect the overall outcome of the struggle. In the fighting the Fencibles from Inverness had lost a dozen men dead as well as weapons and their flag.[9]

Lieutenant-General Gerard Lake, the commander of the British forces, led his men finally to victory on 8 September at Ballinamuck in County Longford. French prisoners were repatriated but little mercy was shown to the Irish who had joined them and hundreds were executed as rebels. On 20 October at Clonakilty Kennedy again took pen in hand to keep his colonel up to date [72.2]. After gossip about individual officers, promotions and movements, Kennedy wrote 'I flatter myself the French will be by this time getting tired of Irish Expeditions and leave us to Eat our Potatoes in peace for this Winter.' A little over a week before, another French force had attempted to land in Donegal but had been overwhelmed by the Royal Navy before a man could be put ashore; the Irish leader Wolfe Tone was taken prisoner in this sea-fight and later committed suicide in a Dublin prison before he could be hanged. Captain Kennedy described the current dispositions of the Legion: 'The Major is stationed with two Companies at Ross-Carbery 6 miles S West of here and Burton with the Grenadier Company at Courtmacsherry 7 miles east from us. The other 7 Companies here at HeadQ^{rs} – This place is something larger than Bantry – and tho' perhaps not the most Eligible Situation in the World, yet as Genl St John says "it is to be considered as the Post of Honour and that it would neither be prudent [hole in the page] Good of the Service to withdraw the C.Legion from it at present." We [another hole] therefore to ensure the Honour put up with the Inconveniency.'

Sir Benjamin harboured ambitious plans for the Legion and kept up a correspondence with the military administration in the War Office in Horse Guards in London. One letter from a Robert Moncrieff dated 25 October 1798 told Sir Benjamin that 'I have His Royal Highness the Commander in Chief's orders to acquaint you in answer to your memorial that His Royal Highness has it not in his power to avail Himself of your offer to add some Troops of Cavalry to the Caithness Legion, under your Command, as it is perfectly contrary to the usual formation of British Regiments …' [68.2.6]. In the following summer, Sir Benjamin was again exchanging letters with Moncrieff, this time on the matter of increasing the size of the Legion to 1,000 rank and file [68.2.5]. The War Office had other plans for the fencible regiments, as revealed in a letter written by James MacBeath at Hempriggs at the end of February 1799 to Sir Benjamin [68.2.13]. 'Dear Colonel,' he begins, '… The unexpected and unmerited fate of your 2nd Batt was communicated to me first by Captain Sutherland who received a letter from you as he passed through Dornoch. It was so unexpected a piece of intelligence that from any other authority we should not have been apt to give it credit – The treatment you have met with is certainly beyond example arbitrary, cruel and ungenerous to the greatest degree …'. The cause of this combination of outrage and flattery – and there is a good deal more in the letter – was the plan to use the Legion as a drafting corps to fill up other regiments. 'You and those who engaged with you are certainly in justice well entitled to redress and many, of whom I am one, stand much in need of it,' wrote MacBeath. There was money at stake. MacBeath owed a sum to Sir Benjamin who, as usual, was not free from debts himself. In October 1799 an Aberdeen merchant called Alexander Duguid brought an action of horning and poinding against him and Captains George MacBeath and John McLean for an unpaid £200 15s, probably for money spent during recruitment [62.3.1].

Those fencible regiments raised for service only in Britain and Ireland were ordered to disband in 1799 but the Caithness Legion and other Scottish units were not amongst them. In June 1800 we find a circular being issued from the Adjutant General's Office in Dublin with the numbers of men permitted to volunteer to join regiments of the line [69.1.9]. Along with the Aberdeen, Elgin, Fraser's and other fencible corps, this figure for the Legion was 100 men; Reay's fencibles were permitted to lose 150 men and the Caithness Highlanders 200, in all 2,300 men to be received into the 21st Foot at Belfast, the 71st at Dundalk, the 72nd at Newry, or the 79th and 92nd at Fermoy. The Legion men were destined to join the last mentioned. Throughout 1800 the companies of the Legion were stationed in various localities in County Wexford, among them Newton Barry, Bandon, Kilkenny, Youghall, Killow, Goresbridge and Graize.

An unsigned report dated 30 November 1800 summarised the state of the Legion at the time in critical but not entirely unsympathetic terms [60.4.?]: 'Lieut Col Monro has been in the command of this regiment the preceding 6 months & appears to have paid attention to his duty as far as circumstances would admit of. The regiment does not appear deficient in discipline but little judgement could be formed of its performance in the Field Exercise Manoeuvres owing to its being seen in so many different places … a tolerable body & many well looking but there are too many old and short men ...'. 'Severe Camp Duty' had partly worn out the clothing supplied in June. The men had paid for their own greatcoats. The officers were 'alert and tolerably well-informed.' No house could be procured to serve as a hospital. The men's messing arrangements were 'As regular as the scarcity and difficulty of procuring proper food will admit of. There are 48 men in this Regiment 40 years of age & upwards, out of which 4 have served 20 years & upwards – There are 71 under 5 feet 4 inches high & 28 reported unfit for service – Much allowance is to be made for the appearance and discipline of this Regiment owing to its being so much divided during the summer & and is at present in 13 different cantonments.'

The Legion was disbanded in 1802 at Enniscorthy in Wexford but that was far from the end of any involvement with military matters for Sir Benjamin. Clarification and settling of debts continued for many more years. In a later section, it will be seen that among the many debts owed by Sir Benjamin when it came to the formation of a trust in 1805 to deal with his creditors, there is the sum of £1,200 owing to officers and others connected with the 2nd Battalion of the Legion.

The Papers also contain quarterly pay-lists for Volunteer Companies for the years 1804–07. These were groups of local men who formed a home defence force and were paid for days spent on exercise. For example, Captain William Gun of Bourtour [sic – for Bowertower] is listed as being owed £43 6s 4d for ninety-two days on exercise at 9s 5d per day for the period from 25 March to 24 June 1805 [66.3.3]. In Gun's company, the position of lieutenant was empty but the others comprised Ensign Hugh Sutherland (he received 4s 8d per day), one sergeant on permanent pay – Joseph Doull, who may have been a Legion veteran, Sergeants Harry Gunn and Donald Mowatt (1s 6d per day), Corporals William Alsherson and William Bremner (1s 2d per day) and fifty-three privates (1s per day). Drummer David Sutherland was on permanent pay of 1s per day, while his colleague Alexander Bain was on the *per diem* pay roll.

Sir Benjamin carried on his correspondence with the War Office in Whitehall over the money which he expected, hoped or was entitled to receive from the government in connection with the Legion with great tenacity. Documents appear to have gone missing. Certificates and tradesmen's bills were appealed for. An agent whom Sir Benjamin claimed had worked on his behalf denied having done so [60.1.2]. The settling of accounts dragged on. Sir Benjamin wrote at length to point out how much he had done for his country in a memorandum dated September 1823, as if hoping to justify expenditure to bureaucrats without any understanding of the real world [60.1.5 probably a draft, 60.1.12 is a better copy]. The Legion had served in Ireland 'during the whole of the rebellion,' he noted, before reminding the government that he had offered to raise a second battalion that could serve in Europe, that he had been the first to make this proposal 'well knowing that he had peculiar facilities for executing this undertaking', a point that may have provoked a few sighs in the War Office. The inspection of the first battalion had been carried out by Sir Ralph Abercromby and most of the recruits had been passed, 518 men in all for a target establishment of 600, 300 more than any of the some fourteen other gentlemen who had been given Letters of Service at the same time as himself. 'In this situation your Memorialist [i.e. himself] felt satisfied that a months recruiting would complete his engagement [for a second battalion],' continued Sir Benjamin, describing how he then sent out recruiting parties while those already enlisted went to drill. '…<u>Arms and accoutrements were furnished by Government together with drums & colours</u>, and the men were immediately put in to slop clothing…', Sir Benjamin underlined part of his case, emphasising how after all this activity in forming the 2nd Battalion it had pleased His Majesty's government at the end of January [1799] to dispense with its services 'at a time when all his other competitors had got time to go forward with their levies …'. The only reason Sir Benjamin could see for this unfairness was the commander-in-chief's not wishing fencible regiments to have second battalions. Sir Benjamin thus felt 'deprived of the advantages of his exertions for the public, a numerous corps of officers … were turned adrift without a sixpence of pay which they had earned by twelve months hard labour in recruiting [and] paying even bounties out of their own pockets …'. Sir Benjamin had also lost money in keeping 16-year-olds expecting them to reach the regulation height to join the ranks. In all the total cost had been 2,000 guineas which he was to have received from Colonel Grant of Grant for the colonelcy. Even Sir Ralph Abercromby on his way to Egypt had backed his case with the Duke of York that he should have been liberally dealt with in the passing of his accounts. He had received assurances, he said, and had returned to duty with the 1st Battalion in Ireland where he had served until the peace, 'cheerfully putting up with a pecuniary loss which materially hurt his patrimonial interest.' The draft has the addition 'not less than 28 years' and also a marginal note: 'I will not weaken this point to state the amount of the loss & it will certainly command more attention.' He goes on to itemise particular amounts that had been disallowed; the list includes a sum for fifty-five men enlisted in Ireland – 'this must arise upon a mistake,' he comments, saying that despite the lapse of time he will be able to 'instruct' that the Irishmen had in fact been enlisted in Scotland and England.

On 30 October 1823 we find a letter to Sir Benjamin from the War Office Department of Arrears and Accounts with the ominous words that, in relation to the absence of any accounts having been rendered in relation to the levy to form the 2nd Battalion in the latter half of 1798, he was requested to pay the sum £1,373 5s 1d to the Bank of England by 24 November; this demand is signed by someone called Palmerston, none other than Henry John Temple Palmerston who later became prime minister but in 1823 was Secretary of War in the Cabinet.

Sir Benjamin did not overlook the opportunity to raise volunteer companies of militia on a local, part-time basis but there was an obstacle to be overcome, as Alexander Miller stated in a letter from Staxigoe to the laird on 15 July 1801 when the latter was in Newton Barry [9.7.3]. 'Donald [his son] and me are surely very much oblidge to you for what you say and intended to do for him respecting two Volunteer Companys on your Estate,' wrote Miller, 'but it is a thing perfectly impracticable at present; in the first place their is not a young Lad on your Estate but who has joined himself to some Volunteer Company or other …'. Not only were all available recruits already signed up to two existing companies, it seemed, but a stop had been ordered to recruiting by the Earl of Caithness who had complained in a letter 'that he had some how or other been ill used and … that he was resolved not to apply for any more Volunteer Companys.' A Major M'Leay, wrote Miller, had been told all this in a letter that he had seen; M'Leay had wished to raise a third company until the Earl had put his foot down. James Sinclair, the 12th Earl of Caithness, was lord lieutenant of the county. Born at Barrogill Castle in May 1766, he does not appear to have added anything notable to the annals of the history of the county but clearly he had felt himself slighted in the matter of volunteer companies.

After the disbandment of the Legion, and presumably after many of the rank and file had returned to Caithness, Sir Benjamin had better luck in his wish to command a volunteer company. A series of printed circulars from the War Office in London came to him in 1806, addressing him as 'Lt Col Sir B Dunbar Officer Commanding 2nd Batt Caithness Volunteer Infantry, Wick, NB.' These contain the various regulations and amendments governing the companies. The Memorandum of 12 July 1806 [63.2.3] brought the bad news that pay scales were being revised downward: for example, the adjutants and serjeant major could continue on permanent pay as before, but officers on full or half pay would receive nothing more after 24 September, and drill serjeants and drummers would likewise get sixpence a day instead of constant pay. The men would receive one shilling per day 'for every Day … present at Exercise, not exceeding 13 for the Half-year ending the 24th December 1806; but no Person entering a Volunteer Corps after the 24th July 1806 will be entitled to any Pay whatsoever.'

Pay lists for the companies in the Caithness Volunteer Infantry survive in the Dunbar Papers and one such [63.2.8] for Captain John Gordon's company between 25 June and 24 December 1806 shows that the contingent comprised Captain Gordon, Lieutenant George Leith, Ensign David Miller, three serjeants, two corporals, two drummers and fifty-three privates, all of whom received one shilling for each day they appeared on exercise. Few missed a day and the opportunity to earn their bob. The total wage bill came to £63 2s 6d, a third of it (£22 8s 6d) to Captain Gordon himself who was on permanent pay at 4s 10½d per day. A note [63.2.2] of money claimed by Sir Benjamin in December 1806 for pay (13s per day) and arms (2s 6d per man) for men 'late belonging' to the Stircoke [sic] Company lists the individuals and where they lived, and gives a snapshot of the social background of the volunteers [Appendix 10].

The volunteer companies, presumably without any further recruitment, continued to meet and drill for a few years. On 27 June 1809, James Waters wrote to Sir Benjamin from Fort George: 'Sir, Having been informed that the Battalion of Volunteers latly under your Command are getting settlement for their Services, I take the Liberty of requesting you will be pleased to order payment of the annex accompt to be made to David Waters, my brother, whom I have by this day's post authorised to receive it. I have the honor to be … James Waters' [63.2.1]. The account that Waters attached came to £25 19s 5d for pay and drill days between June 1806 and March 1808, and compensation for two years' clothing. The address of Fort George suggests that he may have become a regular soldier.

8 | *'he will neither be a good tenant or a good neighbour'*

While the Caithness Legion was in Ireland, the administration of the Dunbar estate was left in the hands of Alexander Miller of Staxigoe. He kept up a steady correspondence with Sir Benjamin, writing long letters at frequent intervals, suggesting hours spent with oil lamp, ink and quill. In February 1801 he was concerned with the leasing of parks at Ackergill to Captain Robert Sinclair of Scotscalder. Captain Sinclair, or Scotscalder as he was usually termed, was corresponding directly with Sir Benjamin and Miller feared not only that he was being kept in the dark about the captain's intentions but that any business with him might prove to be a waste of time: 'I expected to have heard from him [Scotscalder] ... but after waiting until the 30th [January] I began to suspect that Captain Sinclair did not intend to write me. Therefore in case you might blame me in any part for this seeming fruitless negotiation I wrote him a letter ... and I have just now received his answer ...'. Miller included copies of this exchange in his own letter to Sir Benjamin [9.7.9]. Scotscalder had replied curtly to Miller's approach, saying in effect that Miller would be told once an agreement had been concluded with Sir Benjamin; this despite the fact that Sir Benjamin had made it clear that in his absence in Ireland Miller was the man to see about leasing parks. Scotscalder's reputation was not one to inspire confidence. 'I believe from what I hear of his temper and disposition you will be just as well off if the bargain do not take place,' wrote Miller, 'it is generally said that he will neither be a good tenant or a good neighbour ... I do not speak from experience ... but common report is not favourable.'

Farming in Caithness was going through a long, slow revolution at the time, with many changes being implemented under the banner of improvement. The introduction of the potato, the humble 'tattie', was of great significance: Henderson called it the 'best of all roots' and, although for years after its appearance in the county around 1754 it had been cultivated only in gentlemen's gardens, it had now become a favourite food and 'even the farm servants must have a few drills of potatoes each, planted for them, for which they stipulate when they engage.'[10] Enclosure of parks and the cultivation of good grazing, which could then be leased, was part of the pattern of development. By mid-February Miller had heard nothing from Scotscalder and his suspicions about the latter were heightened when another gentleman who had applied for the use of the Bogtoun park revealed that he was doing this secretly on the captain's behalf. In the event Scotscalder did obtain a lease. Miller let to him the grazing of the so-called tenants' park at Ackergill until the end of the year, for which the captain agreed to pay 80 guineas. This, however, was not the end of problems with the troublesome Scotscalder.

As the spring wore on into the summer and as Sir Benjamin had neglected to send clear instructions about the management of the castle park, Miller had taken a decision: '... the season of letting grass drawing towards an end I thought it proper to advertise for takeing in cattle to graze at 20 shillings each; I advertised accordingly at the parishes of Wick, Watten, Bower and Canisbay and I wrote to several persons in other parishes' [9.7.1]. In the letting of grazing, the custom was to set a day when the owners of the cattle would bring along their herds. In this instance it was Friday 12 June, and on the following Tuesday, when he wrote to Sir Benjamin, Miller felt that they would not receive sufficient animals to consume all the grass on the castle park and expressed his intention to keep half of it for hay and roup the standing hay crop later in the season. 'I am hopeful you will approve of these measures,' wrote Miller, 'it ... is exactly what I would have done if I had been doing it for myself,' reminding the laird of his own expression of confidence in his agent. When Scotscalder had heard of Miller's plan to let the castle park, 'he was ill pleased' as he believed that this would interfere with his own occupation of the tenants' park. Apparently Scotscalder had offered Sir Benjamin £150 for the crop of hay from the castle park; 'if he has done so,' wrote Miller in an annoyed tone, 'it surely is with a mischievous intention ... after knowing that I had advertised to take in cattle ... had he wished for the park he might have applied to me when he heard it was advertised ... his writing you ... appears to me in so bad a light that I cannot allow myself to believe it, although one of his confidants told me he heard him say so...'. 'There is few men of my acquaintance that I would wish to be more on my guard with than Captain Sinclair,' concluded Miller.

Miller wrote again about this matter on 15 July [9.7.3], saying that he thought he would earn about £120 from letting the castle park grazing and that he had rouped the hay from the remaining part of the park for £25 sterling 'a very high rent indeed I think.' Miller also managed to sell the grass in the garden for £5 8s and, with £50 from Mr Traill for two other parks, 'makes a very handsome rent, twice as much as you drew out of it before and I think preferable to Scotscalders offer.' He felt he was justifying his actions to Sir Benjamin and hoped for the laird's 'approbation'. This was not quite the end of the business. In August, from one of Miller's letters [9.7.2], we find that a George Dalrymple had also been corresponding directly with Sir Benjamin about the parks. Miller thought well of Dalrymple's offer of £800 and, if Sir Benjamin agreed, would settle with him to take over the tenants' park as soon as Scotscalder's tenancy ended in December. However, warned Miller, Dalrymple was a 'miserable suspicious creature, to tamper with him increases his suspicion' but he did not 'think it a bad scheme to let this park to Dalrymple as I apprehend grass will not fetch so high in Caithness next year as it has done this one.'

Miller was anticipating less demand for grazing, as the war with France had driven up the price of livestock and encouraged the Caithness farmers and tenants to sell 'even … part of their labouring stocking', the oxen they kept as beasts of burden. To Miller the prices being obtained for beef were 'extraordinary … you'll surely wonder when I tell you that Caithness has drawn more than £20,000 for cattle this season.' He had himself sold ten stirks 'of a middling size' at £12 10s each and two 2-year-olds at 8 guineas each. Nothing like this had been heard of in the county before with the result that Caithness was 'bare enough of cattle' to affect the prices that could be expected for next year's grazing. In the middle of June Mr Traill (at Castletown) had rouped his cattle 'generally … at very high prices although scarcely [any of the] appearance of the Ackergill breed was to be seen amongst them' and drovers were now much in evidence in readiness to drive the cattle south to market [9.7.6A].

Miller was still unclear as to Sir Benjamin's intentions regarding Scotscalder but, in view of the captain's propensity to be indecisive, urged a conclusion of the proposed deal with Dalrymple. The saga of the parks continued. Miller thought that Dalrymple had intended to pay rent for his present possession (£70 a year) and another £60 for the tenants' park. It turned out that Dalrymple meant no such thing, as Miller tried to explain in a letter on 1 September [9.7.47] to Sir Benjamin after they had met. Dalrymple really had wished to continue to pay £46 8s as the annual rent for his present possession and £50 for the park. 'However he at last agreed to pay £60 for the park' but would not budge from the £46 8s for his present tack, continued Miller, before launching into a complicated explanation of how the original £800 mentioned as a grassum (the legal term for a sum paid at the beginning or renewal of a tack) also included payment to the outgoing tenant for new houses the latter had built and the further cost of another house and a 'shade' [probably he means shed], to be added to the steading. Perhaps Miller was growing weary for he writes to Sir Benjamin, 'In my opinion this is no bargain for you but you may do as you please' before offering to see to the written tack once Sir Benjamin had made his views clear. As if with relief, Miller adds that 'I hear nothing of Scotscalders motions whether or not he is corresponding with you about the parks.'

The Wick area as depicted on the map by Robert Gordon based on the work of Timothy Pont, c.1590. Telstane, yet to be renamed Hempriggs, is clearly marked. (Reproduced with the permission of the National Library of Scotland. CC-BY 4.0)

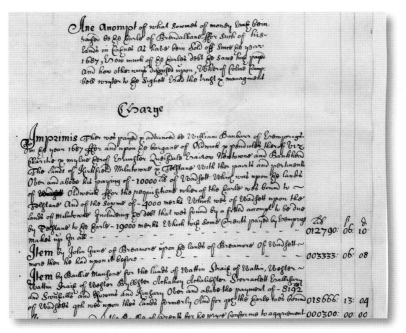

The opening paragraphs of a document in the Breadalbane Muniments describing the lands acquired by William Dunbar in 1687. (Courtesy National Records of Scotland, Breadalbane Muniments, GD112/58/90/2/1.)

Be it Kend to all men by these present letters, me Sir William Dunbar of Hempriggs, Knight and Baronet, heretable proprietor of the lands, baronys, tiends, tenements, mills and others under written, with the pertinents: Forasmuch as, by two several *contracts* of *vendition*, made and past betwixt one Noble Earl, John earl of Broadalbin, and John, Lord Glenurchie his Son, on the one part, and me the said Sir William Dunbar of Hempriggs, therein designed William Dunbar of Hempriggs, on the other part; the *first* dated the twelfth day of August, the twenty day of September, and last day of October, in the year of God one thousand six hun-dred and ninety one; and the *other*, of date the Sixth and twenty third days of November in the year of God one thousand six hundred and Ninty nine; and by a *procuratory* of *resignation* a part, relative to the first of the said contracts, granted by the said Earl and his said Sone to me the said Sir William Dunbar, and to my heirs of taillie therein mentioned, of date the sixth day of November

The first page of the Deed whereby Sir William Dunbar secures succession of his Caithness lands to his daughter Elizabeth, dated 11 October 1707. (Dunbar Papers 79.2.13)

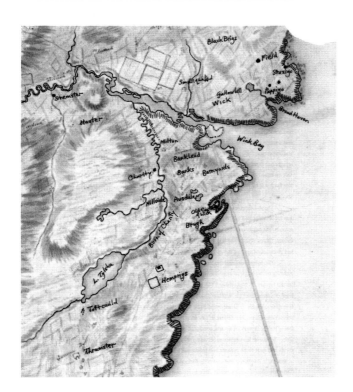

A map of the area south of Wick based on the military survey by William Roy in around 1750.

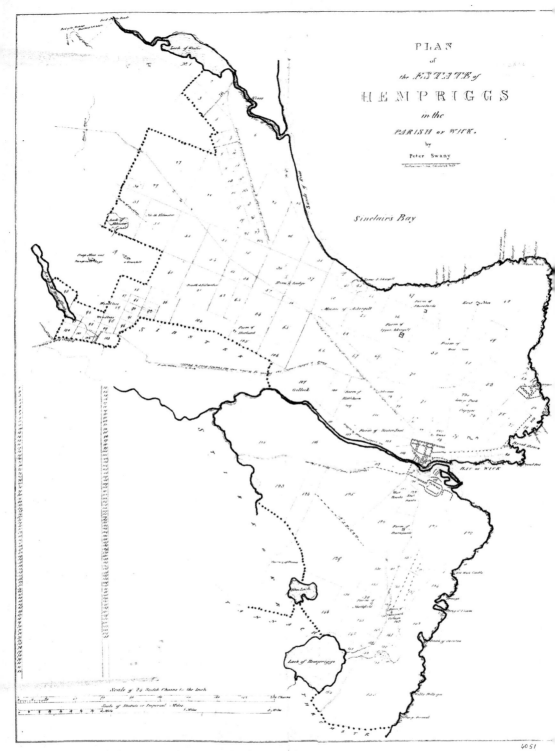

Peter Swany's map of the Dunbar estates in 1837.

The impression of Ackergill Tower made by William Daniell in 1815. In the original tower, the main entrance was on the side facing the sea.

When David Bryce remodelled Ackergill Tower in the mid-1850s, he moved the main entrance to its present position on the landward side and added wings to form the Tower as we have it now.

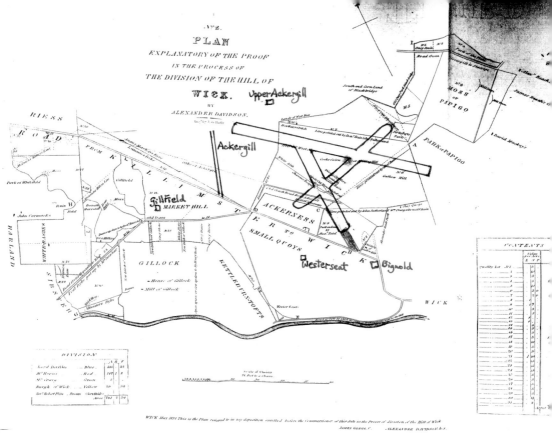

The plan of the Hill of Wick area published after the court hearings on its ownership and use in the early nineteenth century, with the runways of the airport superimposed.

Left: Garden Duff in the uniform of the 79th Regiment.
He was commissioned as an ensign in December 1855.
Middle: Garden Duff-Dunbar.
Right: Jane Louisa Duff-Dunbar with her son George born in 1878.

Wick 19 March 1824

Sir,

 Having occasion to be here, I learn that it is proposed to establish a new Coach betwixt Thurso & Dunbeath, & that you are interested in the management. I have in consequence taken the liberty of offering my services to drive the Coach & take charge of the Horses which I could undertake in a month from this date. From your knowledge of my former employment in that capacity, & my present engagement with Mr Sinclair, I trust I need say little of my qualifications for such a situation: and have only further to request you will favor me with your answer addressed to the care of Mr James Mackay Wick.

I am, very respectfully, Sir

   Your most obed.
   humble Servt.
   John Fraser

George Dunbar Esqre
of Hempriggs.

A decorated arch in Wick, possibly one erected for the arrival of the Duff-Dunbars in 1874.

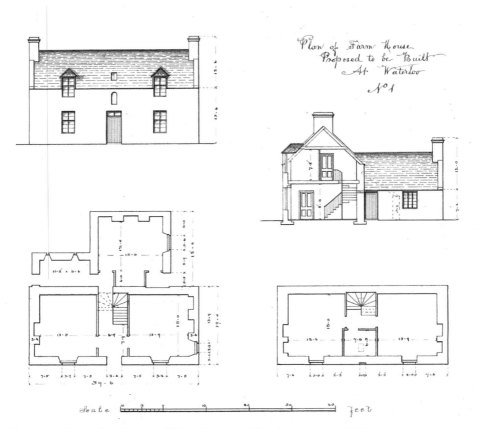

The plans for the farmhouse of Waterloo near Wick drawn up in 1872.

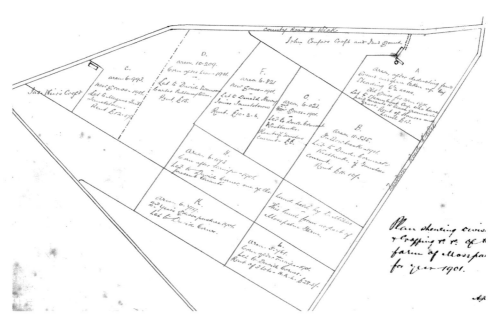

The plan showing the division of the ground at Mosspalm and the letting to different individuals for crops and grazing in 1901.

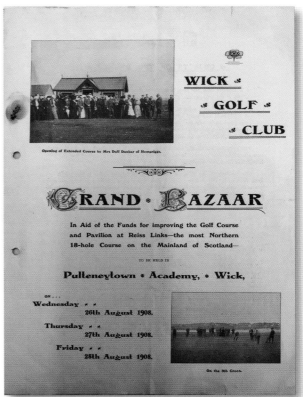

Above: Jane Louisa with the Duff-Dunbars' first son, George, in 1878.

Right: The Grand Bazaar was held over three days in August 1908 to raise funds for Wick Golf Club. (courtesy Roy Mackenzie)

A shooting party with dogs, guns and their bag for the day at the front door of Ackergill Tower. The date is unknown but it was possibly in the 1890s.

Left: The great hall in Ackergill Tower with décor typical of the late Victorian – Edwardian period. (Johnston Collection, Wick Society)

Right: The other end of the great hall. (Johnston Collection, Wick Society)

Hempriggs House, considerably enlarged and modified since it was originally built by William Dunbar in 1692. The two-storey central porch was added in 1875. (Johnston Collection, Wick Society)

Left: Jane Louisa Duff-Dunbar in 1882, at the age of 26.

Right: A much-scratched photograph recording an address being read to George Duff-Dunbar at Ackergill to celebrate his marriage to Sybil Tate in July 1903. Sybil stands behind George, in the checked suit, and on her right are her mother-in-law, Mrs Duff-Dunbar and George's younger brother Kenneth James.

Kenneth Dunbar, in his uniform as a lieutenant-commander in the Royal Navy, his wife Katharine and his brother George with their mother, Mrs Duff-Dunbar, together possibly in Ealing where the couple had their home at the time of Kenneth's death in August 1916.

Above: Kenneth Duff-Dunbar and Katharine Daw on their wedding day in February 1915.

Right: How Kenneth's death was reported in the John o'Groat Journal. (courtesy Roy Mackenzie)

NORTHERN INTEREST IN THE WAR.

NORTHERN CASUALTIES

DEATH OF LIEUT.-COMMANDER DUFF-DUNBAR.

As will be seen from obituary column to-day, the death in the service of his country is announced of Lieut.-Commander Kenneth J. Duff-Dunbar, younger son of Mrs Duff-Dunbar, Ackergill Tower, Wick, and brother of Sir George Duff-Dunbar, Baronet of Hempriggs. The sad intelligence has come on the eve of our going to press, and will be received with the deepest regret in Wick and throughout the country generally.

A member of an old and well-known Caithness family, Commander Duff-Dunbar's brilliant career in the Navy was watched with pride, and honours gained by him in the present war shed lustre on his native county.

Commander Duff-Dunbar, who was in his thirtieth year, having been born on 16th October, 1886, entered the Navy at the age of 15, his first ship being H.M.S. Britannia. He was promoted Lieutenant with seniority in February, 1907, and in 1909 was in charge of a submarine. In November, 1912, he was promoted to H.M.S. Princess Royal, and was on board that vessel in the naval engagements at the Bight of Heligoland and the Dogger Bank. On 25th February, 1915, he was promoted to the rank of Lieutenant-Commander. There was much gratification in Wick and Caithness when in January of this year Commander Duff-Dunbar was awarded the Distinguished Service Order in recognition of a submarine feat of exceptional daring and brilliancy.

Commander Duff-Dunbar was married in St. John's Church, Edinburgh, in February, 1915, to Miss Catherine Bennet Daw, daughter of the late Mr W. A. Daw of The Grange, Ealing, London. There will be much sympathy for the young bride of little over a year in her desolation, and also for the dead hero's bereaved mother, who is so universally beloved and respected.

LOCAL SOLDIER DIES IN HOSPITAL.

The people of Wick will hear with deep regret of the death of Pte. David Campbell, Black Watch, son of Mr David Campbell, railway surfaceman, Francis Street, Wick. As intimated a few weeks ago, he sustained severe injuries to

Ackergill Tower. (courtesy Alan Hendry)

9 | 'the mason is not near done'

During this time Alexander Miller was also overseeing work on the house at Ackergill. Sir Benjamin wanted a staircase built inside the tower to replace the outside stone stair, which would have reached only to the first floor and was a common feature of tall buildings up until this time but was now being seen as distinctly old fashioned. Miller enlisted a wright or carpenter called John Cormack and his two assistants, and an unnamed stone mason to examine how this might be done. What was found was not calculated to reassure Sir Benjamin, as Miller wrote in a letter on 14 February 1801 [9.7.8]: '... after examining everything about making a stair it does not seem practicable to make an inside stair without spoiling one of the low rooms and one of the upper rooms and the wrights are very suspicious as to the sufficiency of the joists that must be cut before an entrance is made from the lower flat to the second storey they seem to be afraid that the joists will not be strong enough to bear bridling for that purpose, they say if the joists is once cut and then found insufficient the whole floor will be irreparably lost in this situation of things I could not pretend to persuade them to begin such a hazardous piece of work; I fear the outside stair must be had recourse to it altho it will no doubt make a very awkward appearance we will however let it alone until we hear from you again.'

To make matters worse, slates had fallen from the roof in the winter and water was getting in. The mason told Miller that the roof was so bad he could not guarantee to make it watertight. Miller set up a long ladder so that Cormack and his colleagues could climb in at a garret window. More bad news – three couples were 'much decayed' and the sarking on the south side had turned too soft to hold a nail. There was nothing for it, in the carpenters' view, but to take all the slates off and fix the roof. There was no point in starting work on an inside stair until the building was once again weather-tight. 'I entreat of you to write immediately and to give your own opinion and directions,' wrote Miller, 'there will be full time for hearing from you before the season come in proper for beginning the roof.' The state of the tower and the need for renovation meant, however, that the house would not be ready to receive Lady Dunbar at the time she had proposed to come north. Miller tried as gently as possible to suggest that Lady Dunbar should stay in Mrs Anderson's house in Wick. 'I have no reason to believe that Lady Dunbar will be fond of residing in Wick but what can be done if her ladyship come to the country in the belief that the house of Ackergill is in order, and when she arrives finds nothing but ruins both you and Lady Dunbar will feel yourselves disappointed without a remedy and I am sure it will be very vexing to me and to some others I thought it best to tell my mind freely leaving it to yourself to do as you please.'

The mason began to take away the outside stone stair but this aroused fears for the security of the exposed wall. Miller ordered a thin supporting wall to be built 'all the way from the entry to the drawing room to the North Gavle; neither the mason or me could contrive any other means to support the old wall and to make it have a desent appearance.' In the letter in which he described this action [9.7.6], Miller added with an impatient tone 'the house is in much worse condition than you or any other person could immagin; I wrote you long since about the badness of the roof and am surprised that you sent no answer, especially as the season is so closs at hand when something must be done if it is to be done at all.'

To compound his worries, the factor's son was unwell and he himself was feeling under the weather. Miller had reached the age of 60, and his energies were understandably not what they had once been, although he was to go on playing an important role in local affairs for many years. All he now had to report to Sir Benjamin, who made things worse by being tardy in replying, was bad news: 'The old house will I see cost a great deal of money and I am much afraid you will have but little satisfaction for it: I expected also to have heard something from you about the house in Wick whether or not it would answer as a temporary residence for Lady Dunbar at least until the house of Ackergill is put in such order as you directed, which I am afraid will not be got accomplished by the time you wish it.'

The work went ahead but, unsurprisingly, took longer than Miller had hoped. In June he wrote to say that 'the masons is not near done with the Tower the work that you ordered to be done at Ackergill will not all be completed the middle of harvest' [9.7.6A]. A month later, the masons were nearing the end of their task. Miller gave John Cormack £50 to settle with them on 15 July, and he was expecting the carpenters to start their work right away [9.7.3]. Cormack seems to have been too slow for the factor's taste, as Miller wrote in August 'we have been spurring John Cormack as much as possible … I cannot say that he is so active or pushing as might have been expected although at the same time I believe he has your interests at heart, but he neither has that skill nor activity necessary for such a charge, I am not sure but he is offended that you have not wrote him on the subject for a considerable time back, please do so now and tell him that you wish everything done agreeably to your former direction excepting the east wing of the house that you had wrote me some time ago to stop the repairing of' [9.7.2]. Further references to the repairs and changes at the Tower have not been uncovered so far but we would like to assume that Cormack did complete the job.

Miller kept Sir Benjamin apprised of other local affairs. He bought canvas for a new sower for almost £35 for the farm, and sent his sloop 'to the south firth', presumably the Moray coast, for lime, to fertilise the soil [9.7.7]. From time to time he mentions the cutting of ware or kelp on the shore. This was a lucrative product during the Napoleonic era when the war prevented the importation of chemicals such as iodine, soda and potash, all of which could be extracted from the ash of burned kelp. Miller thought that Sir Benjamin wanted kelp to be burned and issued instructions to John Cormack to engage a gang of men and women to do this but later ordered him to stop as it turned out to be against the laird's wishes [9.7.3]. Miller included in his letters some news about local people. On 17 August 1801 he wrote that Wester had been 'dropsical for more than a twelve month he is now and has been for some time past quiet [...gap...] seldom knows anybody and believes that his family has [....] away from Wester and exchanged it for another place he is in a most deplorable situation' [9.7.2]. Sutherland of Wester, who held his land on a wadset from the Dunbars, died at last on 21 August. Miller thought the family was hard-pressed and suggested that Sir Benjamin should begin to prepare early to redeem the wadset if that was his intention and give the family 'timeous warning' [9.7.47].

Miller had a considerable financial interest in the fishing industry. On 17 August he included the news that they had enjoyed 'a tolerable herring fishing but the herrings are not of so good a quality as I have seen them; our cod fishing has been good for nothing this season' [9.7.2]. Two weeks later he summed up the season: 'Our herring fishing is now over ... we had a great prospect once and then it took off for ten days so that we thought it was all over ... however after we got a few good hauls so that upon the whole we have had a tolerable good seasons fishing better indeed than it has been for several years past' [9.7.47]. What Miller does not mention in this letter was that plans were now afoot to alter the face of the Caithness herring fishing for good.

10 | 'such a harbour will be of great advantage'

The British Fisheries Society had been formed in 1786 to develop the industry specified in its title. It founded fishing settlements at Tobermory, Lochbay and Ullapool before it turned its eyes on Caithness by asking the engineer Thomas Telford in 1790 to extend a survey they had commissioned of their west coast ports to include an inspection of any small harbours worthy of improvement around the Moray Firth.[11] Telford found that Alexander Miller already had a herring business at Staxigoe and that there were a few other, small-scale ventures in the locality, for example at Keiss, Sarclet and Clyth. Telford recommended to the Society that they should choose Wick as the focus for their plans.[12] Up until now merchant vessels had been using mainly Staxigoe and Broadhaven. Telford's idea was not an original one – in 1793, the engineer John Rennie had also made plans for a settlement and harbour at Wick for the Society[13] – but it lent the concept renewed force.

The Dunbar papers contain an extract from the Minutes of the British Fisheries Society dated 27 April 1792 which reads: 'Resolved that the establishing of a Settlement at Wick in the County of Caithness and the making of a proper Harbour there would be of great importance to the success of the Fishings on the East Coast of Scotland and of general use to the Coasting Trade, the Foreign Commerce and to the Navigation of these Kingdoms.

'Resolved that in the present state of the Funds of the Society, and the engagements they have entered into, the Society cannot engage in any very expensive undertaking, yet, in hopes that the arrears of past subscriptions shall be speedily paid up and that new subscriptions may be obtained for so valuable a purpose, that Sir John Sinclair Baronet be empowered to correspond and treat with Benjamin

Dunbar Esq of Hempriggs, the proprietor of the ground … for the acquisition of any quantity of land, not less than 1500 acres, upon a perpetual feu duty …

'Resolved that all the money subscribed to the stock of the Society by persons residing or having property in Caithness shall be laid out on settlement upon the said lands, if the purchase is made and in improvement of the said harbour at Wick,

'Resolved that all future subscriptions to the general stock of the Society when paid, be applied to this object, not exceeding three thousand pounds …' [90.1.13].

The Society began to negotiate with Sir Benjamin through Sir John Sinclair of Ulbster, who from 1792 became one of its directors. Although not a member of the Society, Sir Benjamin had already established a fishing village of his own at Louisburgh, named after his eldest daughter Louisa born in 1788, on the north side of the Wick River. The Society wished to build on the south side of the river on the Hempriggs estate but several years were to pass before it could raise the funds for the venture and complete other formalities. Alexander Miller remained a keen supporter of the project but was also loyally looking after Sir Benjamin's personal interests, as his letters show.

Negotiations became quite protracted. On 3 October 1801 and again three days later, Sir John Sinclair wrote from Edinburgh to Miller with notes of the agreement to be entered into between the Society and Sir Benjamin [41.5.7]. With his own experience of investment in herring fishing, first from almost forty years before when he had formed a partnership with the Wick merchant John Anderson and John Sutherland of Wester to equip three boats for the Shetland fishing, Miller was keenly interested in the prospects offered by this new development. A secure haven at Wick would allow the extension of the fishing season beyond the summer months of July and August and encourage the use of decked vessels with their superior catching potential. 'The quantity of herring that may be caught by decked vessels on the east coast of Caithness is beyond calculation but nothing in that way can be attempted until a safe and spacious harbour is first made,' wrote Miller enthusiastically in his reply to Sir John on the morning after the all-important communication arrived from Edinburgh [18.5.34].

'[That] Such a harbour will be of great advantage to the country in general won't be denied and without doubt will be particularly advantageous to the estate of Hempriggs because it borders on that harbour,' continued Miller. 'I therefore think Sir Benjamin Dunbar ought to make some sacrifice [but] on the other hand I do not think the Society ought to desire to sacrifice too much of his interest'. The factor immediately began to argue in Sir Benjamin's favour, suggesting plainly that the rent of £40 a year the Society was offering to pay for the ground they wanted on the south side of the river mouth was not enough, although on paper it appeared considerably more than Sir Benjamin was receiving from the tenants who presently used it. In fact, in Miller's view, 'had Sir Benjamin Dunbar the liberty of granting a perpetual feu of the premises to anyone he would have little difficulty in obtaining £100 yearly rent for it, it is of great extent not one foot of it but is improvable, all a good clay bottom requiring nothing but the plough, spade and manure to make it yield good crops of any kind of grain or vegetables this country can produce and there is a good lime quarry and lime kiln on the premises. This with its situation otherwise makes it one of the best, I believe the very best, purchase that the Society has yet made everything considered'.

Miller also told Sir John that his master would not agree to the standard clause 'Together with mosses, muirs, meadows, grazings, common pasturages and other parts, pendicles and pertinents belonging to the said lands' as this would set no limit on the Society's claims on the Hempriggs estate. The factor cunningly suggested that this had surely been included by mistake and that the Society's claim ought to be only to 'the utmost boundary of the … feu without any other claim of servitude.' Sir Benjamin might concede access to some moss, perhaps close by the Hempriggs loch, but he had 'very little to spare'. The laird should also be 'indemnified for any loss he may sustain' when the Society installed a ditch or other means to convey water from the loch across the estate for its own purposes. Miller thought of several other matters of which the Society should be aware – the location of quarries, the rental value of the mills on the Hempriggs burn, the salmon houses and the salmon fishers' lodging on the shore, the leases of the tenants in the township of Harrow, and the value of the timber in their houses. Miller had a keen business sense and was willing to bargain strongly, even riskily, with Sir John, presumably because he sensed or knew how desirous the Society was to have a Caithness base. It was a seller's market and Miller was determined to miss no opportunity. 'If you had leisure when in the country to have gone over the ground and examined it tentatively [attentively] with me or any other person who could have given you the necessary information,' he wrote, 'I am sure you would see the propriety of what I have said with respect to the yearly [letter torn but the missing word is probably 'feu'] and I think other things also, at any rate I do assure you the opinion I have given is perfectly candid according to my judgement of the matter, I [obscure] wish Sir Benjamin Dunbars interest very well and in doing so I could heartily wish that he would agree to dispose of this property to the society on liberal terms because I think his estate will in the end be much benefited thereby.'

Miller lost no time in copying to Sir Benjamin, then in Ireland, his reply to Sir John, adding a covering note to explain the course he had taken and encouraging the laird to accommodate the Society. 'It is what occurred to me as proper …' said Miller, adding '… perhaps he [Sir John] may think the yearly feu I mention too high were you to drop £10 of it better do it than stick the business …'. Miller also warns Sir Benjamin that, should the project of the Society fail, the public would blame him.

Sir John Sinclair redrafted the letter of agreement to take into account Miller's views and sent a copy to the Staxigoe merchant [41.5.7]. As soon as he had received this, Miller took time out from unloading two boats with cargoes of fish to pen his observations and reply on 24 October [12.5.8]. The protagonists in this negotiation appreciated what the Society's plans could mean for Caithness. 'I cannot say what Sir Benjamin Dunbar may do but I shall by Tuesdays post writ him and recommend strongly to him to close with the Society without delay,' wrote Miller. On 30 October, he kept his word, addressing his letter to Sir Benjamin at Newton Barry in County Wexford [9.7.46]. 'Upon the whole it is my serious advice to you to authorise Sir John Sinclair to close with the Society immediately,' Miller urged. 'In his letter to me he says you had wrote him and in some measure had refered him to me, he does not say he had answered your letter but I think he has surely done so and sent you a copy of the minute of agreement with the amendments … I will be happy to be informed that you are to close immediately with the Society, being well persuaded that if you do not close now their [there] will never be such another opportunity in my time, or perhaps in yours; besides the many great advantages that you and your Estate must soon derive from this Scheme takeing place, you will immediately after Whitsunday receive an addition of upwards of £30 Sterling of yearly Rent.' Miller concluded his letter with news of slow progress with work on the buildings at Ackergill.

On 20 November 1801 [9.7.], Miller expressed anxiety for Sir Benjamin's health: 'For some time past I have been in daily expectation of hearing from you I wish you may be well as there is many flying reports through this country of you being very bad but I hope it is no more than the trouble that you had some time ago which is now talked of, only your unexpected long silence makes me fear that there may be some truth in the reports now in circulation I will be glad soon to have my fears removed by a letter from yourself.'

Possibly Miller was feeling left out of things as he continued by saying Sir John Sinclair had told him 'some time ago' that he and Sir Benjamin had 'settled about the new harbour at Wick and the grounds adjacent.' Sir John had sent Miller a copy of the agreement they had signed. One can read between the lines Miller's disappointment that Sir Benjamin had not done the same. 'I am very glad to see the matter so far concluded that it now rests with the British Fishing Society to ratify what you and Sir John have agreed to, whether it come to anything or not the public will no longer believe either of you but I hope it will not now be put off longer I have not answered Sir Johns letter yet Altho I ought to have done it before now but I waited until I would hear from you and know your sentiments fully.' Miller seems determined to maintain his position as a key adviser to the laird – 'care ought to be taken that your meaning be perfectly understood every article' – and talks about ensuring the rights of tenants for pasturage and the use of mills.

More correspondence from Staxigoe to Sir Benjamin followed. Miller sent proposed plans for the new settlement of Pulteneytown in December (unfortunately this plan, if a copy exists in the Dunbar Papers, has not so far been unearthed), with much comment on the content and a cautious reminder that Sir Benjamin should go over the ground with the surveyor, a certain Mr Campbell (probably the same William Campbell, the Keiss schoolmaster, who was involved in surveying for the Hill o' Wick case), in case the Society took more than they said they would.

Sir Benjamin's absence with the Fencibles and his travelling about the country caused delay, as John Mackenzie, the secretary of the British Fisheries Society said in a letter written in London on 14 December 1802 [9.7.40] and sent to Miller to enquire about the present occupiers of parts of the Links on the south side of the river mouth at Wick – '… you will have the goodness to acquaint me, for the information of the British Society for fisheries, who the present occupiers of the Spot of the Links marked G, and of the place called old yards, and marked D and E on Mr Campbell's plan of the Lands designed for the settlement at Wick.' The secretary added that the Society was expecting to hear good news about their application to the government for funding for the Wick project. Miller replied two days after Christmas to say the marked areas on the Links were used by the tenants of the township of Banks but that Sir Benjamin should have 'little difficulty in getting possession when he please of those two parts marked D and E if the Society find it necessary to get possession before the present occupiers Lease expires' [9.7.46/40]

The contract between the British Fisheries Society and Sir Benjamin, by which 390 acres of land on the south side of the river mouth became the site for Pulteneytown, was signed at last on 11 March 1803. On the 25th of that month, in a letter dealing mostly with estate business [9.7.35], Alex Miller expressed his satisfaction. 'I received both your letters of the 8' and 12th Curr, the last brought what I think was not only good news for this part of the Country in general but must be of particular advantage to your own family providing the Society go on in the way we have now reason to expect they will do in makeing a Harbour and placing settlers on their lands; every one who I have seen since I received your last letter rejoices at the Prospect of a Harbour at Wick.'

In her history of the British Fisheries Society, published in Edinburgh by John Donald in 1978, Jean Dunlop noted that the Society agreed to pay a feu duty of £69 per year for their acquisition. Further squabbling over such things as salmon fishing and kelp harvesting rights raised this sum after twenty years to £169. By 1806, the Society had raised through government grants and investment £9,500 and construction at Wick began with the replacement of the wooden bridge over the Wick River with one of stone, designed by Telford and built under the eye of the architect George Burn. The building of the harbour followed. Telford laid out plans for the new settlement to be called Pulteneytown after Sir William Pulteney, the governor of the Society who died in 1805 and was buried in Westminster Abbey.

11 | 'much mischeif is done on the coast'

At the same time as he was corresponding with Sir Benjamin on the negotiations with the British Fisheries Society, Alexander Miller was commenting on other estate business. For example, on 20 November 1801, he described how two farmers from 'near Elgin' came in search of a farm 'in this country' [9.7]. Miller sent them off with his son, Donald, to visit the township of Harland and the minister's farm. The minister of Wick at the time was William Sutherland, a native of Tain who had been ordained in the parish in 1765 after being presented to the congregation by Sir William Dunbar as patron. In 1793 Mr Sutherland wrote an account of the parish for inclusion in Sir John Sinclair's *Statistical Account of Scotland* and mentioned there how the glebe, the land dedicated to providing the minister's livelihood, had been 'exchanged for a sufficient equivalent on Mr Dunbar's estate'.[14] He also declared his stipend to be £97 13s 4d sterling. The two Morayshire farmers were 'well pleased' with the glebe land, thinking the soil 'in general of a good quality' although the place itself was 'in wretched bad order.' This suggests that it had not been cultivated for some time and that the visitors were making an opening gambit in some canny bargaining. Clearly, though, they were interested as 'they looked at it twice afterwards and came here wishing to bargain about it,' said Miller, regretting that he could not conclude the business there and then but had to communicate with Sir Benjamin. Miller told the prospective tenants that the farm had to yield 60 bolls of 'farm' or ferm, a term that meant rent paid originally in kind but now rendered as the cash equivalent of the stipulated amount of grain, and not to be confused with the general meaning of the word farm. The visitors did not like this but agreed to it after Miller had explained that it was used to provide the minister's victual and stipend. They also proposed to pay £30 sterling per year, 'which to be sure in my opinion is a very high rent', wrote Miller.

Sir Benjamin's absence meant the negotiation could not be concluded and the Moray men went away. 'I wished them to bind themselves in writing to the offer they had made until I could hear from you when they might depend on it I would write them but they said that would be tying them down and preventing them taking another farm if such came their way,' explained Miller.

Mr Sutherland the minister, however, had spotted the visitors inspecting his fields and, perhaps suddenly fearing for his possession, wrote to Miller to offer to pay 60 bolls of ferm for a 'lease of his present farm exclusive of Gillock and Gallowhill'. Miller was unsympathetic – 'he never would agree to pay farm out of his possession until he saw Donald and the south country men traversing the lands and now I suppose he may give up all thoughts of it as his offer is a great deal below what others have proposed to give.'

Before Miller could finish the letter in which he described this affair, a better offer for the farm reached him from the Morayshire visitors. They were willing to pay Mr Sutherland's whole victual and money stipend, and take out a lease for eighteen years. '… I really think you ought to authorise me to fix,' urged Miller, '… in case you may have forgot what the yearly stipend be you pay Mr Sutherland is I shall mention it the victual stipend is 59 B[olls] 2 F[irlots] 2 P[ecks and 0] L[ippies] [page torn] money stipend £32 5s 10½d With Gillock and Gallowhill set well you will have a very great increase of rent on Mr Sutherlands present farm at present he only pays £54 yearly for the whole …'.

Miller had also received an offer from a tenant in Reiss of £40 of grassum for a park of Harland but in relation to this he reminded Sir Benjamin that there were several men in the Legion who wished to have farms 'and who are able and willing to pay good rents.' Miller proceeded to outline the advantages in letting to good tenants: 'I would safely recommend it to you to set the farms to people who knows something of the business and who you believe will pay attention to it, its very true you may get persons to take some of your farms who are both able and willing to pay good rents but if they are not attentive although they may pay for a few years in the end land and houses may be allowed to go to wreck and the rent may fall into your own hands in such bad condition at a time when you will have great difficulty in getting it set at a low rent, you know such has been the case before but it would be highly proper as much as possible to avoid the like in time to come, when you return to the country and attend to the affairs of your estate I think it possibly highly gratifying to bring you to see your houses and [obscure] lands occupied by such persons as will keep them in good order and will be able and willing to pay your rents punctually.'

Among the Dunbar Papers is a tack drawn up on 10 April 1801 for the town and lands of Achlipster in the parish of Halkirk between Sir Benjamin and two men in the Legion, Sergeant Benjamin Sutherland and Donald Murray, a private soldier [12.5.40]. The two men were to take on Achlipster for eighteen years from Whitsunday 1806. The wording of the tack seems to be standard. The tacksmen gained possession of the township and lands with the 'houses, biggings, yards, tofts, crofts, grazings, parks and pendicles, mosses, muirs, pasturages' and so on but the laird reserved the rights to 'all mines, minerals, forests, lime, slate and stone quarries if any be within the said lands'. The annual rent was to be £41 19s 6d, and the woodwork on the houses on the farm – in the roof, and including the doors and jambs – was to be assessed at the start and the end of the lease and taken into account in any final settlement. The tack was drawn up at Newton Barry and witnessed by Captain Robert Kennedy and Ensign John Miller.

Alexander Miller took out a tack himself in November 1802 on a half-acre of ground lying below the brae at 'the Broadhaven of Papigoe' [12.5.41]. In the agreement Miller defines himself as a 'merchant in Staxigoe'. He wanted the land primarily for a fish-curing operation. The tack duty was set at 10 shillings per year. Miller undertook to build a dwelling house on the half-acre of sufficient quality as to be worth £10 in ten years' time. The tack was to run for ninety-nine years and bound Miller's heirs and successors to the agreement, with each successor paying an extra year's rent on taking up possession. The document was signed at Ackergill Tower by Sir Benjamin, and witnessed by 'William Mackay of the late Caithness Legion and John Ross gardener'. The Legion had of course been disbanded by this time.

In one of his letters [9.7.39] written from Staxigoe on 10 January 1803 to Sir Benjamin via the Edinburgh advocate Kenneth Mckenzie, Miller mentions shipwrecks. 'Much mischief is done on the coast for some time past, on Friday last a vessel was wrecked at Dunbeath and all hands lost except one man – Another was drove ashore on the Sands of Keiss last Saturday night and of ten people who composed the Ships Company seven was saved and three drowned, I hear James Dow has taken charge of the vessel and crew, an excellent hand for that purpose to be sure.'

An early reference to a shipwreck on the Caithness coast occurs in letters to the Laird of Hempriggs (at the time, Sir William Dunbar) on behalf of an Edinburgh merchant Patrick Wilkie.[15] One letter reads in part: 'Much Honoured, Our Ship now being wracked And the cargo like to be lost I earnestly desyre you will be pleased to assist us with the help of your Countrey people And they shall be honestly payed for their work ...'. The oldest letter on the subject is dated in Wick on 5 December 1699 but it appears that Wilkie had little satisfaction for the same plea was registered with the Court of Session in October 1701.

A letter written by David Murray at Castlehill to Sir William Dunbar on 18 March 1776 shows what could happen to a cargo from any ship wrecked on the Caithness shore in the days when such incidents provided a business opportunity [8.6.3]. Murray had heard from a company of merchants about the latter's interest in a cargo of timber. The vessel is not named but the merchants were keen to buy the wood. 'We were lately informed that a wreck loaded with firr logs was cast ashore near Wick and that the greatest part of the logs (amounting as we hear to about 4000 cubic feet) has been safely landed at Wick,' they wrote, 'If it is not sold before this comes to your hand we would incline to have it purchased for us, providing it can be bought not exceeding 6d per cubic foot in full of the price duties shiping [sic].' In his capacity as Admiral Depute, Sir William had an interest in the wreck that Murray was acknowledging.

Murray gives no indication of where the merchants were writing from, but he quotes their fear that a 'ship of proper burden to carry away the whole wood' might not be able to find a secure anchorage at Wick and that therefore there had to be 'expedition in the shiping'. Murray offered to act as an intermediary between Sir William and the southern merchants. 'If its agreeable to you [that is, to Sir William] and that you have influence with Mr George Sinclair in Bilbster to oversee the measuring of the wood when it is to be Shipt I shall write to the Gentlemen to referr it to him also. Let me know if there will be 4000 feet or more of it, As they may not choose to buy it, if its below that number. I would think if you are to sell it altogether in this manner for ready money you would cause collect what is in other parts of it along the coast. Please to favour me with an answer that suits yourself, that by transmiting of it to the gentlemen with a copie of this letter they may be satifyed I have obeyed their orders. I am [etc].'

Murray added a postscript: 'If you are under necessity to Roup the wood and think you may not make so much of it in that way as the offer made you now in ready money I woud think you might put off the roup for two or three weeks until I can have powers to offer for it at the Roup But I would not purchase it for these Gentlemen to load them with the trouble & Expence of preserving it from the time it is bought until it is shipt, I would only pay for the number of feet shipt. DM.'

New charts of the Pentland Firth, far more accurate than any hitherto available, had been drawn by Murdoch Mackenzie and published in 1750. These, combined with lighthouses constructed at Kinnaird Head in 1787, North Ronaldsay in 1789 and the Pentland Skerries in 1794, and with the threat from privateers during the Napoleonic War, had encouraged an increase in the shipping making use of the Pentland Firth as a shorter route from the North Sea to the Atlantic. In turn this had resulted in a rise in the number of wrecks on the Caithness coast. It also brought to the fishermen who knew the northern waters lucrative opportunities to act as pilots for the dangerous passage between the northern mainland and Orkney. This was a competitive business – with the pilots racing to be first to reach a passing merchant vessel to secure the job – and several men moved with their families from the shores of the Firth to Staxigoe where they could more readily catch passing trade. On 25 March 1803, Alexander Miller in one of his letters [9.7.35] mentions but does not name three Freswick men to whom he had agreed to let Elzie. It is a sad story, as one of the men 'their best hand' had recently died and the other two felt 'unfit to manage the place.' Miller says, 'I told the man that I could not make him free of it now as others might not take it at this late season of the year, but I desired him to return this day.' Fortunately, as Miller relates, a satisfactory outcome was achieved. 'Some days thereafter I was speaking of this matter in the house and rather vexed at the seeming disappointment when Mr M'Pherson asked me the Rent expected out of it yearly. I told him what it was and wished to know if he had any inclination to take such a farm, he did not say much at that time but next day he and Donald went out and examined Ilsie.' M'Pherson offered to take the farm on for six years with an option to extend his lease for nineteen years, for an annual rent of 15 guineas, and furthermore take out a ninety-nine-year lease on three to five acres of the waste ground. 'This in my opinion is as good an offer as you can expect …,' wrote Miller to Sir Benjamin. It is probable that the pilots from Freswick were released from any obligation without penalty.

Miller thought more about the number of wrecks on the Caithness coast and told Sir Benjamin, who was then in London, in a letter on 22 February 1803 that he had sent to Sir John Sinclair a list of 'vessels wrecked or stranded between Duncansby Head and Dunbeath since I first remember' as a further encouragement to the British Fisheries Society to build a harbour at Wick [9.7.36]. Miller recalled thirty-one such incidents. Unfortunately he did not include with the letter a copy of this list but the story of the wreck of the *St Nicholay* (see page 172) may have been all too typical.

In his letter on 25 March 1803 [9.7.35] Miller told Sir Benjamin about another idea: 'It had occurred to me that you have one of the best opportunitys you possibly could look for to get a large track of your waste ground near the Killimsters Peopeld [sic].' This was in the context of a deal Sir Benjamin had struck with his agent, a lawyer called K. M'Kinzie, whereby M'Kinzie would take possession of a farm at Killimster from the forthcoming Martinmas, i.e. November 1803. Miller astutely suggested to Sir Benjamin that he could make use of this time gap to turn to advantage his possessions at Reiss – 'you must have the grass, houses and kaileyards of Reiss to dispose on from Whitsunday to martinmass next, also the Straw of the ensueing crop to dispose on.' 'These are the best materials you can be possessed of for forwarding a new settlement on the waste ground near the Killimsters,' continued Miller, 'such of the Reiss people as are willing to treat with you, you can accomodate them with their present houses, grass and kaileyards until Martinmass next, against which time if they are active they may have new houses built on the new settlements and at Martinmass they may carry their corns, chaf and straw to their new habitations which will give them plenty of provender and be the means of providing some manure for their new lands.'

'I believe very few of them have taken houses any where yet,' explained Miller, 'and from what I learn Mr M'kinzie has bargained with only a very few of the very worst of them; indeed I do not see much that Mr M'kinzie is doing either one way or other, however I have nothing to say as to that. No doubt the tenants will now be looking about for shelter some way or other; if you think well of what I have suggested [sic] it would be of advantage how soon you come to the Country to make proposals to them: You know it is near the time of planting kaile, a thing of consequence to poor people, it is likely they will be more hurried in looking for places of residence on this acct than they otherwise would have been.'

It is not at all clear which 'waste ground near the Killimsters' Miller had in mind. The Killimster Moss is now a broad tract of low-lying, boggy ground around two lochs draining sluggishly to the valley of the Wick River. The wetland and bog were probably more extensive in 1803, and Miller may have been talking about the drier acres on any side of the wetland. The letter is also significant in that it shows that in lowland Caithness Miller and possibly others were looking to increase the number of tenants as part of the general drive to improve agriculture and bring more land into useful cultivation. Further south in the Highlands the shifting of tenants from their land to allow the consolidation of sheep farms to be let to incomers, the series of changes normally referred to as the Clearances, had barely begun but were soon to attract notoriety.

Notes

1. Caithness Monumental Inscriptions, Vol 2, p. 25.

2. A.R.B. Haldane, *Three Centuries of Scottish Posts*, 1971, p. 96. In the 1790s, the Thurso postmaster was allowed £47 4s per year to pay the runners who carried mail between Thursoa nd Dunbeath.

3. The Inneses of Sandside were an important Caithness family. In *Ane Account of the Familie of Innes* (Aberdeen Spalding Club, 1864), Duncan Forbes says that an Alexander Innes received a crown charter of the lands of Dunbeath, Reay and Sandside on 8 August 1507. Dunbeath was later acquired by the Sinclairs, and the Reay properties by the Forbes family. R. Innes-Smith explains in his history, *The House of Innes* (1990), that William Innes, a descendant of the original Alexander but born on the wrong side of the blanket, worked as a factor on the Caithness estates of Lord Forbes from 1610 until he became the first laird of Sandside in 1626, and also acquired Isauld and Borlum in 1637. Innes-Smith says that Lord Forbes was regarded in Caithness as an incomer (shades of what befell Glenorchy) and was so harassed by the locals that he was glad to get shot of his property to his factor, who may incidentally have been robbing his employer in any case. The alleged embezzling apart, the rise of the Inneses and the slightly later settlement of the Dunbars show some interesting parallels.

4. See Billy Kay (with Cailean Maclean), *Knee Deep in Claret: A Celebration of Wine and Scotland,* 1983.

5. James T. Calder, *Sketch of the Civil and Traditional History of Caithness*, 1887, p. 213.

6. Ian H.M. Scobie, *An Old Highland Fencible Corps*, 1914. This is an account of the Reay Fencibles, also known as Mackay's Highlanders but not to be confused with the similarly named regiment raised to fight in the Thirty Years' War.

7. Sir John Sinclair's *Account of the Rothsay and Caithness Fencibles* is a slim volume that does its best to promote the image of a military unit that never saw action. For an unknown reason, Colonel David Stewart does not include the Caithness Legion in his famous work *Sketches of the Character, Manners and Present State of the Highlanders of Scotland* (1822) but has a section on the Rothesay and Caithness Fencibles.

8. A letter written on 24 April 1798 by Captain Alexander Macpherson to the Wick merchant Harry Bain describing the same incident was published in the *John o' Groat Journal* on 23 March 1876.

9. J. Firebrace & A. Rawlings, *His Majesty's Fraser Fencible Regiment of Foot 1794–1802*, 1993. Other Fencible histories include those by H.B. Mackintosh: *The Northern or Gordon Fencibles 1778–1783*, 1929; and *The Grant, Strathspey or First Highland Fencible Regiment 1793–1799*, 1934.

10. John Henderson, *General View of the Agriculture of the County of Caithness*, 1812, p. 123.

11. Jean Dunlop, *The British Fisheries Society 1786–1893*, 1978.

12. NRS GD9/32/2.

13. NRS GD9/259.

14. *OSA*, Wick, X, 1793.

15. NRS RH 15/13/19.

Part 4

Trustees, travel and common land

1 | 'as to my creditors shall appear proper'

When he was in London in March 1805, Sir Benjamin drew up a list of his properties and their rents in Caithness, 'from memory ... and is not far wrong', as he added for whomever this document was intended [41.5.10]. He also listed what increases in income he could expect from various properties, which suggests that he was compiling the list to satisfy existing or would-be creditors. It gives a succinct picture of the extent of the Dunbar estate.

Rental of the Estate of Hempriggs as at Martinmass next 1805. (The amounts are in sterling.)

Reiss, West Park and links	£600
East Noss	130
Upper Ackergill	180
West Noss, Field, Quoystain and Elzey	80
Papigo and the Park	150
Hillhead including the Rockhead	200
South Killimster	250
North Killimster	250
Shorelands	105
Upper Park	42
Lower Papigo and Mill	100
Wick Staxigo & Louisburgh	160
Ministers farm	106
Harland and Gillock & Whitefield	120
Salmon fishing, Mills, Quarries, Fews of Commons and Kelp Shores	200

Wester	100
Windlas	70
My own Domain (Ackergill Tower and home farm)	400
Total North side of the Water of Wick	**£3243**
Hempriggs Mains	250
Moss palm & Newtown	40
Milltown	30
Moss Edge	50
Joint Stock Society [Feu duty from the British Fisheries Society for Pulteneytown]	62
Small tenants	300
Total South side the Water	**£732**
Latheronwheel estate	£186
Ditto Mains	20
Dalnaglaton	100
Achalibster	42
Dalnavullan	8
Badgillisried & Tollichen	12
Westerdale	5
Shinvall & Acharascall	50
Total Highland estates	423
Do North Side the Water of Wick	3243
Do South Do	732
	£4398

Sir Benjamin expected changes in rental agreements and leases to raise the value of the estate by another £2,035, bringing the total to £6,433. This is a substantial sum and, although it can be misleading to seek a modern equivalent, it equates to several million pounds in today's currency[1].

Sir Benjamin, in fact, was mired in financial difficulties for many years. A list of his debts was compiled in December 1809 during the establishment of a trust to administer his affairs. The document detailing this resolution to a long-standing problem runs to 47 pages, bound with string in the Dunbar Papers, every page signed by the lawyer Kenneth Mackenzie, and generally exuding an air of uncompromising thoroughness as if Sir Benjamin's creditors were determined to overlook nothing [90.1.19]. It is a daunting piece of legalese and begins as follows: 'Be it known to all men by these presents that I Sir Benjamin Dunbar of Hempriggs Baronet Considering that I stand indebted to different persons herein after named and referred to, in different sums of money constituted by bonds, bills, open accompts and other documents all which sums I am desirous shall be paid off and discharged as speedily as possible'.

The creditors are listed. It is worth quoting this, as the names and occupations give a clear indication of the pattern of consumption of the baronet:

'to the Representatives of Humphry Donaldson Esquire late army agent in London the sum of [left blank]

To Neil Ryrie brewer in Edinburgh the principal sum of [£360] [the sums are written out in words in the original] contained in my bill to him;

To George Hunter Clothier in Edinburgh the sum of [£386] also contained in my bill to him;

To Messrs Eagle & Henderson seed merchants in Edinburgh the sum of [£250] sterling;

To Peter Lawson seeds merchant in Edinburgh the sum of [£192] sterling;

To William Trotter upholsterer in Edinburgh the sum of [£90] sterling;

To Misses Christina & Janet Stewart fancy dress makers in London the sum of [£88] sterling;

To George Napier writer in Edinburgh the sum of [£44] contained in my bill to him;

To Alexander Mackenzie banker in Inverness the sum of [£900 sterling];

To Messrs Miller & Bain & company, merchants in Wick the sum of [£300 sterling];

To the proprietors of the society or company of agents and insurance brokers called the Royal Exchange Assurance Company the sum of [£720 sterling] and of that over and above the annuity of [£800 sterling] due by me to them as herein particularly after mentioned;

To Edward Fletcher [blank gap] the sum of [£280 sterling] exclusive of the annuity of [£625] also herein aftermentioned;

To Case China Merchant in Edinburgh the sum of [£30];

To [gap] Blackwood merchant there the sum of [£45];

To William Child china merchant there the sum of [£20];

To [gap] Schultze merchant there the sum of [£26 sterling];

To Miss [gap] Cringle mantua maker there the sum of [£16 sterling];

To Miss [gap] Catullo milliner there the sum of [£14];

To John Sinclair linen draper there the sum of [£48];

To [gap] Macpherson seed merchant in London the sum of [£18 sterling];

To the officers and others connected with the Second Battalion of the Caithness Volunteers the sum of [£1200];

To William Couper upholsterer in Edinburgh the sum of [£52];

To Mark Duncan merchant there the sum of [£35 sterling].'

These sums total £6,539 sterling, an amount almost equal to his rental income as detailed four years before. To make matters seem worse, a page was left blank after the list in full expectation of additions. Indeed Sir Benjamin admitted he was indebted 'to sundry other persons in different sums of money'. The agreement to form a trust was probably masterminded by Kenneth Mackenzie and was not an unusual way to manage debt. It may not have been an especially humiliating experience for the baronet and he may have felt some relief that his affairs were under some kind of control at last.

It seems to have been drawn up at a meeting presided over by James Gibson, writer to the signet. Sir Benjamin stated that he had no funds for the payment of his debts beyond the rental income from the entailed estate of Hempriggs. This was part of the problem. Because the estate was entailed Sir Benjamin was forbidden by law from selling parts of it to redress his losses, and had to pass it on intact to his heirs. Many a landed family was brought into difficulty through being rich in land but poor in cash as a result of the law of entail. Charles Ferrier, an Edinburgh accountant, was named as the principal trustee for Hempriggs on behalf of the creditors.

The document describes the estate in considerable detail, much of it couched in ancient legal terminology, already referred to in Part 1. These include reference to multures (the owner's proportion of the grain or meal processed at a mill), sucken (the obligation on tenants to use a certain mill; or the payment due in kind, service or cash for its use), knaveship (the proportion of the grain or meal processed at a mill paid to the miller's servants), sequels (the amounts of grain or meal or cash in lieu given to the miller's servants by tenants obliged to use the mill) and bannock (the small quantity of meal sufficient to make a bannock due to a servant of a mill from each person using it). These customs and laws relating to the mills emphasise their importance as a rural institution and also explain why millers were often unpopular and suspected by the rural poor of cheating.

The areas of the individual properties on the estate are given in the old units based on the concept of the pennyland, with its fractions of half, farthing and octo, a system that recognised the supposed productivity of the land rather than its area. There are also references to old practices, drawing on the wording in the charters from the beginning of the eighteenth century, such as in the description of 'Telstane now called Hempriggs' where it is noted that the owner had the 'fowling and fishing of all the rocks and caves of Telstane & stacks thereof with the maw nests thereof with the harbour and haven called the Burgh of Telstane and liberty of fishboats therein with wrack, ware and other pertinents of the said lands of Telstane used and wont as the same was possessed by Alexander Sinclair of Telstane and of his tenants and cottars'. The reference to the old name of the property before the Dunbars changed it to Hempriggs in the 1690s suggests either that the old name was still being heard or, more likely, that the lawyers drawing up the document were leaving nothing to chance.

This determination to avoid any possible loophole, and possibly to impress and reassure the disgruntled creditors with their thoroughness, comes through again and again, as in the following: 'And suchlike all and haill the one penny land called the Lairds penny land lying at the east side of the town of Wick with one farthing and one octoland called Crooksquoys which is a part of the lands of Wick and Papigoe with the halfpennyland of Rainnies barns, which is also a part of the foresaid lands of Wick and Papigoe together with the salmon fishings upon the Water of Wick from the top thereof to the outmost bounds of the same where it falls to the sea and upon such parts of the shore of the said lands above described, where salmon fishing used to be fished and which of before were reputed part of the salmon fishing of the said Water, with liberty of cobles nets & places for drawing of nets and cruives as the said salmon fishings were possessed by the former tacksmen thereof conform to use and wont with the haill manor places, castles, towers, fortalices and particularly the Castle of Old Wick & houses biggings yards orchards mosses muirs thack flash wrack, wrath, ware, peat, peat stacks turf, feal and divot, grazings, shealings, pasturages, parks, havens, harbours, loans, leisures, freedoms, outsells, nests, tofts, crofts, dovecots, cunningheanes, skleats, skleatheughs, quarries of free & rough stone, tenants, tenandries & services of free tenants, freedoms, commonties easements priviledges parts pendicles and righteous pertinents as well under the ground as above the same which do or may anyways pertain or belong to the foresaid lands and others above written …'. There may have been few orchards or cunningheanes [rabbit warrens] in the vicinity but even the remote possibility was recognised. Presumably the word 'nests' refers to the harvesting of wild birds' eggs.

The place names as given in the agreement are of great interest. It is clear, for example, that Latheronwheel is a modern version of the older Latheronfuilzie or Latheronfuilzy. The 'wheel' element in the name has been treated often as a mystery and solved by ingenious folktales. Some have suggested that it comes from the old Scots for filth or dubs, in reference to the miry nature of the strath, but it is rather a rendering of the Gaelic a'Phuil, 'of the pool', a straightforward reference to the burn in the strath or to the harbour area.

The section dealing with the burgh and barony of Hempriggs, erected under the Great Seal of Queen Anne 'of blessed memory', mentions weekly markets and 'the two yearly fairs … to be holden the one at Kettleburn tofts above the town of Wick upon the penult Tuesday of July yearly called Margarets Fair and the other at the Banks of that pendicle of Wick called Harras upon the first Tuesday of November called Elizabeths fair; with the tolls of the said mercats and fairs'. In his *General View of the Agriculture of the County of Caithness* in 1812, John Henderson makes no mention of these in the list of fairs he states are held annually in the county; perhaps by then the Margarets Fair had merged with the Hill Fair held on the Hill of Wick on 1st August. In cribbing from old documents, the Edinburgh lawyers may have included reference to practices already obsolete in Caithness.

Charles Ferrier and his fellow trustees became in effect the landlords of the Dunbar estates, with the power to collect all the rents, evict and place tenants, grant tacks and appoint factors to run the business. Sir Benjamin could not revoke the Deed of Trust until all his debts were paid, and the order in which these were to be met was clearly laid down – first all the public and parochial burdens, thus ensuring that the minister's stipend and other necessary local services were taken care of, then the interest and arrears of a debt of £2,000 incurred by Sir Benjamin's father and now a burden on the entail, then several annuities secured on the estate, and so on. Fifth on the list, and only fifth, appeared 'payment of such allowances as to my creditors shall appear proper and necessary for the support of me and my family'; this may have been a hard pill for Sir Benjamin to swallow, a sad blow to his prestige, to live on what numerous merchants thought fitting.

As the news of the Trust spread through the newspapers, other creditors made themselves known. On 13 August 1810, a Mr A. Taylor wrote from Tain to Kenneth Mackenzie to pursue what he was owed – 'I … inclose an Acct due to James and Andrew Glass Plaisterers in this Town amounting to £22 – I wrote to Sir Benjamin several letters for payment of this acct & and he promised to settle it tho he never did – I will thank you to say when payment may be expected …' [1.4.9].

2 | 'the want of good roads'

As we noted earlier, Sir Benjamin married Janet Mackay, the daughter of George Mackay of Bighouse. The wedding was held on 10 December 1784. Their first child, Louisa, was born in 1788. Another daughter Henrietta followed in 1790 and a third, Elizabeth, in 1794. Known as Lady Betty, this Elizabeth succumbed to consumption as a young woman of 20 in 1814, and a poignant undated letter survives among the Papers from a Dr Law in Edinburgh acknowledging payment of a two-guinea fee and reminding Sir Benjamin that £4 5s 10d was still owed for medicines [1.4.6]. Henrietta married William Sinclair Wemyss of Southdun and had four children, the youngest of whom was named Benjamin, before she died in 1820. The eldest daughter, Louisa, married Garden Duff of Hatton in Aberdeenshire on 17 September 1805, a union to which we shall later return (Fig. 9).

Sir Benjamin and Lady Janet also had two sons, George, born in 1799, and Robert, born in 1801. The two boys were sent away for their higher education in York, as is confirmed by a letter dated 22 August 1814, when William Turner in Newcastle, a classmate of Sir Benjamin's when they had both attended school, wrote that he would be able to meet George and Robert on their way south. He was pleased at the opportunity of 'renewing our personal acquaintance and retracing many of the scenes of our youth', and 'as Newcastle cannot fail to form a stage from Edinburgh to York I shall probably be enabled to give the young gentlemen some useful previous information respecting the customs of the place and the fellow students they are likely to meet with' [1.1.14].

Turner was in the habit of attending the annual examinations at the school and had lately started to draw up 'Historical recollections of our former Alma Mater' which, he was clearly proud to relate, had formed 'a series of Essays in a London

Fig. 9 The family of Captain Benjamin Duff of Hempriggs, 3rd Bt, and the link to the Duffs of Hatton

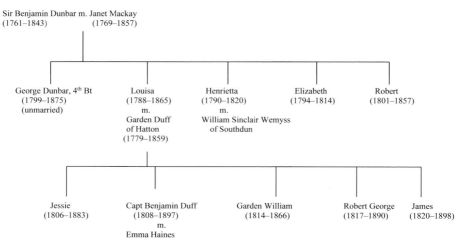

periodical publication entitled *The Monthly Repository* during the last and current year …'. What the Dunbar boys, aged 14 and 12, made of their encounter with the solicitous William Turner when they stumbled tired but probably also excited from the stagecoach in Newcastle can only be guessed at. *The Monthly Repository* was a magazine closely associated with the Unitarian Christian movement.

At some point, George Dunbar formed a friendship with James Easton, an Edinburgh solicitor who will figure prominently later in this narrative. Letters from Easton to George survive from 1821. The first, written from Edinburgh on 19 January [1.4.13], is interesting for the light it sheds on the possible problems with buying a horse for a servant of the Dunbars to bring to Caithness, problems associated now often with second-hand cars.

'My Dear Sir, You cannot imagine what a bother we have had about a horse,' it begins. 'Johnnie only starts tomorrow morning.' After acquiring a horse from Roxburghshire for £60, Johnnie found he was too small, presumably for riding on the long journey to the north. The first horse was sold again for £60 and another bought for 60 guineas. 'Johnnie when about to start with him last Saturday thought he discovered a hurt on his knee. This we knew not to be the case but as a horse not liked by a servant never does well we told the owner that your boy was not pleased with him. He readily agreed to take him back & we in the meantime allowed him to remain in the stable until another purchaser should cast up.' The search for a third horse proved fruitless but in the meantime Johnnie changed his mind about the second horse and 'wont have anything else.' By now, however, the owner of the second horse had been offered a higher price for it and would not drop below £65 'but in consequence of our having kept the horse a week he is to take that sum. We are therefore obliged to pay £2 more than we might have had him for last week'. Easton assured George he would find the animal 'excellent'. 'The price is long', admitted Easton, 'but it cannot be helped and you should not mention it to anyone. I never saw anything like the scarcity of good horses. There is not another in Edinburgh worth sending you.'

George's travail over procuring a horse was an echo of the old days when land travel in the north relied on foot and hoof. In the early 1800s a transport revolution was underway. The construction of the new harbour at Wick by the British Fisheries Society was the largest infrastructure project of its day in the county but before that there had been some making of roads and bridges. The public body in charge of road-making in each county was the Commissioners of Supply, a committee of the major landowners established by an Act of Parliament in 1667 originally to collect taxes but later charged with additional duties. The Commissioners had the power to call out tenants to perform statute labour for six days each summer, work that could be deployed to maintain roads. The first major road-building effort in the Highlands, begun in 1725 under the direction of Lieutenant-General George Wade, was confined to the south of the Great Glen and had no impact on the northern counties. There were local efforts in Caithness such as in 1726 when Patrick Dunbar of Bowermaddan, the proprietor of Latheronwheel House, had a stone bridge put over the Latheronwheel Burn.[2] In November 1753, a group of 'substantial' people in Wick met to consider the best site for a new harbour, 'whether Staxigoe or Broadhaven would be most convenient' (80.1.8). As they could not agree, they chose John Anderson, the merchant we have already met, to write to another merchant in Banff for his opinion. Sir William Dunbar, who was in Forres at the time, was kept informed of this by Hugo Campbell, who also added that Lady Hempriggs had declared a willingness to contribute £50 towards a harbour in Broadhaven, where it would clearly be in the family interest, but 'would not concern herself with Staxigoe'.

The justices and the heritors met in Thurso in November 1755 to consider the state of the Caithness roads. John Sinclair of Freswick, the sheriff-depute, was chosen to be the president of the group and John Gibsone acted as clerk. At this time Sinclair had been in post for less than one year and his dispute with the justices was still in the future. The group was unanimously agreed that it would tend much to the advantage of the county to have good roads; that such roads should go from Sutherland over the Ord along the Latheron coast to Wick and thence to Thurso, through 'the CaswayMyre to the Bridge of Halkirk and from thence to Thurso', west from Thurso 'by the confines of Lord Reay's country, and to the ferry at Skarfskerry; and that bridges should be built over the Waters of

Berriedale and Dunbeath [90.1.7]. The heritors would fund this network by paying two months' cess each year, thought likely to amount to around £100, along with a stent or tax of 2 shillings for every head of family on their estates; supposing there were around three thousand families in the county, this would raise some £300 to be portioned by the heritors according to people's circumstances.

There soon arose disagreements over how to proceed, where the roads should go, which should be built first, and how the work should be funded. Sir William had not attended the Thurso meeting but had submitted some observations shortly afterwards, on which the group in turn had recorded some remarks [90.1.8]. The group felt it unreasonable to agree to Sir William's proposal that the road from the Ord should first be carried to Wick: 'severall Gentlemen of large property about Thurso and the middle of the country insist that Thurso is the most frequented town and blest to contribute to any publick Work.' The road to Wick was 'already tollerable' and the Causewaymire route should be tackled first. There was also disagreement over the road to the Orkney ferry landing at Scarfskerry; in Sir William's view, this would be 'almost totally for the Ease of Orkneymen' who would never contribute anything towards the plan. At a further meeting in January, someone proposed that bridges at Thurso and Wick should be included in the network [90.1.9].

The heritors often hesitated over committing their own money towards the cost of public goods. Because the access to Caithness was often retarded and very dangerous when the rivers at Langwell, Berriedale, Dunbeath and Reisgill were in spate, a scheme was put forward in January 1767 to construct more bridges (90.1.30). Captain Robert Sutherland of Langwell donated £100 in the hope that his generosity would encourage others to follow suit. Apparently they did not. A scheme was concocted to raise money in instalments, and those who gave £20 or more would have their names commemorated on the new bridges. Again, little appears to have come from this.

Wick Town Council on 19 March 1776 discussed 'how extremely insufficient and dangerous even for foot Passengers the present Bridge over the Water of Wick is' and, as a cargo of timber from a wreck lay on the shore at Sarclett, decided to ask the gentlemen and tenants of the county to buy it, estimating that £80 would be enough to pay for an 8-foot-wide bridge fit to carry a horse and carriage [88.3.]. Sir John Sinclair famously called out his tenants on statute labour in around 1790 to cut the road from Latheron to Georgemas, the road known as the Causewaymire. Thurso eventually acquired its bridge in 1800, while Wick had to make do with its wooden structure until a stone bridge was completed in 1806. In his letter to Sir William on 15 December 1767, James Sinclair of Tister mentions finding funds for bridges [6.2.7], and Colonel Scott also refers to a bridge in a letter in November 1766 and a discussion that somehow had become mixed up with the dispute between the sheriff and the justices (see Part 7): 'Langwell himself has made it impossible for me to decide that the hundred pound shou'd go solely towards building his bridge for he has shown my letter or the paragraph to Freswick, it appears highly improper for me to give a partial decision how it shall be apply'd but to be sure the majority of the justices and freeholders that direct the making of the roads may dispose of it as they please and for the reasons you mention may very properly begin with ye bridge of least expence' [143.4.15]. This probably refers to the bridge built just before 1770 in the bottom of the Berriedale strath spanning the confluence of the Waters of Berriedale and Langwell.[3]

In 1792, when he wrote an account of his parish, Joseph Taylor, the minister of Watten, could still observe that 'the want of good roads' was greatly retarding the improvement of the parish. The routes had been marked and a little work had been done, 'reluctantly, by the statute labour of the people', noted Taylor, but rain and frost played havoc with the surface and in winter and spring not even the best horses could drag a cart along it with safety.[4]

Progress became more rapid with the establishment of the Commission for Making Roads and Building Bridges in the Highlands of Scotland, the body instituted by an Act of Parliament in July 1803 with the task of bringing the transport infrastructure of the north into the nineteenth century. It began work with a government grant of £20,000 and appealed for 'the moiety of the expense', a contemporary term for what would now be called match-funding, from the landowners in the various sections of the proposed highway network. Funds may have been slow in coming forth, and the appeal was reinforced for Caithness in July 1806 by the passing of the Caithness Assessment Act, obliging the heritors to pay half the cost of roads. It was a charge that Sir Benjamin could not evade although it did present him with some difficulty. Sir Benjamin was beset with financial problems, as we have seen, owing money to various creditors. Among them were the Road Trustees for Wick and Canisbay who were charged with raising and managing public funds for local road construction.

The Dunbar Papers has a copy of a report made by Thomas Telford on the Dunbeath road on 13 July 1812 [100.2.19]. Telford, with the engineer Joseph Mitchell, Robert Greenfield the resident inspector, and Mr Leask the contractor, examined the whole section and found that 'Excepting the 2 Divisions where a variation has been proposed a beginning was made on each of the other divisions and, in some, a very considerable quantity of work has been performed.' Soon, however, Mr Leask was to prove troublesome and there were delays with the work on this, the main artery up the east coast, and on other roads. When the Commissioners published their seventh report in April 1815, the Dunbeath–Wick road was still unfinished and there was a melancholy note that Mr Leask had 'deserted the work much indebted to the County Workmen employed by him'.

Despite this setback, it was expected that the road would be finished by the end of the year. No contractor had yet come forward to do the Wick–Thurso stretch but Mr Traill was expected to undertake the Thurso–Huna road along the north coast.

A new Highland Road and Bridge Act in July 1814 widened the Commissioners' fund-raising powers. Now the government would put in one quarter of the costs of road repairs and the locals would make up the balance according to assessments made by the Commissioners of Supply. It was estimated in March 1817 that it cost £2 10s to keep each mile of road in good repair but by March 1821, when the Road Commissioners issued their ninth report, this had risen to £3 10s for each mile of the Dunbeath road and was still rising. The ninth report also presented the gloomy news that the estimate for the Wick–Thurso road, reckoned to be £12,072 19s 0d, was too high for the government to consider and that the local heritors would have to pay for it by themselves. Faulty materials had made resurfacing necessary at a further cost of £1,300. The road, now the A882, was eventually finished in July 1819 but surface problems raised the maintenance costs to £7 per mile in 1820. The Commissioners acknowledged their debt to the heritors for seeing the work done, but this compliment probably did little to alleviate local grumbling among those who had to foot the bill.[5]

On 17 March 1825, William Steven and Alex Leith submitted a tender to George Dunbar to build a section of the road to Wester 'commencing at William Donaldson's Quarry and ending at the feal Dyke a little North of James Georgeson's Barn ...', a distance of about 630 yards (99.2.20). The two men laid out the specifications they would adhere to: the road to be 18 feet broad, with side drains 9 inches deeper than 'the bed of the metal', 15 inches wide in the bottom and sloped on the sides at the rate of two [inches] horizontal to one perpendicular, the stones of the road metal to 'roughly but regularly broken to the depth of seven inches in centre and four at the sides ...' and so on, all for the charge of threepence per yard for forming, and 15 pence per yard for the metalling and finishing. If the job was not completed satisfactorily or in the time allowed, the contractors agreed to 'forfeiture of one third of the prices as stated'. William Steven also tendered to construct the embankment at the north-east end of the Bridge of Wester (99.2.22), an offer accepted in November 1826. Thomas Spence, the consulting road engineer, inspected and passed the bridge embankment on 1 June 1827: 'I have this day examined that embanking ... & found it executed in a workmanlike manner' (99.2.23).

Caithness was now enjoying much better communication with the south. A coach or diligence began to run daily between Inverness and Thurso. It normally carried three passengers inside, three outside, and a driver, a guard and the mail at an average speed of 6 miles per hour. The service normally left Inverness at 6am and rattled into Thurso between 11am and 12 noon on the following morning, a

159-mile trip in almost thirty hours with the pair of horses being changed twelve times. The southbound coach left Thurso at 7am and reached Inverness shortly after noon on the following day. In the summer the journey could have been tolerable but in winter it could at times be very uncomfortable: accounts are rare but there is one striking eyewitness testimony in a letter written to George Dunbar by a Major W. Mackay on 10 November 1825 (16.3.16): '...I was almost starved to death on the outside of the Coach from Tain to Inverness. William Horne his wife and two sisters having the inside – My wish was that they had been inside of a whale's belly.'

'It would be unreasonable to expect that occasional snowstorms and sudden thaws ... and (more than any of these causes) the inexperience and want of accurate habits in the persons engaged in such an undertaking, should not sometimes delay the arrival of the coach,' warned the Road Commissioners.[6] Nevertheless the Thurso coach appears to have maintained a good record for not missing the connection to the coach southbound from Inverness.

The want of accurate habits in the drivers and coach handlers was one thing. The Road Trustees in Caithness were more concerned with extracting necessary contributions from the local landowners. Sir Benjamin fell into default. Four of the trustees, William Sinclair of Freswick, Kenneth Macleay of Newmore (the convener), William Horne the younger of Stirkoke and John Sinclair of Barrock, met on 1 October 1822 to discuss this problem of funding [100.2.]. They noted that Sir Benjamin owed a lot and resolved to tell him that they would be under 'painful necessity of reviving the judicial proceedings in the Sheriff Court' if no arrangement were made in the next fourteen days. 'Reviving' makes it clear that this was not the first time that the Ackergill laird had failed to provide his share. One month later, the trustees, now including James Innes of Thrumster, George Sutherland Sinclair of Brabster and James Waters, the 'eldest' [senior?] bailie of Wick, considered Sir Benjamin's case again [100.2.]. Sir Benjamin had not responded to their letters but they resolved to make one more effort to avoid court proceedings which 'could not fail ... to be extremely unpleasant' for the defaulter. The trustees were clearly reluctant to act against one of their neighbours, and sent William Horne of Stirkoke to visit Ackergill to persuade Sir Benjamin to do something, threatening that if this failed they would initiate legal action.

Road money arrears continued to accrue to Sir Benjamin's account. The sum stood at £249 16s 11½d on 26 January 1825. In October that year the trustees and heritors met in the new town and county buildings in Wick 'as a more convenient place' to consider obtaining a new act from Parliament to allow the raising of money from the commutation road assessments of the county at their own discretion but not to exceed in any case £4 10s per £100 Scots valuation. This was to be levied on all proprietors and tenants with a rent equal to or more than £4 sterling per year. For rents below £4 the old rate of commutation of 3s would pertain. By this time the new roads had expanded or been improved to cover much of the modern network: Thurso to Wick via the Killimster Moss, the Causeymyre [sic] from Rougie (near Georgemas) to Latheron, Wick to Huna, Huna to Thurso joining the Wick–Thurso route at Castletown, Bridge of Wester to Castletown via Barrock, and Thurso to Drumhollistan by Forss.

In 1827 Sir Benjamin became the sixth Lord Duffus after his cousin, the fifth Lord James Sutherland, died unmarried.[7] It was therefore to Lord Duffus, then residing at 8 St Vincent Street in Edinburgh, that J.A. Waters on behalf of the Caithness road trustees addressed his letter of 10 February 1831 seeking payment of the road money. A further £186 8s 6d had fallen due in the three years since 1828. Waters, who had the hapless task of collecting road dues, was polite: 'The money is wanted immediately to meet claims incurred under the new Road Act and I have been censured and threatened with a prosecution for not having long ere now collected & deposited this sum in terms of my instructions.' [100.2.].

3 | *'when wicked people gets into power, the peaceable gets trouble'*

Alexander Miller continued to correspond frequently with Sir Benjamin, habitually sealing his letters with black wax. The last one uncovered so far in the Dunbar Papers is dated 18 November 1824, when he was 84 years of age. At times his handwriting is sprawling and clumsy and he seems in the later years to have occasionally employed someone to produce better-looking manuscript.

On 30 March 1810, as the developments at Pulteneytown and the construction of the new harbour were in progress, he was still vigorously commenting on what was taking place, still concerned with the interests of the Dunbar estate. The work was proceeding at Pulteneytown under the direction of George Burn, a local architect and builder who was described to the British Fisheries Society as 'a skilful workman but not in affluent circumstances'.[8] If that were the case, Burn would have been very grateful to the Society for an opportunity to ply his profession on such a challenging project. In 1808 he finished the construction of the new stone bridge over the Wick River and in 1810 he was making progress in constructing the new harbour. There was a pressing need for building stone and Burn was treading on some toes to fulfil this requirement, as Miller records: 'I am now informed by John Ross the Mason that during the late bad weather when he and his hands was absent from the work, Mr Burns Carts had carried all the stones away John Ross had in the quarry, either to the Pier, or else to extensive buildings Mr Burns has engaged for erecting in the town of Wick' [7.1.67].

The stones which Burn's men had carried away had been earmarked for the repair of the boiling house where the salmon fishermen processed their catch. This was a Dunbar property – the salmon fishing at the mouth of the river was a valuable estate asset. A Major Williamson, in an official capacity for the Society, had sought an interdict on its repair, a needless move in Miller's view. Miller also thought that Burn had taken over all the quarries: 'It seems he [Burn] has either with or without your consent taken full possession of all that quarrys and disposing on the stones in any way he thinks proper: I hear he has a mind to carry stones by sea from Old Wick to Helmsdale to assist in the work he has undertaken there...'. Sir Benjamin was now living at Hempriggs and Miller was unsure about any possible agreement between him and Burn but still felt that to prevent the repair of the boiling house was going too far, especially as the damage to it had been caused in his view by Burn's men in the first place.

Miller sent John Ross to ask leave to fetch enough stone from the quarry on the north side of the river to finish the boiling house. The quarry had been leased by a Wick man called William Sinclair who was naturally keen to earn as much as possible from it as long as the building boom lasted. 'William Sinclair told John Ross I could be allowed quarry leave, but not under Twenty Shillings of Rent whatever stones would be needed for the house, whether less or more,' grumbled Miller in his letter, 'but that he must not begin to quarry a stone until the Twenty Shillings was paid; no doubt I thought this a hardship but as there is a necessity of geting [sic] the Boilhouse ready, I thought it best to pay...'. Miller also anticipated difficulty in finding carters to bring the stone to the boiling house.

Caught in the throes of sudden change, some of the locals were finding it hard to adjust to the impact of the developments. 'When wicked people gets into power, the peaceable gets trouble,' lamented Miller, 'I am sure neither my son or I ever did any thing with an intention to offend or to disoblige either Major Williamson or Mr Burns [sic]; with the former we wished to live on terms of freindship [sic]; the last mentioned I have obligd in different ways, sometimes at expence but a more thankless gentleman I never did a favour to.'

At some point relations between Alexander Miller and Sir Benjamin had cooled. The reasons are at present unclear. Perhaps the laird had simply grown weary of the Staxigoe man's ways and wished to control his own affairs himself, or perhaps he suspected shortcomings in the way Miller had been dealing with him. There is evidence in the letters described below that this may have been the case. The last two paragraphs of Miller's letter on 10 March discuss financial business.

'You will receive with this, Copy of the two years accounts between you, my son and me that you wishd to have; you thought it would not take much trouble to make out those accounts, but it has taken a great deal; after you examine the account, please return it so that it may be Docqueted [sic], but before it be so, I wish to give you credit for the money I receivd from your Tennants on the south side of the Water, in part of Grassum payable by them to you; but I cannot give you credit for it until the people come here with my receipts as I find it not so distinctly stated with me as it ought to be; I expect the tenants here tomorrow and Monday in terms of what I wrote you last.

'In my statement of rent with Mr Trail for Martinmass 1807, I find I am short paid £25 10 8¾; I think he retained this on your account besides what he retained for the Minister of Latherons stipend but as I cannot be sure of this until Mr Trails return, I have not charged it against you but will afterwards if I find it ought to be so. I remain [etc.]'

The response to this letter is unknown. Possibly an indication of it exists in the Dunbar Papers. The letter from Miller dated four months on, on 14 July, is from a man who is distinctly upset [7.1.71].

'Dear Sir

I wish to answer your letter of yesterdays date in my own hand, but my hand is unsteady as my mind is unselded. I am sorry indeed to find you write to me now in a <u>Strain</u> you never did before. You tell me [obscure phrase – dryly?] you are sorry to give me troubles! I never was [expecting?] to take trouble for you, no doubt I have had a good deal of trouble sometimes when it answered little, of [?] no purpose to you, but that was no fault of mine; I was always happy when my services answered any good purpose to you, and I think they sometimes did so, you have said they did: I am indeed come to that time of life now that my personal services cannot answer any great purpose to any account I believe none at all to you, but whither your mind is changd towards me or not, my good wishes to you and your family has not abated.

I remain [etc]'

On 16 July 1811, Miller wrote a long letter to Kenneth Mackenzie, the Edinburgh lawyer [7.1.45]. He began with condolences on the death of Mackenzie's son before going on to express a desire to reach a final settlement with Sir Benjamin. Disagreement had arisen over the payment of a debt for the substantial sum of £91 8s. Sir Benjamin's stance was that Miller owed him this money after Sir Benjamin had paid it to a Mr Stewart on Miller's behalf. Miller's own case was that Sir Benjamin was mistaken. As we have seen, Sir Benjamin had put his affairs in the hands of a trust with Charles Ferrier as the trustee. There was inevitably much correspondence about this but Miller was adamant: 'Notwithstanding it being perfectly clear to you and (I hope) to Mr Ferrier that I myself paid the debt to Stewart of London I hear Sir Benjn gives it out to his friends in the country that I did not pay it and that he will make it appear that he paid it. These assertions are of little consequence, only it is an additional proof among many others that Sir Benjn will pay me as little as he can; but as our affairs are in the hands of an honest man and a man of judgement and discernment, I think I have nothing to fear notwithstanding all Sir Benjamins plausibility in the way he represents his own matters.'

Relations between the laird and his erstwhile factor had reached a low ebb, a situation compounded by Miller's doubts about Sir Benjamin's plans for the future of the Trust formed in 1809. This involved a Mr Smith of Olrig: 'There seems to be strange things going on: Mr Smith of Olrig you know becomes surety for £2000 of Sir Benjamins debts payable by instalments at different periods: for this he gets a lease of the Lands of Latheronwheel for fifteen years at Six Hundred Pounds yearly Rent; he is to pay £100 Rent yearly, also the interest of Twenty Thousand Merks Scots which is the Wadset sum; likewise the Ministers Stipend and Schoolmasters Sallary [sic] yearly; all the rest of the £600 yearly rent goes to extinguish gradually the loan of £3000, so at the end of fifteen years when the tack expires, the £3000 is extinguished likewise! This appears to me to be a new scheme differing from every one else I have yet heard of; and I think not a very wise one either for Sir Benjn or Olrig.'

We can imagine Miller, now past his seventieth birthday, sitting at home but alert to every piece of gossip flying about the countryside, chewing over what he hears and exploring in his mind what others may be up to, while at the same time harbouring some resentment that he is no longer involved in things. 'It seems Sir Benjamin and Olrig is on a new bargain about the loan of £3000 now,' he wrote to Mackenzie, 'if this take place, Olrig is to be appointed Trustee and Mr Ferrier will be allowed to retire; Olrigs security as I hear is to be the rents in general out of which he is to retain ten per cent for the £3000 during Sir Benjamins lifetime! If this take place, nothing but a desire to make money as fast as possible can induce Olrig to come into such a wild scheme; I realy think him a man by no means fit for such management, but so is the news of the day; as for Sir Benjamin I get none of his news; we have had no kind of communication for a long time past, were our accounts settled and on a fair way of being paid, I could not care much if our intercourse should pass away silently: I sincerely wish him and his family well, but his plans and schemes are daily more and more (in my opinion) contrary to his interest in every sense of the word.'

Mr Smith of Olrig was James Smith. Originally from Aberdeen, he married the daughter of a Thurso merchant and held several properties in the town before he bought Olrig in 1791. Miller was right to be wary of Smith. In 1848, when he was in his late eighties and might have been thought to be at ease, Smith demonstrated that he had lost none of his obvious business acumen and brought a case before the Court of Session to establish an instrument of sasine over the barony of Hempriggs. The Dunbar family owed him a large sum of money, contended Smith, nothing less than £23,900. A settlement was reached with Benjamin's son George, who was head of the Dunbar family by then, and in November 1849, only four years before he died, Smith gave up his claims.[9]

The appeal to Mackenzie produced no immediate result. On 28 April 1812 [7.1.44], Miller wrote directly to Sir Benjamin to protest that 'It has always been my desire to be usefull to you and your family when it lay in my power but at present I am so circumstanced that I cannot comply with your request. It is twenty months and upwards since (at your request) I lodged my accts with Mr Ferrier and from the strain of your letters about that time I had every reason to expect our accounts would have been adjusted in a short space of time.' Miller said he answered all the 'obstacles' preventing settlement, sending everything to the arbiter Mr Ferrier through Kenneth Mackenzie, agent for both himself and Sir Benjamin. Miller went on to say that he expected Sir Benjamin to answer questions from Mr Ferrier which would result in settlement and the fixing of the final balance due to him. Now it appeared that Sir Benjamin wanted to lay a plan before his creditors at a meeting advertised in the papers, but Miller refused to sanction this 'especially as I have been told that the intention in part is to choose a new trustee for the management of your affairs.' Miller wanted Mr Ferrier to stay, as the appointment of a new trustee would mean going over everything again and another twenty months' delay, 'a prospect very unfavourable for an old man like me.' Now Miller was having second thoughts about retaining Mackenzie to handle his affairs, as he was also Sir Benjamin's agent, and told the laird that he had written to Mackenzie to say he hoped he would be excused for employing another agent.

Charles Ferrier stayed in his position as trustee, as in November 1815 we have a letter written to him by a lawyer called William Henderson [7.1.39]. Ferrier was in Wick to receive the Dunbar tenants' rents. Enclosed with the letter is a statement of the rent and other sums payable by Alexander Miller. The statement was for £10 for the rent of Field, the farm Miller held for most of his adult life; £7 for the rent 'of a house and pendicle of land, part of the Field subset to Alex Reiach'; and £33 15s 4½d for various items. This broke down as £31 15s 6d for parcels of land Miller rented in and around Staxigoe and Louisburgh, and the following:

To proportion of ½ school salary, Crop 1809, 10, 11, 12 & 13 of the estate of Hempriggs effeiring [pertaining to] the rents payl by			
Mr Miller at Marts 1810, 11, 12, 13 & 14	-	13s	-
To ½ Assessmt for Militia Men's wives 30th April 1810, 12 and 14, effeiring to rent Marts 1810, 12 & 14		7s	4½d
To road money effeiring to the above stated rents for service of 1815		8s	6d
Interest on the above from Marts 1814 to the 17th of March 1815		11s	
	£33	15s	4½d

This is interesting in that it shows how Miller, as a prominent tenant, had to bear a share of the costs of the schoolteacher's salary, the welfare of the wives of militiamen, and road money. The latter, the assessment laid on landowners to help to fund the work of the Commissioners for Roads described previously, was in this instance passed on to tenants.

Henderson's letter is puzzling. The heading says it was written in Staxigoe and it reads as if it had been taken down from Alexander Miller's dictation. If the words are Miller's own, he claimed that he had written to Ferrier 'some time ago' as he was desirous 'that our differences should have an end' but Ferrier had not replied. Miller learned from the ground officer of the Dunbar estate that the trustee was to be in Wick and took the opportunity to send with the letter a statement of the rents for which he was liable. This is the statement described above. He also raised other points: was he responsible for payment for a piece of land which had been leased to an Alex Reiach, as he thought his own lease had expired the previous Whitsunday; and could the interested parties agree on a fair rent for the mill at Papigoe? There is a complicated explanation behind the latter request, in which Miller appears to address Sir Benjamin himself. Further exploration in the Dunbar papers may throw light on these mysteries.

4 | *'your worthy father and my real friend'*

At some point after 1815 Miller and Sir Benjamin reached an understanding. On 8 May 1818 we find Miller in a mollified and respectful tone [7.1.38]: 'Sir, In your letters to me lately you mention the trust or confidence Sir William Dunbar your father placed in me. He no doubt had great confidence in me, I think I never deceived him. It was gratifying to me indeed to have his own testimony to that effect when he left the country and resigned everything to your hands, and afterwards when he and Lady Dunbar came to the country on a visit, I found his affection for me had no way abated, and spoke in the same warm friendly manner towards me as formerly: This was gratifying in the extreme.' The second part of the letter suggests that Sir Benjamin had approached the old merchant for some background information on his father's dealings with the Wick magistrates about the placing of mooring posts in Staxigoe harbour. Sir William had never taken anything to do with them, said Miller.

In December 1821, Miller wrote in a reflective tone, 'Sir … I was not well yesterday but am tolerable today. I thank you for your expressions of good wishes. I am now far past that time of Life that the World and the things of it feels that Relish than it does to those far less advanced in days but I ought to be very thankful that I am as I am' [7.1.10]. Clearly replying to a letter he had received from Sir Benjamin, he went on: 'I was very glad to find that you feel Comfortable, especially so at the pleasure you have in the two young gentlmen your sons. May the Lord take care of them; And as they hold Respectable Situations in Privat Life, May their Conduct through Life add Laurels to their Respectability: it is then that they will be respected indeed.'

Once again, though, Sir Benjamin had been neglectful about estate business. Miller reminded him that he had not signed and returned a receipt for the

Martinmas 1819 accounts: 'You wrote to me you was then busy but woud send it afterwards and woud make provision for a balance due to me after payt of the rent … perhaps your other engagements put it out of your mind.' The unsigned receipt still exists in the Dunbar Papers [7.1.19].

The Staxigoe merchant had by now passed his eightieth birthday but he was still being sought for his opinion in local affairs. Letters from the latter half of 1822 show that Sir Benjamin asked him for his views on a dispute over the right for boats to take ballast from the shore at Staxigoe [7.1.9; 7.1.8; 7.1.7; 7.1.6]. In December 1822, Miller had to break off from considering the beach to deal with some matters arising from his sister's death. The matter of the unsigned receipt for the 1819 accounts resurfaced at this time, as Miller explained in his letter to Sir Benjamin on 12 November: 'My son told me lately he had seen your Ground Officer who was calling in your tenants to settle with the Curt Marts Time; The man told him he was forbid to call on me as you was to send Mr Swany here to settle with me: I am obliged to you for that as I am not able to ride now far less to walk as far: I have neither been at the Braehead of Staxigoe or at East Noss for thirteen months past' [7.1.5].

The almost-housebound Miller continued: 'The last Receipt I have for Rents from you is for Marts 1818: At Marts 1819 I sent you by Donald Reach in Papigoe a State of that Marts Rent as usual and some money; their was the receipt wrote on a stamp & joined to the foot of the Account for you to put your name to as you was in the practice of doing in former times: I expected you would have returned it by the man but I did not get it: I imagined you might have been busy counting with the tenants, but afterwards thinking you had forgot it I wrote to put you in mind, but got no Answer. I only mention these particulars to put you in mind of the circumstances. When Mr Swany come here it will be necessary to send with him the State I sent you at Marts 1819 and the letter I sent with it as I kept no copy of either, a thing I am but seldom forgetful to do, but being in a hurry at the time, and expecting it back again, I happened not to do it. If Mr Swany comes so prepared I think we can soon make out clear States of all unsettled Rents.'

Peter Swany must have come and some kind of settlement was reached. In February 1823, Miller wrote to Swany to acknowledge and comment on 'an account of all bygone unsettled rents payl [payable] by me to Sir Benj Dunbar up to Marts last 1822 inclusive' [7.1.4]. He went into detail on several sums of money, including an amount of 6s 2d 'agst me for Road Money' that irked Miller who thought it 'more than any just proportion is, but I could not mend myself without going to Law', an approach Miller accepted would 'soon have cost me twenty times the overcharge' and so decided to 'let it alone' as it was 'but trifling'. Miller ended his letter with a complaint: 'You are just now like the most of my old friends who does not think me worth notice, but it has been the way of the world in time past as well as now. I certainly thought on hearing you was often in the neighbourhood & that you had even gone close past the house, that you would have called for a few minutes were it only to shake hands with an old acquaintance who continues to wish you well. Then I look round me and begin to think of ancient times, I find myself placed like an old tree in a cut down forest whose old acquaintances is all gone and the few that remain of the second generation seems almost to have forgot me so that I may consider myself as a wanderer in a strange country.'

A similar sentiment of regret and nostalgia, possibly self-pity, colours the last letter in the sequence, written by Miller to Sir Benjamin on 18 November 1824 [7.1.2]. The writing is hard to read. 'I must acknowledge my warmest feelings was [obscure] in reading your letter, and calling to remembrance many circumstances very pleasant although (alas) long since buried in the field of neglect if not worse. One thing my conscience desires me to say is, That [obscure] since your worthy father and my real friend took his leave of the House of Ackergill I was amongst the very [obscure] of your friends in promoting your interest to the very utmost of my power and in doing so sometimes even overlookd my own. It is needless for me to say more on this score. Only be said that I ever did [obscure] I hope [obscure] will [obscure] feel happy on hearing of you and your familys prosperity.'

Alexander Miller was to live for several more years, eventually dying at Field in February 1833 at the age of 93. He was buried with his parents in Wick Old churchyard.

5 | *'the rights of common pasturage'*

The Hill o' Wick is no longer to be found on maps of Caithness. This stretch of pasture and moss has been subsumed under Wick airport but for a time in the early nineteenth century it lay at the centre of a lengthy law suit. Back in 1800 in the days before agricultural improvement got up speed, for as long as anyone could remember, the people of Wick had been in the habit of freely using the Hill o' Wick to pasture livestock, cut divots and feal to build dykes, and dig clay. A drove track, a 'caa' in the dialect, led from the town along the north bank of the river and up what is now the road to Westerseat Farm to provide access for herds and flocks to the Hill, which was otherwise surrounded by land occupied by Dunbar tenants. No one, including the Dunbar lairds, bothered much about this common use of the Hill until the tenant of Blackbridge, a certain Benjamin Waters, the tacksman of Harland, began to cut a ditch to enclose a large piece of what had hitherto been considered common land or commonty. Blackbridge lay to the north of the Hill, between Upper Ackergill and Noss, and is one of several long-gone place names in the area.

Alarmed by the prospect of losing a valuable resource and confident that the law was on their side, the Wick magistrates and town council approached Sir Benjamin to resolve the problem. On 21 July 1802 he replied 'proposing to treat with the Magistrates, Council and Heritors concerning a settlement … by arbitration' [91.3.6]. The council was unanimous that an amicable adjustment 'on fair and equitable principles' would be 'most desireable'. The council minute also records that 'Several heritors of the Burgh' were of the opinion that Sir Benjamin had 'of late encroached upon the rights of common pasturage, fuel, feal and divot' and that measures to prevent or settle differences would be in everyone's interest.

Two of the heritors, the burgesses Baillie William Macleay and none other than Alexander Miller of Staxigoe, were charged with meeting Sir Benjamin and reaching agreement. They may have been sanguine about the outcome for had not Sir Benjamin himself written to them of the need to ascertain and fix the boundaries, servitudes and claims of the parties as 'while they remain unsettled the rapacious attempts of individuals will, under the mask of public exertion, appropriate to their present advantage every thing they can filch …'. These had been the laird's own words. On 10 September the council approved Sir Benjamin's suggestion that the Hill be divided and the rights of the various feuars ascertained by arbitration, with John Campbell Sutherland of Forse and Benjamin Williamson of Banniskirk acting as arbiters. James Traill of Hobbister, the sheriff-depute of the county, a great improver in his own right and founder of the important flagstone industry, was appointed 'oversman' with the power of the casting vote should Sutherland and Williamson fail to agree.[10]

That must have appeared to have been that, but for reasons so far not unravelled the case hung unresolved until in 1812 Sir Benjamin was listed as a pursuer with four burgesses who were also feuars in an action raised in the Court of Session. The burgesses were William Macleay, by now the provost of Wick; his son John who with his brothers Kenneth and Alexander and his father founded the Caithness Banking Company that same year[11]; the lawyer James Horne; and the merchant Harry Bain. The Summons of the Division of the Commonty is dated 1 February 1813. It states that the Court of Session should form a commission to investigate the case and appoint surveyors to settle the boundaries. The flaw in the case was that Sir Benjamin had apparently not agreed to being included as a pursuer.

In a legal petition dated 10 March 1818 [90.3.9, an appendix attached to a reclaiming note of 29 August 1833], Sir Benjamin states: 'It would appear that, on the footing of verbal communications or of correspondence, the petitioner [i.e. Sir Benjamin] does not recollect which, to this effect, the feuars instructed their agent to raise an action, concluding for the division of the Hill of Wick, as common property; and by a very singular arrangement the petitioner was classed as a pursuer of this action of division, with some of the Magistrates and feuars of the burgh, while the great body of the feuars were called as defenders.'

Sir Benjamin went on to claim that the order to grant to the sheriff the commission to divide the Hill had been issued before he had been informed what was going on. 'Upon hearing the shape of the proceeding,' reads the petition, 'he immediately stated to the opposite party that he could not consent that the matter should be proceeded in in his name, as a pursuer of an action of division of that which he claimed as his exclusive property.' Sir Benjamin was arguing that he could hardly be called upon to participate in the division of land alleged to be common that was all his in the first place. The only claim that the feuars in the burgh could point to, Sir Benjamin argued, was a burden of servitude – the people could use the land but did not own it – that survived from the time, at the end of the seventeenth century, when the Earl of Breadalbane had sold what had belonged to the Earl of Caithness to the Dunbars. When Sir Benjamin called on the feuars to present their titles to the land, they did not respond and, as the legal documents have it, 'the process fell asleep.'

It was reawakened in 1817. Sir Benjamin petitioned the Court of Session to be 'sisted', the Scots legal term, from being a pursuer in the case to become a defender. The entire estate including the Hill o' Wick did after all belong to him, he argued, and was entailed; he had no right to, indeed could not, alienate or dispose of any part of it. The Lord Ordinary decided against Sir Benjamin's petition for this change of status but his appeal to the First Division of the Court was successful and, in March 1818, he became the sole defender, his defence being that all the land was his.

On 4 June 1818 in Wick, one day later than originally planned thanks to a request from Sir Benjamin for a brief delay, Sheriff-Substitute William Henderson at last convened the first hearing of evidence, to 'take the proof'. Alexander Miller and George Wares appeared on behalf of the feuars after having been chosen at a general meeting in the previous September; and two writers Patrick Thomson of Wick and Robert Mackay of Thurso represented Sir Benjamin.

After the Sheriff had appointed Thurso writer John Gunn to be clerk and had administered the oath, the first witness was questioned. This was James Bremner, a 74-year-old widower and pensioner who lived in Louisburgh, the first of a string of elderly men who spoke about the use of the Hill as they remembered it up to some sixty years before. Bremner, for example, had in 1755 been given the job at Westerseat of herding the cattle belonging to the townspeople, receiving them from the children who brought them out to him in the morning, watching them all day and delivering them back into the hands of the children who in the evening caa'ed them home to their respective owners. It was perfectly normal for the feuars of Wick to own livestock, often a single cow. Bremner testified to looking after a herd of between forty and forty-three animals. He had started doing this at the age of 11, quite a responsibility for a small boy but the common custom in Scotland before the days of fences and compulsory education. Some feuars also kept sheep and in summer they were also grazed on the Hill under the care of Donald Swanson of Gallowhill and his son John. The Swansons housed the sheep at night 'and … got the dung for their trouble' [97.1.1]. In winter the sheep were allowed to forage along the shore where presumably they lived on the banks of seaware. Bremner testified to no knowledge of any restriction on the numbers of animals on the pasturage and described the boundaries of the common land as he understood them to be: '… from Gillfield above Gillock on the west, to the Girnels of Staxigo on the east, and from the loaning dyke of west Noss on the north, to the dykes of Ackerness, Gallowhill and Clayquoys, Kettleburntofts, and the loaning dykes of Gillock on the south.' A loaning dyke stood between a field and a loaning, a track used by animals. James Bremner had tended the town cattle for two years and later at the age of 17 he had gone off to enlist in the army.

Three other locals gave evidence on the first day: William Swanson, aged 80, George Oald from Papigoe, 75, and Alexander Cormack, 72, from Louisburgh. Swanson said that when he had been eight or nine years old the people had 'upwards of 80 head of cattle and from 300 to 400 sheep pasturing on the said commonty.' The witnesses' memories differed slightly as to the boundaries of the common land but there was general agreement on the usage. Swanson recalled that no part of the commonty had been improved except the Rape park but that several parts had been kept by surrounding tenants as exclusive pasture. Alexander Reid had appropriated and improved a piece of ground near Gallowhill; and a field between Kettleburntofts and Gillock, called the Burnt Park, had been taken from the common. People had also cut peat from the mosses of Bronzie and Hayland. George Oald had been employed by the tenants of Upper Ackergill and Reiss to herd their sheep and he had seen the livestock of the Wick feuars coming and going each day; at first he mentioned cattle and sheep but then recollected that there had been no sheep which, he understood, used to be sent to country places to graze. He said that cattle and sheep from West Noss and Gillock had also been pastured on the Hill. Alexander Cormack thought that the offending ditch at Blackbridge had been cut about fifteen years before, and he also recalled peatcutters being interrupted in their work by Dunbar men. He added that he had been 'told by several of the people of Wick that they had been sent home from cutting feal, divot and turf-peats in the said commonty, and their spades taken from them by Sir Benjamin himself, who made them replace the feal, divot or peats in the delfs from which they took them….'.

When the hearing continued on the following day, the schoolmaster in Keiss, William Campbell, was appointed as land measurer. A small party led by the sheriff and including George Oald and Alexander Cormack, witnesses on the previous day, set out to perambulate the commonty. This took all day and further proceedings did not begin again until ten o'clock on the morning of 6 June in the house of John Oald, a Wick vintner, where George Oald and Alexander Cormack were taken through their testimony again and went into great detail on the locations of boundaries. The written evidence runs to over four pages of printed discussion of grey or white stones, old steeths (foundations of dykes), ditches and other markers. 'A grey stone fixed in the ground westward of the said white stone, and about a gun shot above the old corn land of Gillock,' reads one item; 'The said old dyke, being the next to the outermost dyke on the south end of the said park, from the said west side dyke to Angus Mackay's byre,' reads another. Mr Campbell's map, if he produced one, must have been very necessary.

The hearing adjourned to Thurso and opened there on 20 June. Captain John Henderson, a banker aged over fifty, was the first to be examined as a 'haver', that is a person possibly in possession of a document or property relevant to the case. The captain testified that he had no writings or title-deeds relating to the Hill o' Wick or the mosses of Hayland and Bronsy [sic] but that he recalled coming upon by accident many years before – 1789 or 1790, while searching through a chest of papers left by the deceased sheriff-clerk Hugh Campbell, a document that said that 'the right of common property of the town or feuars of Wick … extended to a coal shaft in either the hill of Sibster, Harland or Wick.' This was to the best of his recollection, he stated, and he felt that Sibster had been the place. What made him recollect seeing this paper was that the thought had 'struck him forcibly' at the time that the paper 'might be useful to the feuars of Wick'. But where were this chest and this document now? Isabella Campbell, the daughter of the late sheriff-clerk, testified that she knew of no chest of papers that her father had left in her mother's possession. She did know that he had left a large chest with papers in the old house of Carsgo 'where it lay until the year 1781' when it was brought to her mother's house in Thurso to be searched for papers needed for some family business. Then the chest had been sent to Thurso East to Lady Janet Sinclair in 1782. Lady Janet had since died and Isabella had not seen the chest again. Nothing has been heard again about a coal shaft in the vicinity of Wick.

The search for written evidence brought the third witness of the day to the stand. This was the 60-year-old laird of Freswick, William Sinclair. He did not know the limits of the commonty at Wick, he said, but he had seen a tract of land there pointed out to him as such. He had a handful of documents relating to Wick in his possession, all copies of legal documents, but none of them related to the common land and he had no idea of where any such paper could be found.

No further hearings were conducted until the end of October 1818, when more witnesses gave accounts of the use of the alleged common land. John Harper from Staxigoe, aged in his sixties, told how the livestock from the town used to pasture among the animals belonging to the farming tenants. The tenants found it difficult to keep 'their working oxen from running after the cows, and leaping on them, to the no small injury of the oxen,' said Harper. This animal behaviour naturally resulted in rows between the herd-boys but the town animals had never been driven off the Hill. Harper's father, who was a tenant farmer, and John Miller in Papigoe had complained to Sir William Dunbar about the Wick cattle coming on to the pasture. Sir William had taken no notice of this 'further than to desire them to beat them off the best they could.' The next witness, a Staxigoe man called David Bain, had herded sheep on the Hill but could add nothing new about the practices with cattle. On the following day, Harper and Bain perambulated the ground with the surveyor and the Sheriff to point out the boundaries of the common as they remembered them. William Cormack, a farmer in Humster, testified on 31 October that the tenants and the Wick feuars had 'cast' [cut] peat on the moss of Hayland, as far as he knew without restraint, and had paid 'some consideration to the moss-man or moss-grieve' for this. Some had taken peats from the moss without paying anything. The tenants of Charity had cast their peat on the north side and the tenants of Banks, Barnyards and Humster had taken their peat from the south side of the so-called Blindburn flowing from the Dow Loch, the Dhu Loch between Hempriggs and Stirkoke. Cormack knew of the ditch that Sir Benjamin had recently cut through part of the moss to the north of the old burn. The moss-man of Hayland was next to give evidence. He was John Malcolm, aged 70 and living in Wick at Bankhead, and his father had been moss-man before him. '…As many of the feuars of Wick as had pieces in the said moss, which they claimed as their property, cast peats there without paying any consideration for the liberty to do so,' he said, 'and others of the said feuars paid money to the moss-grieve who was accountable for it' to Sir Benjamin. Malcolm named eight feuars who claimed property in the moss. He had always considered the parts of the moss not so claimed or used by the township tenants to belong to the Hempriggs estate. Later witnesses, John Whier and Axwell Cooper, testified how some of the Wick feuars, themselves among them, had cut peat on the moss of Bronzie without restraint.

6 | *'some obliterations on the ground by improvement'*

After the conclusion of the taking of proof, the parties apparently agreed to remit the whole business to James Traill in the summer of 1819. Traill, however, declined to act. There also took place some legal wrangling over expenses. The upshot was that nothing eventually happened to resolve the dispute and the case fell asleep again. By the time the matter had its second reawakening in the summer of 1830, Sir Benjamin had become Lord Duffus although for the sake of clarity we shall continue to refer to him by name. Sheriff-substitute James Gregg had now been appointed Commissioner and opened the proceedings in Wick on 4 August, appointing Allan Roberston as clerk and a Thurso surveyor, Alexander Davidson, to take the place of William Campbell, the Keiss schoolteacher who had surveyed the Hill twelve years before but was now deemed too old at 65 to serve again except as a witness. The hearings began at last on 6 October in Leith's Inn and immediately the lawyer George Sinclair lodged a protest from Sir Benjamin that in essence argued that he objected to the whole business because a commission should not proceed to treat as common property land that was not in fact commonty. His protest referred to 'this intended invasion upon his property' and argued that 'no proceedings under this commission shall … affect his rights or titles, which shall be held equally free, entire, and secure, as if no such proceeding had taken place.'

Sheriff Gregg led a perambulation of the alleged commonty on the morning of 7 October, with a procession of lawyers and feuars, accompanied by the two witnesses William Campbell the schoolteacher and the Pulteneytown feuar Robert Mulliken. The feuars were over two hours late for the appointed start of nine o'clock and it was not until near noon that the party at last set off. Campbell had not unreasonably brought along 'a paper or plan', probably of the survey he had made on the previous occasion. Objections were made to this, and to Campbell and Mulliken perambulating together. The sheriff was of a mind to dismiss these objections but, in view of Campbell having a plan and Mulliken not being so equipped, agreed that the latter should withdraw. The party then set off from Kettleburntofts around the boundary, apparently repeatedly stopping and starting as an uncertain Campbell strove to recall the route, until they reached the vicinity of the ditch that Benjamin Waters had cut nearly thirty years before. Now Campbell admitted that he was not quite certain of the precise direction of the march; the paper he had brought was only a hand sketch not to scale and not to be relied upon; the measured plan was in the sheriff's house, still wet from having been pasted on to linen. It was too late in the day by this time to finish the perambulation and the sheriff called the proceedings off until nine the following morning.

When they reconvened, the Edinburgh lawyer Alexander Stuart, acting with his legal colleague Robert Rose of Wick on behalf of the pursuers, objected to the presence of George Dunbar, Sir Benjamin's son. George had been there from the start and had tagged along on the previous day's excursion. The Dunbars' lawyer, George Sinclair, argued that 'Mr Dunbar was no party to the present proceedings' and could stay. The sheriff then dismissed a long protest from the Dunbar lawyer about the way things had been done the day before on the Hill. After these and other exchanges, the Keiss schoolmaster was again called on to give evidence. Campbell explained that his confusion had been the result of 'some obliterations on the ground by improvements' since the previous survey and deponed that with the proper plan he thought he would be able to point out the line of the boundary. Thereupon they set off to complete the interrupted perambulation of the previous day.

On the 9th, Campbell was again cross-questioned in considerable detail before the court adjourned to the home of Alexander Miller of Staxigoe, in his eighty-ninth year and too infirm to leave the house. Miller gave an exhaustive account of the Hill, with its boundaries, dykes and enclosed parks and the changes he had seen in his long life. Over the next sixteen days, with breaks for the Sabbath and a few days when the court did not sit, but on occasion in proceedings extending into the evening in Leith's Inn, the Commission heard from over forty witnesses, both men and women, some of them more than once being called to answer questions.

Much of the questioning was about boundaries and named features in the landscape. Some of the witnesses gave detailed accounts of these, speaking about dykes, stones, mosses and ditches, and who could go where. Far from being bare windy acres of heath and grass, the Hill comes over as having been a complex pattern of named places recognized by everyone who regularly frequented it. Among these were Alexander Bain, a tenant in Kilimster who had spent all of his 81 years in the district bounded by Ackergill, Kilimster and Keiss, and John Sutherland, 83 years old, born in Sibster and now living at Gillfield. They spoke of Barney's dam and Whiterashes and Lummie's dykes. John Sutherland testified that Lummie had occupied a piece of ground before the time of Sir William Dunbar (who had died in 1793); '... and he wrought till he could work no more, and then fled away; and this was the same person the dykes were called after, as far as the deponent [Sutherland] ever heard.' The dams penned back water to feed a mill at Gillock. Later in the hearings Lummie was identified as a John Lummie who had held a tack from Sir William from September 1737.

As in the 1818 hearing, several of the witnesses had worked as herd boys, looking after the cows that belonged to people in the burgh. William Mackenzie, now the miller in Sordale, had come to Wick from his native parish of Halkirk to be a herd in the summer when he had been fourteen, driving the twenty cows in his care to graze in various spots between the dykes of Ackergill, the park of Papigoe, sometimes as far east as Staxigoe, up to Clayquoys, and at the foot of the brae up to West Noss – 'there was no stop if they kept out of the corn,' he said, a piece of evidence confirmed by all the others. As long as crops or other property were not invaded or damaged, the herds were allowed to drive their charges where they were wont to go. Robert Mulliken from Pulteneytown also had sheep to look after but likewise he suffered no interruptions. Janet Craig, now 82 years old, used to take her father's cow to the Hill when she had been twelve and had never been stopped from going to the places she frequented. John Phimister in Louisburgh said that he could have up to fifty cattle towards the 'fall of the year' that he pastured on the Hill all the way over to the cornland of Noss. At times, though, there was trouble – as a lad, John Davidson from Louisburgh had worked as a herd for Alexander Bain, then in the farm of Whitefield, near which lay a good patch of ground known as Whiterashes; Davidson used to drive his cattle, and particularly a blue ox, towards the Wick cows, if they came near, to start fights among the animals. The vivid experiences of the teenage herds had implanted the details of their work in their minds. Several recalled at such length who lived in which tenement and who owned which cow or how many that one wonders now how the sheriff and the lawyers kept their eyelids apart. George Bain from Pulteneytown, was a cooper and at the age of 25 one of the youngest witnesses; he had worked as a herd to the parish minister who had sent not only cows but oxen, sheep and geese to the Hill.

The testimony also includes some references to the annual Hill Market. In 1830 this was held at the junction of the roads from Wick to Reiss and Gillock (now the A99 and the B874), the place known locally now as Lochshell, at least sixty years before the market had taken place at another location, though still in Dunbar territory. John Sutherland was still employed by the Dunbars to collect the 'customs' or market fees. Alexander Bain related how he had heard his father say that Sir William Dunbar had been 'struck on the market' and had made a promise that never again would it stand in his day. The Hill Market held on the first day of August was one of a series of twenty fairs that punctuated the year, drawing rural people from a wide area to socialise, buy and sell: the first was the Candlemas Market in Freswick on 3 February, and the last the Magnusmas Market in Watten on 27 December. Most, including the Hill Market, were concerned with the buying and selling of livestock, although Candlemas and the Rood Fair at Larel on 15 May also specialised in woollen goods.[12] Thurso and Wick had weekly markets, on Fridays and Tuesdays respectively, but for most of the folk in the countryside the fairs would have been the all-important highlights of their annual round. It may seem extreme for someone to have taken a swing at Sir William Dunbar but some of the fairs acquired notoriety for drinking and fighting and the Hill Market gave rise to a proverbial saying for a situation of chaotic confusion.

The evidence presented to the Commission includes references to some of the improvements in cultivation that were under way. Alexander Reid, the tenant of Whitefield, described how he 'took in' a triangular area between Ackerness and Gallowhill twenty-six years before, a piece of ground still known after him as his park. Reid said that he had not considered the triangle, which had been covered in heath, to have been part of the Hill or any common ground but the people in Wick had disputed his right to claim it and he had stopped labouring it for two or three years. Then the principal tacksman, Mr Sutherland, had told Reid that he held the ground from him and had to pay for it, and Reid had started to use it again, this time without any further interruption.

An important improver had of course been Sir Benjamin himself. According to the Revd Charles Thomson, the Wick minister who wrote the description of his parish for *The New Statistical Account of Scotland*, published in 1845, Sir Benjamin had embarked on changing the local system of agriculture when he had inherited the estate from his father. Thomson gives this date as 1782 but the date from the Dunbar Papers is clearly 1793, unless Sir Benjamin initiated changes before he inherited from his father. Thomson was all in favour of what had been done – 'The result of this enlightened procedure was most advantageous'[13] – but, as we shall see, in a later part of the text, the process created social casualties. William Craig, the bowman or cattleman at Sibster, told the Commission how Sir Benjamin had improved the tract of ground called Whiterashes, stretching from Whitefield and Harland east towards Gillock, by paring off and burning the vegetation. Donald Harrold, the tenant in Gillock, testified how he had rented some of the Whiterashes ground from Sir Benjamin after it had been pared and burned, and after a crop of oats had been sown in part of it. Harrold's neighbour, William Miller, had also occupied a part, about fifty acres, of Whiterashes.

From Sir Benjamin's point of view, some of the testimony presented to the Commission must have been unwelcome. The first was that of William Craig, the Sibster cattleman, who said that 'he knows that the people of Wick, who sent cattle to the hill [above Ackerness], had pieces of land for grazing from Sir William Dunbar at the loaning shade …', by which he meant possibly the end of the loan. He named them as Donald Cormack, Captain Kennedy, Christian Mullikin, Harry Craig 'and a good many more' all living in Wick. A few minutes later in his testimony, he revised this remark 'That it was not from Sir William Dunbar but from Lord Duffus that they so had lands …'; Craig could not be sure how many had land in this way but it was 'a good many'. Robert Mulliken confirmed that he remembered from his teenage period as a herd that it had been common for people in Wick to have pieces of land at the loaning shade from Sir William Dunbar. It was common to have farthing lands in those days, he stated, but whether people had such land or not they pastured their cows all together. Alexander Sutherland from Keiss gave similar evidence, that people in Wick who sent cows to the Hill had farthing lands from Sir William. 'They called them octos of land,' he said. A man called Craig 'who had five octos, sent 9 or 10 cattle to the hill, and five horses'; and Alexander Bain sent six or seven cows 'and there were a hantle of others who had octos … and considered that it belonged to them.' Sutherland further testified that those who had octos paid land-rent to Sir William, 10s for each octo and one and a half bolls of bere. Buried in the recorded statements of all the witnesses are some nuggets of information that give us a glimpse of a world now gone. Henry Rosie, aged 76 and living in Wick, spoke of the cattle from the Hill going down to the Wick River to drink, of a ford there and cruives, wicker fish traps, in the water. He too said that people held octos or farthing lands from Sir William, and named many who had owned cows, where they had lived and, for some, whether or not Sir William owned the house in the burgh in which they dwelt.

The hearings were concluded on 27 October. The evidence taking was followed by compiling and presentation of inventories, and valuation of the ground. Two maps were drawn. At last, at the end of May 1831, Sheriff James Gregg produced his Report accompanied by two maps and an appendix with an extended analysis of the subject [97.1.1]. More than once he spoke of difficulty in reaching a conclusion. He identified six claimants in the division of the commonty – he had concluded that a commonty did indeed exist, as proved by promiscuous pasturage – and these six were Sir Benjamin Dunbar, William Horne of Stirkoke whose lands at Sibster abutted the Hill, Mr Craig of Whitehouse, Mr Phin the parish minister, the superior and magistrates of the burgh, and individual feuars. By far the largest claimant was Sir Benjamin who had title to 558 of the some 761 acres in contention. Alexander Davidson had produced a detailed plan of the Hill, measuring the total area with great precision at 761 acres, two roods and 39 falls. Horne of Stirkoke claimed just over one hundred and fifty-five acres, Mr Craig a modest eight acres comprising one rectangle of ground adjacent to Gallowhill, and the feuars forty acres next to the burgh on the eastern edge of the Hill. The sheriff went into some detail in a theoretical consideration of division based on the principle of contiguity (whereby a claimant already held land touching the area in contention) and whether or not it was a necessary ingredient in a claimant's position. This was important in so far as it affected what the superior and magistrates would get. This no doubt gave plenty of gristle for lawyers to chew on but would have been of less interest to the others. In the event the sheriff rejected Sir Benjamin's claim of exclusive ownership of the commonty, sustained Horne's claim for the 155 acres to go to Sibster, agreed that Mr Craig could claim a right of servitude for his patch, but doubted whether the claim of all the burgh feuars could be sustained. He named ten feuars as having produced evidence of rights of servitude, defined as being for divots and pasturage for one cow. The minister of the parish was deemed to have right of pasturage. With regard to the claim put forward by the superior and the magistrates for the community of the burgh, the sheriff confessed to have 'not been without very considerable difficulty in forming a conclusive opinion ...' but 'On the whole, my views on it, at present, are adverse to the claimants. I have great doubts,' he continued, 'whether a claim, such as is urged by the burgh, can be at all legally sustained.' In any case, he concluded any claim was not sufficiently supported by evidence.

That was not quite the end of the Hill o' Wick affair. The magistrates persisted in their campaign to secure what they saw as the rights of the townspeople but their appeal failed. In July 1833, the court finally ruled that the burgh had no title. The expenses of £580 had to be paid by the burgh council and feuars.

7 | *'the sea making a complete break over her'*

George Dunbar features as the salvor of a ship wrecked in Sinclair Bay in 1828. The story of the incident and the subsequent roup of the wreckage and much material from the vessel is told in detail in surviving documents in the Dunbar Papers [44.3]. The proceedings were typical for this sort of event, one repeated often on the shores of Caithness in the days of sail.

The *Saint Nicholay* – the name is variously spelled in the Papers, as are the names of the Russian protagonists – set sail from Kronstadt, the port of Saint Petersburg, on 14 November 1827 with a cargo of 'red wood, deals, deal ends, hemp and iron' for Liverpool merchants. A brig of 240 tons, she was described to the legal authorities in Wick a few months later as 'tight, staunch and strong, well manned, rigged and tackled, the masts and pumps well bound, the hatches properly secured, and in every other respect well provided and furnished for the seas'. Bad weather in the Baltic forced the Saint Nicholay to seek shelter in Sagendal in Norway, where she had to lie for ten weeks before the wind shifted to allow her to proceed on 16 February. During the stay on the Norwegian coast she gained an extra man – an English seaman called Robert Anderson who found a passage home after he had been shipwrecked in the Gulf of Finland while serving as the mate on the London brig Harriet. Anderson was able to support the Russian officers in their sworn testimony in Wick as to what had happened on the next leg of the voyage.

On the morning of 21 February, in hazy weather and before a strong breeze from the east north-east, the Russian brig made a landfall. Ione Petahoff, the captain, and Cosma Tuleve, the sailing master, identified a headland about a league (3 miles) away as Duncansby Head and set course for the Pentland Firth. They made the same error of judgement as many another navigator in the days of sail; what they thought was Duncansby was in fact Noss Head and before they realised the truth the brig was within Sinclair's Bay, trapped on a lee shore, the sailing captain's nightmare. 'Several tacks made to get her out of the Bay but the wind blowing right in … and a heaving sea,' reads the testimony. At five o'clock in the evening, the *Saint Nicholay* 'missed stays' – failed to complete going about on to a new tack – and had to 'wear' – turn downwind, a manoeuvre that increased the leeway. Soon she was in among the breakers and drifting towards the shore. She struck the ground at eight o'clock and 'continued to strike all night whereby she became completely waterlogged and the sea making a complete break over her.'

Long before the fall of darkness and the grounding of the brig, the locals would have become aware of the ship in danger and many would have gathered on the shore. In this instance the crew were all saved but the *Saint Nicholay* herself became a total loss. The Russian captain signed a note to George Dunbar recognising him as salvor of the wreck 'of my vessel', in the poignant wording of the document drafted for him. The later testimony acknowledged that the Russians had done all in their power to save the ship. As the main local landowner and the proprietor of the coast where the ship had struck, and also as admiral-depute for the area, the designated officer responsible for the local jurisdiction of the law of the sea, George Dunbar was now the man responsible for the wreck under the jurisdiction of the Scottish Admiralty Court. This body was shortly to be subsumed into the Court of Session and the sheriff courts, and the wreck of the *Saint Nicholay* may have been the last vessel to fall under Dunbar jurisdiction according to the old regime.

George wrote at once to the Liverpool merchants James and Peter Bourne to let them know of the *Saint Nicholay*'s fate. On 26 February, only four days later, they replied, addressing the letter to 'The Hon. George Dunbar, Wick, NB', i.e. North Britain, as Scotland was frequently called in those days. The Bournes said they feared that the vessel was not insured and could give no instructions as to how to deal with all the cargo – only thirteen bundles of hemp had been consigned to them by the shipowner, a Mr Ivan Savin of St Petersburg. They were able to say that 'The deals are for Messrs Joseph Leigh & Co and the Iron for Messrs Richard Rimmer & Son of this town'. The Bournes also gave the good news that a Russian captain called Tchigoreff was about to sail for St Petersburg on the schooner *Wolga* which also belonged to Ivan Savin and would call to pick up the Russian crew at Stromness 'which they can of course reach with facility from Wick'. The Bournes asked George Dunbar to inform Captain Tuleff [sic] and 'let us hear from you or him, by return of post, whether this arrangement for the Crew's passage is satisfactory; it is approved of by the Russian Consul, whom we have consulted in this business.'

The roup of the wrecked ship and the perishable cargo went ahead promptly, taking place, as was the custom, at the site of the stranding only four days later. On the day after the wreck James Bremner, the famous salvage expert and shipbuilder from Wick, had come to inspect the wreck at George Dunbar's request; he had found the brig 'scattered in small pieces' along the sands, and had recommended immediate sale. The Articles and Conditions of Sale survive. These specify that the lots would go to the highest bidder 'when the word thrice is pronounced by the Judge or Auctioneer', that the purchased goods had to be removed by the buyer within eight days, that buyers failing to settle their account by the conclusion of the sale would have to pay 25 per cent of the value of the purchase and forfeit any further claim on the goods, and pay for any loss sustained during later sale of the goods. Allan Macfarlane Esquire of Reiss was made Judge of the Sale, John Sutherland of Wick the auctioneer, and George Forbes the clerk on whom fell the bulk of the work in advertising the roup, recording the sales and completing the accounts [44.3.1]. The publicity included an advertisement in the *Inverness Journal*.

It took three sales to dispose of the *Saint Nicholay* – on 26 February, and 13 and 24 March. The lots and buyers – a considerable crowd gathered – were fully listed by the assiduous George Forbes. Many lots of wood and hemp went under the hammer and some valuable maritime stores were also to be had. James Bremner himself paid £3 6s for an anchor. Individual ropes went for 2s each and upwards. Simon A. Manson bought three large sacks of ship's biscuit for a total of £6 8s 9d. In all, the sales realised £1,009 19s 1d for, as the Conditions state, 'the benefit of the Underwriters and all concerned'. It was not all profit, as the proceedings incurred considerable expense. George Dunbar had to recruit and pay considerable numbers of men for various tasks, including '129 men for saving the crew' at 2s each (£12 18s), 44 men for watching the wreck on night of 23 February at 3s 6d each (£7 14s), 14 men for raising ropes from the sand (£4 11s), boarding the Russian survivors for ten days at Ackergill and another ten days in Wick (£46 15s), the expense of 40 fathom of rope lost at the wreck (12s), a boat 'wrecked in endeavouring to save the crew' (£5), a surprising 'spirits to the men employed at the wreck' – clearly cold work in February (£8 13s 6d), and much more [44.3.10]. George Dunbar gave £2 to the Russians to tide them over in Stromness and William Manson and his crew received 3 guineas for taking them there from Wick. It is to be hoped that the *Wolga* was able to give these reluctant, lucky guests a safe passage home.

Notes

1. The relative values of money in different historical periods can be obtained from websites such as www. measuringworth.com .

2. 'Latheronwheel', p.13. *Geographical Collections relating to Scotland*, Walter Mac Farlane (Sir Arthur Mitchell, ed.) vol. 1, p. 163

3. J.B. Craven, *A History of the Episcopal Church in the Diocese of Caithness*, 1908, p. 249.

4. *OSA*, Watten, XI, 1792.

5. *Commissioners for Highland Roads and Bridges*, 7th Report, 1815; 8th Report, 1817.

6. *Commissioners for Highland Roads and Bridges*, 9th Report, 1821.

7. The restoration of the title of Lord Duffus, forfeited when Kenneth Sutherland, the 3rd Lord Duffus, fled to Sweden to escape retribution for his support of the Jacobites, had to be approved by Parliament. Kenneth's son Eric was known as the 4th Lord but this was only a courtesy. The so-named Duffus Restoration Bill endured a few delays in its passage into law – at one point the King did not sign it in time to meet the Session deadline, as told in a series of letters in the Dunbar Papers (49.5.36 – 43), but on 25 May 1826 James Sutherland of Duffus officially became the 5th Lord Duffus. When James died in the following year, Sir Benjamin inherited the title, becoming the 6th Lord Duffus. Restoration did not come free: the steering of the Act through Parliament cost £200.

8. Jean Dunlop, *The British Fisheries Society 1786–1893*, 1978, p. 159. The story of Wick Harbour has been often told, in Dunlop's work and also notably in Iain Sutherland's two books, *Wick Harbour and the Herring Fishing*, 1984; and *From Herring to Seine Net Fishing on the East Coast of Scotland*, 1985.

9. Scottish Record Office B02390/4; http://freepages.family.rootsweb.ancestry.com (accessed 8 July 2014).

10. James Traill (1758–1843), born in Dunnet where his father was minister, became sheriff-depute of Caithness in 1788. His contribution to the economic development of the county was immense; he oversaw large-scale improvements to his Castlehill and Rattar estates, including the construction of Castlehill Harbour, and initiated the flagstone industry.

11. The Caithness bank issued its own notes but fell into difficulty after the Macleays died; it was acquired by the Commercial Bank of Scotland in 1825.

12. James Henderson, *General View of the Agriculture of the County of Caithness*, 1812, p. 304.

13. *New Statistical Account of Scotland*, Wick, 1841, v.15, p. 147.

Part 5

Evictions, renovations, sport and war

1 | 'enlightened procedure'

Farming in Caithness, as in the rest of northern Scotland, went through a revolution in the early decades of the nineteenth century. One man who was especially influential in this great shift from the farming practices of the past to a new emphasis on improvement, investment and greater returns on capital was Sir John Sinclair of Ulbster. His list of achievements is exhaustive, and there seems to have been hardly an economic or social pie in his day in which he did not dabble at least a finger. 'Agricultural Sir John', as he was nicknamed, was born at Thurso Castle in 1754. After qualifying for the Bar in Scotland and England, he was elected to Westminster as MP for Caithness in 1780. He became a Baronet in 1786, established the Board of Agriculture and became its first president in 1793, oversaw the compilation of the *Statistical Account of Scotland* in the 1790s, changed the map of Thurso and of a goodly part of his native county, and did much else besides – we have seen how he led the negotiations for the acquisition of land at Wick for the British Fisheries Society.[1]

Under his leadership, the Board of Agriculture commissioned a series of surveys of the agriculture of the northern counties. Captain John Henderson wrote the Caithness account, which was published in 1812 in London and contained a description of the improvements Sir John introduced to his own estates and the plans for Thurso.[2] It is virtually a textbook on the new agriculture. Sir John's Ulbster estate was listed as the biggest in the county, with a valued rental of £7813 1s Scots, with the Freswick estate in second place (valued rental £4259 4s 4d) and the Dunbar estates in third place, with a valuation of £3624 16s 10d. Henderson gave prominence to what Sir John was achieving and wrote next to nothing about the Dunbar estates, although Sir Benjamin was no laggard himself in the improvement business.

In his description of the parish for the *New Statistical Account of Scotland*, the Wick minister, Charles Thomson, gave Sir Benjamin high praise for the way he tackled improvements on his estate after he took over from his father in 1782. 'He found all the townlands … comprising the half of the parish, under lease to middle-men who paid him only the money rent payable by the small tenant for the grassland, and 6s 6d for each boll of eight stone and a half, paid by them for the cornland,' wrote the Revd Thomson. Sir Benjamin abolished the middle men, converted all the rents and services of the tenants to money, and granted leases at a fixed rent. The advantages of this 'enlightened procedure', continued Thomson, was an extension of tillage, better methods of cultivation, land improvement, delivery of tenants from their 'former degrading vassalage and their comfort and respectability greatly promoted', and increased rental income to Sir Benjamin himself. Thomson also says that when Sir Benjamin took over, the estate had few farmhouses built with stone but now there were few, if any, built of turf. The minister goes on to say that in 1792 there had been 'not a cart in the parish', an exaggeration, as we know that Eliza wrote about carts from Moray in her letters in 1775.[3]

In his own book on agriculture in the north, Sir John Sinclair argued that a landowner was 'properly a Trustee for the public, invested with the possession of a certain tract of country, partly for his own, but principally for the general benefit.' He listed the duties of a laird as (1) to cultivate to the best advantage; (2) to encourage farmers and the peasantry; (3) to share in the defence of the country; (4) to fulfil his public obligations – that is, support the kirk, the poor, the maintenance of roads and bridges, etc.; and (5) to inform the legislature of all proper information regarding his property. Sir John thought that the laird knew best, and almost all his neighbouring lairds would have agreed with him.[4]

A valuation of the Dunbar lands, this time representing the older system of agriculture, was drawn up in June 1793 [41.5.9]. It is a complex document laid out as a spreadsheet listing the various properties with their valuations given in quantities of both grain and money. The areas of the properties are measured according to the old system of pennylands, assessments of the productive capability of the land rather than the actual area. The first entry for the parish of Wick encompasses 'East Noss Quoystain Nossedge and Cantsquoy' and notes that this land is possessed and occupied by Alexander Harper and others. The land is valued at 8 bolls, 3 pecks and 2 lippies of grain per pennyland. One firlot is deducted to pay the 'smith and officer', resulting in a net total valuation of 134 bolls, 1 firlot, 3 pecks and 2¼ lippies, worth £21 17s 9d Scots. The same group of tenants also shared the 'Park of Castle Sinclair' where, as the name suggests, an area of pasture had already been enclosed.

All the properties on the estate are listed in a similar fashion. Several of them mention place names that no longer feature on local maps. One entry in particular is a striking example of this – of the places of 'The Lands and Mills of Gillock and Knockdry also Smallquoys Kettleburntofts Westerseat and Skinnerscroft possest by Mr William Sutherland', only Gillock and Westerseat remain distinct. The mills of Gillock probably existed along the burn of Gillock but of these buildings and of the others mentioned in 1793 no trace remains on the Ordnance Survey map of 1907. Interestingly Sutherland's possession was valued in cash only – a net figure of £37 3s 7d, after deduction of £20 for the rent of the two mills.

The enclosing of land and its division into farms to be let to single tenants left no room for the large numbers of cottars who had tilled their rigs in a system of shared ownership. Their views on the new agriculture with its emphasis on investment and cash return were never sought and hardly ever recorded, although we hear a few voices in the testimony to the hearings on the Hill o' Wick. How they felt when they were told to quit when their leases expired can only be imagined although, in Caithness, this flight from the countryside may have been ameliorated by the opportunities offered by the contemporary growth of the herring fishing and the expansion of Wick. There seems to be no lasting folk memory of eviction in the lowland parts of the county, in contrast to the situation in other parts of the north such as Sutherland and Wester Ross, but it did occur. Sir John Sinclair himself recorded how he turned land along the Thurso River from country occupied by eighty-two tenants into 'regular' farms for only twenty-five; the evicted families formed new townships and 'cottage farms', flitted to Thurso or Wick, or emigrated from the county.[5] In their study of farm buildings, Glendinning and Martins say that the creation of the 'showpiece Caithness farms' by such men as Sir John Sinclair, Sir John Anstruther in Watten, and John Traill in Rattar involved the relocation of many small tenants to marginal crofting land.[6] The witnesses who testified before the Napier Commission in 1883 stated that 35 crofters were evicted to make room for the farm of Rumster, 17 for Reaster and 15 for Rattar. Some of the evictees settled on waste ground; at Reaster there were two such hamlets, brutally called Beggars' Town and Paupers' Town. In the 1841 Census, there were 61 families living in Reaster and Greenland, representing 280 people, and in Reaster alone there were 25 inhabited houses, although it is unknown if any of these were linked to the squatters who had occupied the waste ground on the edge of the mosses.

The Dunbar Papers do contain lists of tenants to be 'removed' but they have to be interpreted with care and do not necessarily indicate wholesale eviction in the manner that has come to be associated with the excesses of the Clearances. One document [49.1.8] has the names of twenty-six people to remove at Whitsunday 1813. They are scattered across the estate from Papigoe to Latheronwheel and to Tulachan in the upper reaches of the Thurso River. Two of the people are clearly stated to have died. Neither are they all farmers or cottars, as among them is

William Sutherland described as 'Innkeeper in Weeke from lands in Louisburgh', and 'Alex Miller Staxigoe from Miln of Papigoe'.

As could be expected, the Dunbar Papers contain many lease and letting agreements. For example, in April 1812, George Phimster took on the ground to the south of Wick formerly let to Donald Farquhar at the same rent of 23s per acre [48.1.2]. Another lease shows that the traditional practice of paying rent in kind and service did not altogether disappear. This lease is dated at Hempriggs on 20 November 1810 (although not signed until the following March) and details the agreement between Sir Benjamin and John Sutherland, a tenant in Killimster [90.1.8]. Sutherland took on 125 acres on a three-year lease from Whitsunday 1811, agreeing to pay £50 per year in 'money rent' along with 'six hens, 12 dozen eggs and 18 chickens at any time called for in the course of each year with four days cutting hay four days winning hay and four feet of custom peats at the usual periods.' John Sutherland signed as accepting these terms and, interestingly, another man Donald Bain signed as being a co-possessor of the farm.

2 | *'totally unfit for such an undertaking'*

In 1820 Sir Benjamin became involved in what we can call the Wester affair. This was a complex, long-running legal saga, involving a long list of personalities and ramifying into a few sub-plots, and what follows is a summary of the main thrust of the story. Twenty years before, William Sutherland, who had served for years as Sir William Dunbar's factor and had been granted a liferent tack of the property, had held the lands of Wester and Killimster. After William Sutherland died in 1801 or 1802, his son Alexander, with Sir Benjamin's agreement, took over Wester on a tack set to run for eighteen years. Killimster was given up to Sir Benjamin's possession. The agreement between Sir Benjamin and Alexander was later quoted as follows: 'The sum of 14,000 merks, presently secured upon the lands of North Kilmster, to be added to the wadset sums over the lands of Wester, and the said lands to be thereafter redeemable, upon payment of the sum 16,900 merks. The lands of Wester to be held from and after Whitsunday 1802, for the interest of the said sum of 16,900 merks …' [85.3.4].

In 1820, when the Wester tack could be expected to run out, Sir Benjamin was looking forward to regaining the land and adding it to the acres already in his personal possession. But there was a complication. In around 1809, because he had fallen into debt, Alexander Sutherland had been forced to 'leave the country' and move to London, and had placed his affairs in the hands of a trustee. This was Major William Innes of Sandside, the grandson of Harry Innes of Sandside and Janet, Sir Benjamin's great-aunt. Innes, who at this time was also Sir Benjamin's trustee, sublet Wester to Captain Robert Kennedy for an annual rent of £120. Although Sir Benjamin would have preferred to have chosen the subtenant himself, the Captain was an old friend – they had been in the Legion together – and Sir Benjamin acquiesced in Innes's action.[7]

When Kennedy gave up his sublet in 1816, Sir Benjamin saw an opportunity either to become a subtenant himself or put someone of his own choice – James Smith of Olrig was mentioned as a possible candidate – in on a short let. It may seem odd to wish to be a subtenant on land that already belongs to one, but the idea behind it was that Sir Benjamin would work Wester and Killimster until Alex Sutherland's original tack expired, paying the rent to Innes, and then simply continue in possession as the proprietor. Sir Benjamin put this plan to Innes, writing to him several times when no reply was forthcoming from Sandside. Whatever the reasons for his reluctance to agree to Sir Benjamin's plan, Innes avoided replying and instead granted the subtenancy to the brothers John and Charles Davidson. Sir Benjamin was to claim that this had been done 'in secret' to disappoint him [85.3.5].

Sir Benjamin did what all the Caithness lairds did when their plans were thwarted – he went to court. In his view, the Davidsons were 'two small subtenants who in point of capital and skill were totally unfit for such an undertaking' as running a modern farm and that by the time the tack would run out the land would have been 'laid absolutely waste.' In November 1816 Sir Benjamin sought an interdict to keep the Davidsons off Wester but delayed its implementation when Innes told him that he was about to proceed to Edinburgh where he would direct his agents to arrange everything to Sir Benjamin's satisfaction. This he did not do, and a Summons of Removing was eventually issued against Innes and the Davidsons on 28 April 1817 [85.3.4].

Further legal wrangling ensued until on 11 March 1820, the Court of Session agreed that Sir Benjamin had the right to the land, that the trustee should receive the rent he would pay as a subtenant and that, as the original tack was about to expire anyway (18 years had passed since Alex Sutherland had first taken over Wester) there was no need for a formal decision on the subletting. The Davidsons were told that they had to quit their possession by Whitsunday 1820. There then ensued a row over what – removal, or settlement of rent – should happen in which order. Sir Benjamin lodged the money – 16,900 marks, equivalent to £938 18 shillings, agreed with Sutherland for redemption of the wadset – with the Caithness Bank and sought a warrant of eviction.

Sir Benjamin's lawyers, the Edinburgh firm of J. & D. Horne & Easton, continued the struggle in the face of further delays. [He] 'is compelled to notice another circumstance which characterizes and he is sorry to say disgraces the complainers [Innes's and the Davidsons'] proceedings,' reads part of one legal document [85.3.5]. 'They were bound to remove from the house and grass at Whitsunday … but now that their immediate removal has become unavoidable they have consumed destroyed or carried off the whole of the valuable natural grass … and the whole of the fuel [peats] … and are now busily employed in removing their straw and committing every possible waste and damage they can contrive to injure the respondent [Sir Benjamin] so that the lands have already been nearly rendered waste and untenantable.'

Yet further delays and court proceedings meant that it was not until nearly the end of October 1820 that the Edinburgh lawyer David Horne was able to tell Sir Benjamin that he could now request the Caithness sheriff to proceed with the eviction [110.1]. But again there was obstruction as more legal objections were heard and rejected. On 16 November, Horne's partner James Easton, whom we have already met as a friend of Sir Benjamin's son George, wrote to Sir Benjamin with the news that he had sent the notice of ejection and a horning to Robert MacKid, procurator fiscal in Caithness, for execution.

In the last week of November, the court's messenger-at-arms, Alexander Farquharson, with a party of followers rode to Wester to implement the eviction of the Davidson brothers. Farquharson was prevented from carrying out his duty, according to one account being 'violently obstructed and deforced by John Davidson his family and several of the cottars on the estate [85.3.3].[8] This document also alleged that the cottars had been misguided by instructions sent by William Innes. This was deforcement, 'most atrocious' deforcement said Sir Benjamin who immediately sought the assistance of the fiscal in what had been a criminal act [7.4.1]. As MacKid sought more information, he confessed to James Easton that he had been 'placed between two fires, a threatened complaint to his Majesty's Advocate on the one hand … and the Sheriff's Veto on the other.' Apparently no warrant for the ejection had been issued, hence the fiscal's fear of incurring the sheriff's displeasure [110.1.31]. David Horne was of the view that the case should be considered a straightforward breach of the peace, as Farquharson had acted under written authority.

January found the Davidsons still in residence at Wester. James Easton's impatience began to show in his letters to Sir Benjamin: 'I begin to be annoyed beyond what I can express at the want of the execution of ejection,' he wrote on 6 January [7.4.5], '… Robert MacKid today puts us to 4 [shillings] of postage with inclosures about his miserable complaint …. I begin … to be quite alarmed that the execution may not be forthcoming … & that the case may be ruined in consequence of this unaccountable tardiness on the part of your law officers.'

In February, Innes and the Davidsons brought in another Bill of Suspension, this time citing as a co-tacksman a certain James Mowat. 'I never before heard of Mowat the third potential subtenant,' noted James Easton on 12 February [7.4.9]. Sir Benjamin advised the lawyer about this man's real status – of which more below. Easton also complained that he had not received from Farquhar a copy of the sheriff's warrant, although he had written for it twice, and he would be required to produce it in court. On the 21st Easton wrote again to say that 'The Wester case was taken up on Saturday & after a great deal of angry discussion was continued until yesterday [7.4.10]. The Court had no problem with defining the status of Sutherland and the Davidsons – 'The difficulty then was with Sandside.' Easton and his colleagues maintained he was a 'mere' trustee but 'They again shifted their ground' and 'averred that he was not Trustee but assignee to the Tack of 1802' and that they could prove this by producing his own assignation and Mowat's tack. The document in question proved, though, to be a conveyance of the old tack acquired by Sutherland's grandfather – Sandside was not an assignee. The Court, however, passed the Bill of Suspension in Sandside's favour – absurdly in the view of the Dunbar counsel – on a technical interpretation hingeing on Sir Benjamin's wish to be a subtenant until 1820 and a landlord thereafter. 'There is a strong combination against you in this business,' warned Easton, hinting that mysterious others, Sinclair of Freswick among them, might be in the background. He also warned of the expense of lawsuits but acknowledged 'If necessary we must proceed with the action before the Sheriff which concludes against Mowat & I shall raise a new action of multiple poinding declanaton [he probably means 'declination', the refusal to perform one's legal duty] & damages against all concerned & particularly against Sandside for the violation of the Lease 1802.'

On 3 March Easton told Sir Benjamin that, in answer to his 'amicable' proposal to the opposing party's lawyer 'to put an end at once to all proceedings in Court about Wester as there never could be any dispute about the rights of the parties', he had received a request that Sir Benjamin give up possession and allow the Sutherland tack to run for thirty-one years in place of eighteen [7.4.12]. 'This is a piece of the highest assurance I have met with,' growled Easton. Three days later he was writing to state that as long as he had management of the affair Sir Benjamin would never be dispossessed: 'I consider your family & my professional honour to be involved' [7.4.13]. Towards the end of the month, Easton told Sir Benjamin that he had 'everything arranged for bringing John Davidson & his sons & their accomplices to trial on the ensuing circuit at Inverness for the heritors deforcement … This will cool these gentry a little and will be attended with a good effect in the county' [7.4.15].

3 | 'We who subscribe this paper'

James Easton died unexpectedly shortly before the end of April, 'an event which has thrown us all into the deepest affliction,' wrote David Horne in a letter to Sir Benjamin on the 30th of that month [7.4.18]. A few days later, another Bill of Suspension and Interdict against the eviction at Wester was served on Sir Benjamin, this time at the instance of four subtenants [85.3.3]. By this time it appears that the Davidsons had up sticks and left. The case had never been simply a matter of getting the Davidson brothers out. There were also cottars, dependants and other subtenants to consider. This is a clear reminder of how complex rural society could be at this time in terms of landholding and land use, throwing light on the repeated references in estate rentals to 'others' with some claim on patches of ground.

In the previous autumn when the letters of ejection had been issued to get rid of the subtenants, Sir Benjamin's lawyers pointed out that 'his feelings revolted at the idea of turning a number of families out of their houses at so inclement a season' and he had allowed them to stay over the winter [85.3.3]. He had, however, asked them to sign an agreement to leave at Whitsunday 1821.

This agreement [49.1.9] shows that thirty-two subtenants promised to 'remove peaceably at the said term unless a new written agreement is made with us to continue'. They all signed it, possibly feeling they had no choice, five of them with an X and William Bryce with his initials WB, all witnessed in the act by their neighbours. John Bremner signed 'for myself and my father', Christy Gray for herself and her daughter, and William Oal for himself and his two sons Alex and John. This was a mass signing, all done at or almost at the same time, and one page, with fifteen names, listed everyone as residing at Wester, where there must have been a small hamlet, presumably now to shift lock, stock and barrel. It is worth listing in full the inhabitants of this 'lost' community, all described as cottagers or tenants except for the few others noted below: Betty Doull, William Gow; Christy Gray and her daughter Betty Williamson; James Harold; Alex Brock, weaver; William Gilbertson; Henry Craig, weaver; Alex Brock junior; John Farquhar; John Sandison; William Oal & Alex & John Oal his sons, tenants & weavers; James Cormack; Catherine Cormack; Ann Farquhar, the widow of Hugh Brock; and Margt Mowat widow of John Land. These names of course are of only those who signed the factor's paper; we do not know of any spouses, offspring and dependants.

Three of the householders described themselves as being weavers. In the 1790s when the reports were being compiled under Sir John Sinclair's direction for the Statistical Account of Scotland weavers appear in many parishes; for example, the descriptions of Latheron, Reay and Thurso state there are twenty, eighteen and seventy-three weavers respectively. This does not indicate textile production on any scale but rather the existence of cottage-based weaving of cloth for home use or for limited sale. A weaver had a trade or skill that was one among many skills he might deploy in a year's work to earn a living. By the 1820s this kind of weaving was becoming outdated, losing out in competition with cheap manufactured cloth from the industrial south.

Four of these subtenants appear as the names on the Bill of Suspension and Interdict already mentioned [85.3.3]. Sir Benjamin's lawyers argued that this had happened at the instigation of William Innes. No evidence was produced that James Mowat, earlier cited by Innes and the Davidsons as a co-tacksman, had had any share in the sublease and he was described as 'a quiet inoffensive man' who had been 'improperly made use of by others'; he removed himself without resistance at Whitsunday, asking only for eight days' grace as his wife had newly recovered from childbirth, grace that was granted. He had in fact signed a letter with his mark on 16 March 1821 at Reiss to state that he had no intention to carry out any legal 'step' against Sir Benjamin. Mowat apparently took over, at least for a time, another farm on the Dunbar estate in Killimster at a rental of £20 a year. James Cormack left on the day of ejection but came back to petition Sir Benjamin successfully for leave to labour a croft which he had held, seemingly as long as he did not resume possession of anything he had held under the Davidsons. This suggests that some of the subtenants may have been breaking hill ground into cultivation on the margins of the Wester lands. In the 1851 Census, Wester was occupied by a John Gallie from Ross-shire, and his brother Abner Gallie was also there as farm manager.

Another list of people exists from 1822, this time of tenants whose leases were due to expire on Whitsunday that year [49.1.10]. The list was drawn up at the beginning of January, five months before the crucial date, and contains the sentence 'We who subscribe this paper acknowledge that the lease of our land is out at the term of Whitsunday first and we promise to remove ourselves, our families and stocking [livestock] at the usual term without any summons of removal or other order of law unless a new agreement be made with us in writing before that term.' This time, with the seeking of prior agreement to remove, Sir Benjamin was probably trying to avoid what had transpired at Wester. With ninety-six households, all named apart from '8 small tenants' at North Killimster, this was a long list. It would seem to comprise a large number of the rural poor – 39, 40 per cent, are marked as illiterate or semi-literate – but it also includes the Revd Mr Stuart, the smith at Reiss and a schoolmaster.

The place names mentioned span the Dunbar lands and include places on both sides of the Wick River. A few localities are, however, disproportionately represented: with eight people from Newton, nine from Wester that included seven named the year before but who were clearly still there, nineteen from North Killimster, and twenty-two from Winless, of whom fourteen are noted as illiterate. The particular circumstances of some of the individuals are also noted, giving the impression that this document may be for administrative convenience and does not preclude recognition of special cases. The lists are evidence for the early 1820s having been years of upheaval, a time in Caithness when the rural hamlets of subsistence cottagers and even squatters in some instances were being cleared as large farms were enclosed and let to 'big' tenants.

4 | 'Not many however have left the parish'

A third list of tenants survives from a decade later [21.4.20], in Thurso on 18 June 1831, and accompanies a letter from a certain Robert Mackay to George Dunbar, who had succeeded his father Sir Benjamin at Ackergill. Before considering the list, however, it is worth devoting some attention to the first part of the letter.

'Sir,' writes Mackay, 'I called on Robt Mackay the Boat Skipper, and mentioned your terms to him – but he said he and his crew would not go to Ackergill to reside on anything less than those terms I had at his desire formerly stated to you, which he added are below what Sandside allows in a similar case, and that the coast there is better for fishing than that of Ackergill. He said he had been informed that other fishermen had been applying to you – but from what I know or can learn none would give you more satisfaction than Mackay & his crew.'

George Dunbar wanted to encourage the growth of the fishing at Ackergill and the best way to do that was to induce fishermen to move there from other parts of the country. Many of the fishing villages around the Moray Firth were founded in this way.[9] This letter also shows that fishermen, unlike their landward neighbours, were in a much better position to defend their own interests. They had skills that were in demand and were unafraid to negotiate, unlike the illiterate cottars who scraped an existence on the sufferance of their betters. That there is no Robert Mackay in the 1841 Census return for Ackergill suggests that George Dunbar's inducements were not enough to persuade the fisherman to move home.

The second part of Mackay's letter deals with the less favoured. 'On Thursday I forwarded by the Mail Coach the Ejection, summonses etc against the tenants of Dalnaglatton & their sureties to John Gun Sheriff Officer Dunbeath with instructions…'. Although Dalnaglaton lay in the parish of Halkirk, upstream from

Loch More, it was much closer to Dunbeath from the point of view of travel by horseback. In any case, wrote Mackay, the sheriff officer in Thurso was 'otherwise much engaged' and the Dunbeath man was 'active and accurate'.

The list of names falls into two parts – one part with twenty-seven households gives the names of individual tenants in a range of properties across the estate, but the second part concentrates on the neighbouring upland townships of Dalnawillan and Dalnaglaton. Four families or heads of families are noted for the former, and twelve for the latter.

There exists a letter written five years previously on 8 May 1826 by one of the twelve men named in the 1831 list [21.4.29]. This was Adam Gunn, and on the earlier occasion he was writing to George Dunbar to say: 'Sir, As I understand that Dalnawillan we now Set; and as I am become bound cautioner for the south part of the rent, for William Mackay – and as I am so, I hope that you will do me and him the favour of granting William Mackay his own house and Barn as he is the only one that any strangers that may come the way do lodge with – and as John Gunn has as good as he has; and that John Gordon may be accomodated [sic] by removing John Gunn to his brothers house who I understand is to be removed may answer all parties fully as well.

'And as I understand that some of the neighbours has being writing complaining on to you of Willm Mackay being a bad neighbour; which I know myself that there was some disputes between them two or three years ago; and as I have been sent often for by them to settle some disputes between them – and that as the whole of the arguments between Willm Mackay and his neighbours has often been laid before me I can really say that the rest of the neighbours has been in the fault oftener than him; and that I can get good many of the rest of the neighbours to know that, as well as myself.'

Gunn may have already sensed the precariousness of the occupancy of the tenants in Strathmore. Here he was clearly speaking on behalf of one of them, William Mackay, and defending him against complaints made to Ackergill Tower. In the long run, though, all the tenants, Adam Gunn included, were removed from Dalnaglaton.

By 1841 the population of the valley of Strathmore Water was much reduced. In the Census that year, only two families appear to be living there: those of Alex Cluich or Cleugh and Peter Gibson, both aged 45 and both listed as 'Ag Lab', in this instance probably shepherds. In 1851 there were two Cleugh households at Dalnaglaton, one headed by a shepherd, Andrew, aged 45, and the other by Davina, a shepherd's wife, aged 42, and her five children; probably she was Alex's widow. Peter Gibson was still there, and is described as having been born in Coldstream in the Borders. Upstream at Dalganachan resided another shepherd from the Borders, James Oliver from Roxburghshire. Two more shepherds, both Sutherland born – William Polson from Kildonan and John Macleod from Farr, lived at Glutt and Rumsdale respectively. The names in the 1831 list of people to be evicted are familiar and local – four Mackays, five Guns, two Sutherlands, a Sinclair, a Gordon, a Mcpherson, a Matheson and a Reid. William Gunn the Census enumerator noted, 'a considerable number of families have of late years been removed from this district in consequence of the introduction of sheep farming – Not many however have left the parish – The houses in general are of so fragile a construction that if unoccupied for a few years they crumble into dust and soon disappear which may account for so few being marked uninhabited.' The advent of sheep farming did lead to evictions in Caithness although on a lesser scale than in Sutherland and some other counties.

For the lowland parts of the Dunbar estate, the 'home territories' close to Wick, the 1841 Census recorded 'no decrease or unusual influx of inhabitants' and stated that only one person had emigrated in the previous six months. On the other hand there had been 'a small decrease … of about 50 persons' on the Hempriggs side of the river. The enumerator for Winless counted twenty-four 'farmers' (the Census does not distinguish large farms from small crofts), twelve agricultural labourers, two families of 'tinkers', an army pensioner and a miller. The range of surnames is much the same as for 1831 – some may represent the same families, people who had extended their lease or found some other way of staying on.

Of those who left the rural townships, many may have found new work and new homes in Wick, now booming as the herring fishing grew from year to year, and to a lesser extent in such villages as Keiss and Staxigoe. According to the figures reported by the Revd Charles Thomson in his account of the parish, published in 1845, for *The New Statistical Account of Scotland*, the population of the parish of Wick grew from 5,080 in 1811 to 9,850 in 1831, a space of only twenty years (Appendix 11). In this context, the Census enumerator's conclusion of little movement in population in 1841 may be misleading, as the movement may have already largely happened.

5 | *'the County Gentlemen and respectable Farmers'*

In June 1841, at the time of the Census, Sir Benjamin Dunbar and his wife, recorded as Lord and Lady Duffus, were staying at Hempriggs House. Sir Benjamin was now 81 years old; he was to die in 1843, and Lady Duffus, aged 73, outlived him to pass away in 1857. Resident with them was listed a widow called Mrs Pearce, aged 45, probably a companion for Lady Duffus. Four servants – James Sutherland, Janet McDonald, Elizabeth Cormack and Margaret Hannie – lived in the House, but another lived with his wife and seven children in a servant's house. George Dunbar was living at Ackergill where he was noted as having a guest of independent means, Sinclair Wemyss aged 25. This was George's nephew, son of William Sinclair Wemyss and George's sister Henrietta. Five servants lived in the Tower, whereas three times that many were active out and about as gardeners, labourers and so on.

The engineer Joseph Mitchell, who was chosen by the Caithness heritors in 1830 to build some roads in Caithness, wrote a memoir in which he recalled meeting George and his brother Robert. 'Both the Dunbars were very handsome men in their youth,' recalled the engineer, 'George was particularly so; and when seeing him on horseback, as I have frequently done, riding about Wick, he reminded me, from his graceful and manly bearing, and his solitary and desolate residence at Ackergill Tower, of the Master of Ravenswood in the romance of the Bride of Lammermoor. He ... devoted himself exclusively to farming and the improvement of his estate ...'. His younger brother Robert, wrote Mitchell, lived at Latheronwheel on a small estate worth some £500–600 annual rental.[10] George's existence at Ackergill was far from the 'desolate' state imagined by the road engineer and he seems to have played a lively and full part in local life.

In 1846, the family was successful in obtaining the passage of a private Act of Parliament (9 & 10 Victoria I, c.2) to enable them 'to sell such parts of the entailed Lands and Estates of Hempriggs lying in the county of Caithness ... as may be necessary for the payment of the debts and obligations ...'.

The Census suggests that George's ambition to settle fishermen in Ackergill had met by this time with some success, as it lists as 'Whitefishers' three households of Thains and one family called Flett, all of whom hailed from the Inverallochy – Cairnbulg area of Banffshire on the other side of the Firth. That George also had a keen interest in the latest ideas in agriculture is borne out by his response to an invitation to attend the founding meeting of an agricultural society in Caithness on the last day of 1829 [8.2.28]. A public meeting on Hogmanay would be a most unusual occurrence now but in the 1820s it was presumably one day of the year when many people would be free from their normal duties to come to town, and enjoy a few drams into the bargain. 'Although unable to attend the meeting today I nevertheless am anxious to express my conviction of the beneficial tendency of its object,' wrote George, '... Something of this sort is now highly requisite to nurture the rapidly increasing exertions of a numerous, and important class of the community into a regular system by which individual energy may be assisted by more general information.'

Although he could not be there, George felt free to send in his ideas at some length – the society should include as many as possible of 'the County Gentlemen and respectable Farmers', it should meet quarterly at stated times, and it should encourage not only markets for farm produce but 'the better regulation of servants, and the awarding of prizes for best stock, samples of crops, and ploughing matches'. The new society should also combine in some way with the old County Farming Club 'whose funds to a considerable extent have lain so long dormant', and it should be recognised as a horticultural as well as an agricultural body. George ended by emphasising his fondness for thorn hedges for enclosing fields, a method by which 'the appearance of the county will be very materially improved'. Many of the fields around Ackergill sport hawthorn hedges, presumably the legacy of George's enthusiasm. The Society was indeed born, for we find in April 1830 the minutes of their March meeting being forwarded from Thurso to George at Ackergill with the news that there were now over forty subscribers. Unfortunately the minutes themselves are no longer attached to this letter (8.2.23).

The new farming methods were being taken up across the county and many documents in the Dunbar Papers are devoted to the management of the land. Some of these are of great charm such as the lists of the names of two herds of cows under the care of Donald Campbell, who probably wrote out the lists, at Shorelands and Ackergill in October 1825 [8.2.]. The names themselves give an insight into folk culture and a glimpse of a practice that has had a long pedigree – a few would not be uncommon today but others seem strange (Appendix 12). The lists also have a purely practical purpose, distinguishing cows to be kept from those whose future is doubtful, although they are in calf, and those who are 'to be cast', i.e. sold.

The new farms provided plenty of work for the construction industry. New steadings and new drystone dykes were built across Caithness and many survive to show to us the expertise of the masons who worked with the local stone. In March 1825 an unsigned offer was submitted to repair part of the Shorelands steading or square [8.2.2]. Another offer, almost identical and for the same job, is signed by a Mr Liddle and Son. The work included taking off injured or broken tiles [presumably this refers to slates rather than baked tiles] on the roof of the long byre, kiln and kiln barn, replacing them and 'pointing the Rooves [sic] carefully on the inside with Haired lime, and on the outside with haired lime'. This was costed at 5s per rood. The rood was the standard measure for masonry or slatework and comprised an area of 1,525 square yards, one quarter of an acre. The tiles on the roofs of the barn, stable and small byre were also to be taken off, bored and nailed back on again carefully, a task that would cost 16s 6d per rood, the higher price reflecting the amount of time that would be needed. 'We will build if required the walls of a horse track for a thrashing mill,' continued Mr Liddle, for 2 guineas per rood, and 'Any other plain mason work we will do at the rate of [36s per rood] girth measure – and joint harling at [2s 6d per rood]'. 'We will pave any part of the Barn you may wish with properly laid and squared and jointed flags at the rate of threepence per square yard – and causey the stable if required at the same price' … all to be done by the middle of August under penalty of forfeiture of one-third of the price.

The same Mr Liddle offered in September 1825, probably after the completion of the work at Shorelands, to build for George Dunbar a small shed of some kind on the same property (8.2.1). The letter includes a brief protest from the mason that 'it is imposable [sic] for us to carry stones to it and to finish it as soon as you mentioned to me' but Mr Liddle says he will help to fill the carts himself to speed things along. George accepted the offer on the grounds that the building, 10 feet long by 16 feet wide, would be built within the next ten days.

James Gair submitted an offer on 16 June 1826 to 'quarry and build a dike … within the farm yard at Riess [sic], four feet high above the toestones two feet broad at bottom and one and a half at the top, which is to be carefully tabled with properly squared and jointed flags each at least two inches thick' [21.4]. Gair agreed to finish openings where George Dunbar wanted them, and to dig the stones from one of the quarries beside Mr Liddle's house at Reiss. The job was to be completed by the next market day on the Hill o' Wick under penalty of one half the value, a sum to be determined on completion by James Williamson of Upper Ackergill 'if not previously mutually agreed upon'.

One of the tenants on the Ackergill estate – John Craig who had Kettleburntofts – fell into arrears with his rent, and his goods and gear were sequestrated. By early 1836 Craig had failed to pay the rent of £31 10s sterling due at Martinmas, the previous November, and an action was raised against him through the sheriff court. There is a considerable body of correspondence dealing with this unfortunate affair but one document is of particular interest as it lists farm equipment, produce, livestock and furniture confiscated for sale by roup, and thereby affords us a glimpse of a Caithness farmer's possessions at this time [88.2.20]. Craig had one grey horse, one grey mare, six cows, one 'white bull Pold' [polled], seven quoys [heifers], one calf, two black pigs and one white pig. The implements included carts, harness, one iron and one wooden plough, and wooden harrows. The grain in store, either as thrashed grain in the barn or in stacks, amounted to 55 bolls, comprising 'din' oats, 'white' oats, bere and barley. There was also about one hundred and fifty stone of hay. The household furniture included an eight-day clock, a writing desk, three meal barrels and a weather glass. It seems that Craig had had a fairly comfortable life with a modest level of possessions. Sadly we do not know what he had left after the roup or what became of him. The action was brought by the trustees of the estate – most of them were identified as residing in London – and Sir Benjamin, whose hands were tied by the trust he had been forced into in 1809, would have felt that he had no choice but to allow the law to take its course.

6 | 'carting the harvest shearers home'

The large farms on the estate kept a record of the working year – the so-called Farm Book. The one for Harland for 1850 is a large leather-bound volume filled with detail [233]. For example, on Tuesday 11 June and Wednesday 12 June, it records that Joseph Mackenzie, George Angus, William Horne and James Angus were harrowing while Daniel Bain was carting on Tuesday and rolling on Wednesday. Presumably Bain was rolling the fields where the others had newly harrowed in the seed for that year's grain crop. Another employee, Alex Waters, was the herd and he is noted as herding every day, looking after the cattle to make sure they kept to the fields where they were meant to be. The farm hands also included day labourers. They spent the whole second week of June in trenching, carting and spreading dung and gathering 'Weds', which we can take to mean weeds. There were twenty such labourers, seven men who were paid 1s 4d per day and thirteen women who received 7d for their labour. Thus we can see that, for example, Margaret Swanson gathered weeds for five days and was paid 2s 11d.

In July the main tasks were thinning turnips, making hay, gathering in peats and 'scuffling', weeding the turnip and potato crops by horse-drawn scuffler. Also, it was noted that houses were being repaired for the harvest shearers, a temporary and often itinerant workforce. On many farms in Caithness they would have included Gaelic speakers from Sutherland but it is not known if this was the case at Harland. The harvest was the busiest and most crucial time of the year, a race to get the oats and barley cut, dried and safely stored before the autumn rain threatened to ruin the crop. It was a time when there was plenty of labour for all who wanted work, as the grain had to be cut by scythe, and bound into sheaves and stooked by hand. The cutting of the corn was recorded in the Farm Book as the shearing. Harland was busy with this task in September. On Wednesday 18, thirty-four were recorded as shearing and six as binding. They continued on Thursday and Friday, but on Saturday they had an easier time, all of them making simmons, ropes of plaited straw. Perhaps the Saturday was too wet for work in the fields, or perhaps it was necessary to ensure an abundant supply of simmons for the rest of the harvest. All the following week was devoted to the harvest and then in the first week of October the Book notes the carting in and building of the corn, in stacks or 'scroos', to use the Caithness term, in the stackyard. On Tuesday 15 October Joseph Mackenzie and George Angus had the presumably pleasant job of 'carting the harvest shearers home', although unfortunately there is no mention of any destination. 'Thatching screws' is noted for the following week. The Book contains a printed receipt from Wick Steam-Mills on 1 November for 20 quarters of oats, weighing 37.5 lbs per bushel.

After the harvest the permanent hands turned to ploughing as their main activity before leaving the ground bare over the winter in readiness for the sowing in the spring and the next round of the endless cycle of years. At Martinmas, the servants received their wages for the previous six months. Joseph Mackenzie got £4 4s, George Angus £4 10s, and the herd Alex Waters only £1, a sum that implies he was only a lad who, in a time when education was not yet compulsory, found a simple but still useful role in society until he was old enough to join the men.

Some tenant farmers became quite prosperous. Such a man was William Gunn. When he died on 13 July 1864, he was occupying Glendhu, near Kylestrome in Sutherland where he is listed as a sheepfarmer in the 1861 Census, and also shared the tenancy of Greenland and Sibster, in Caithness, with his brother James. Presumably it is because of the Sibster connection that a copy of the inventory of his assets came to rest at Ackergill among the Dunbar Papers [112.4]. The Gunns were not poor tenants by any means. The inventory of William's personal estate gives a picture of the wealth of someone who could be termed a 'big' farmer. He had only £15 18s in the house at the time of his death and was owed £5 by James Oliver of Ardvar, but his assets also included the worth of crops, implements and livestock, and investments, as follows (all the account balances include due interest):

Account at the Commercial Bank, Tain	£13	8s	2d
Account with the Aberdeen Town & County Banking Company, Golspie	£88	1s	5d
Joint account with his brother James in the Commercial Bank, Tain	£762	13s	
Joint account with James in the Commercial Bank, Wick	£767	14s	6d

William's half of the stock, implements and crops on Greenland and Sibster, as valued by Alexander McBeath, a licensed appraiser from Thurso, and George

Brown, a Watten farmer, was set at £2,307 2s 3d. McBeath and Henry Hall, a farmer from Coul near Skelbo in Sutherland, appraised the deceased's half of the Glendhu assets and valued them at £4,630 13s 11d. William's personal possessions in his home were valued at £176 3s 1d, and he also had title to half of the value of seventeen Cheviot wedder lambs – £15 11s 9d. On top of this, though, William had shares in the Inverness and Aberdeen Junction Railway Company (the Ross-shire Exclusion), worth £180, and shares worth £4,887 10s in the Capital Stock of the Commercial Bank. With dividends on these, his total estate amounted to a tidy £13,250 16s 6d (equivalent to an economic power of £970,000 in the present day).

William Gunn's worth stands in stark contrast to the wages earned by farm servants, such as the sums listed for the farm labourers at Reiss Lodge [93.1.10]. For the year ending on 26 May 1875, the nine men and women engaged for the six-month summer term had a cash wage of between £4 5s and £9 each. The lowest wage – £4 5s – went to a William Harrold, suggesting he was a young lad at the beginning of his working life. The highest wage – £9 – was earned by John McLeod. As well as money, the workers were given milk and meal, valued in the account book at £14 1s 3d and £25 14s respectively. The grieve also received the keep of one cow, valued at £4. For the succeeding six months of the winter term, the payroll swelled to twelve men and women, and the wage bill rose accordingly to £70 16s, not including the proportional increase in the milk and meal allowance. William Harrold does not appear in the winter list – had he gone back to school? George Cormack was given a rise from £8 15s to £9, to match that earned by John McLeod. The lowest winter wage – £1 15s – went to a Margaret Miller, but for her as for the others there are no indications of specific duties. Five extra servants were hired during the harvest for between £3 15s and £4 5s plus milk and meal, and the accounts also include varying sums listed as paid to 'Hirers', taken to mean extra workers brought in for short periods and special tasks.

The farms of Upper Ackergill and the Quoys of Reiss had similar wage bills, but the accounts for Ackergill Farm include wages for two shepherds – John Coghill who got £9 per six-month term, and James Campbell, presumably in a subordinate role, who received £7. Ann Sutherland and a Mrs Sutherland were paid £4 5s and £3 10s respectively for their work in the dairy.

The revolution in farming that saw the end of the old township-based system of cultivation and its replacement with tenancies of large, consolidated, enclosed acres brought other changes in its wake. Evidence for some of these exists among the Dunbar Papers. One was the imprinting of ownership on the land, as exemplified in this warning notice issued from Ackergill Tower on 28 April 1858, ominously addressed in bold capital letters 'WARNING TO ALL WHOM IT MAY CONCERN', a salutation reinforced by having been printed at the office of the *Northern Ensign* in Wick [31.4.27]. 'TRESPASSES by Persons LEAPING DYKES and CROSSING the FIELDS of ACKERGILL and the FARMS of Shorelands and Reiss have of late been so frequently and recklessly practised as not to be longer tolerated,' it thundered. 'Notice is therefore hereby given that promt [sic] and stringent Legal Proceedings will be instituted against all Persons detected in future indulging in such unwarrantable practices,' it went on, before ending in a somewhat lamer fashion, 'It is hoped this Warning may suffice and that the habit will be discontinued.'

The lairds and the big farmers also had time for fun, and their servants often shared in this. The 37th livestock competition of the Caithness Agricultural Society was held at the Georgemas market ground on 6 August 1867 [31.4.21]. There were entry classes open to draught horses, polled Aberdeen or Angus cattle (at the time a recently developed breed), pure Highland cattle, short-horned cattle, crosses of short-horned cattle, Leicester sheep, Cheviot sheep, swine, poultry and dairy produce. In these competitions, the forerunners of the modern county agricultural shows, the men and women who laboured in the byre and the dairy could show off their skills and share in the glory.

7 | 'an intractable old building'

The oldest, detailed description of Ackergill we have was written by Robert Forbes who was elected bishop of Ross and Caithness in October 1761. Forbes embarked on his first tour of his diocese in the summer of 1762 from Leith, and his account of the weeks he spent travelling from one big house to the next and attending to his flock gives us a picture of the lives of the lairds at the time. On 12 August he rode from Wester for his first close look at Ackergill. '… We set out by 10 o'clock and travelled over one of the finest Links I ever beheld, to the Castle of Ackergill, which is a grand lofty tower of 7 stories at least … The wall of Ackergill Castle is at least ten feet thick. You enter first into a Grand Vault, equal with the Ground in its floor, now a Kitchen, where formerly there has been a large Draw-Well, now filled up, but the Circumvallation at Top is still entire. Above this a lofty Hall, 32 by 18 feet, and 26 feet high, of an arched Roof, in which Sir Wm Dunbar has cut out some large Windows, and is doing it up in a very pretty and elegant manner. There are 32 steps of a Turnpike [spiral stairway] before you get on Top of this Hall, where Rooms go off at Right and Left. I went up to the Top of the Castle, and walked round the Roof, there being a Balcony or little Turret on each corner, and had a commanding view … We … dined upon many good Dishes, particularly a very large One, in which there were three or four Kinds of Fish, elegantly dress'd in a rich Sauce.'[11]

Another visitor was the artist William Daniell, in the autumn of 1815. Sir William was dead by this time and his host at Ackergill and Hempriggs was Sir William's son, Sir Benjamin. Daniell was alarmed by the ease with which the boys climbed the natural bridge – the Gote o' Tram – linking the stack of Hempriggs to the cliffs. His colour plate shows Ackergill Tower as a four-storey keep with a small wing adjoining the east side. The surroundings are very plain and bare with cropped grass extending right up to the walls and no garden evident.[12] The Tower is described by the Revd Charles Thomson, minister of Wick, in the *New Statistical Account of Scotland*, published in the early 1840s, as being 'in excellent repair' and the 'residence of the Honourable George Dunbar, Master of Duffus'. It was a 'noble and impressive' landmark, '… perfectly rectangular, eighty-two feet in height, and battlemented … The walls are extremely massive, upwards of thirteen feet in thickness; and the whole building is venerably grey with the hoar of great antiquity.'[13] The perfect rectangularity and the hoar of antiquity were soon, however, to be disturbed through the work of David Bryce, architect.

Born in Edinburgh in 1802, David Bryce was to become one of the most eminent architects and designers in the country. His vision was responsible for the appearance of many prominent castles, country houses and public buildings, the style we now know as Scottish Baronial. Probably in 1850 George Dunbar commissioned Bryce to work on Ackergill Tower for, in mid-March 1851, we find the architect writing from his address in George Street, Edinburgh, to George with initial designs [151.6.5 – 6.6]. Two months later, Bryce had good news [151.6.2]. '…The working plans of Ackergill are now all ready for being put in ink but before doing so I thought it better to send you the enclosed tracings to show what effect your suggestions when last here, have had upon the design …'. George was in the north but a relative, Mrs Wemyss, was on hand in the capital for Bryce to consult. She clearly had a considerable say in the future of the Tower. Bryce wrote that she seemed quite satisfied with the design, 'only remarking that there ought to be a bathroom in the house so that a hot bath could be had in the event of sickness …'. Bryce added the bath to the WC adjoining George's dressing room.

'The coal house is intended to be below the servants' hall, and the beer cellar below the pantry – the ash pit below the knife and shoe place and next to it the tank so that a cart could be backed in to be filled,' continued Bryce, 'I think also of making some additional … men's rooms over the scullery & pantries – And the ladies maids rooms will be placed in the garret over the nurseries …'. He concluded with a request for some measurements and a reminder that any suggestions from the client should reach him in a day or two.

George replied at once [151.6.1]. 'I have received … the supplementary tracings of the proposed additions … have examined them most attentively, and find you have carried out to perfection the alterations I suggested when last in Edinburgh as regards the main body of the House, but I much fear that the servants appartments [sic] and other minor portions of the structure are too extensive, and would cost more money that is at present intended to be expended.'

Possibly writing quickly – some of the letter is difficult to read – George feared some 'engineering difficulties' that might prove to be impractical and, mindful of the cost, expressed a wish to take more time – '... would it not be the better way, if you can have the time, to come over and take another look at the premises before completing the working plans ... I hope persuade you to come down by the steamer of Friday the 6th of June.' The Tower, reminded George, was an 'intractable old building'.

Bryce came to the north in June but not by sea. He had another project, at Castle Leod in Strathpeffer, and after he called there he came up to Wick by the mail coach. He wrote to George to say that he expected to arrive on Saturday, late in the evening, and that he would stay in the inn until the following morning [151.6.3]. In the meantime he was sending by steamer the half-finished working drawings so that Sir George could have time to look them over before he arrived. We can assume that this visit took place for we find Bryce on 18 June back in the south, writing to Sir George to say he will be pleased to see him when he reaches Edinburgh, adding 'With regard to the change of the House Keeper and Butlers Rooms in the design, this can be very easily, and I believe, advantageously managed, but I am not quite so sure about the change of the kitchen' [151.6.4].

The work on the Tower went ahead during the 1850s. The interior of the existing house was remodelled and various extensions were added, to give the battlemented, turreted appearance of the modern building. The carpentry and joinery work was done by Messrs James Buyers & Co – a note from Bryce dated 17 October 1855 certifies the completion and the balance due to them of £110 17s 3d [152.4.49]. A man called John Smith appears to have acted in a supervising or surveying role for Bryce. In August 1855 he was issuing instructions to the carpenters at Ackergill [152.4.50] and a note from him, dated at Kinnaird Castle (another Bryce project) near Brechin on 12 January 1856, to Sir George acknowledges receipt of a draft for the 'full amount' of £26 2s 6d for some aspect of the work [152.4.28]. In August that year Sir George was anxious to have the freestone work of the east and west fronts done before the wet weather set in [152.4.47]. The panelled lining of the dining hall was finished in 1859 – again Bryce certifies the completion, by Messrs Wm Dodds & Sons, and that £100 is still due to them [49.2.7].

Bryce carried out other commissions in Caithness, at Latheronwheel House in 1851 and Keiss Castle in 1859–62. He also had an influence on other architects and masons who imitated his style, for example in the construction of Stirkoke House in 1858–59. His nephew, John Bryce, carried on the tradition in his remodelling of Dunbeath Castle in 1907.

8 | 'the States are yours'

Sir George Dunbar died at Ackergill Tower on 28 August 1875, without any direct heirs, and was buried in Wick churchyard on 3 September. His younger brother, Robert, who had died in 1857 also had no offspring. On 7 September, just over a week after George's death, a telegram was sent to India, addressed to a Gordon Duff at Numale Kulu in India. The message, preserved in the Dunbar Papers on a telegram form stamped Amritsar reads in an abrupt unpunctuated manner 'Sir George Dunbar is dead the States are yours Arrange to leave India finally' and was signed by Helen Duff in London [119.3].

'States' means of course estates and the Gordon was a mistake for Garden, made by some telegraph clerk and unsurprising in view of the unusual nature of this first name. This Garden Duff was the grandson of Sir George's younger sister Louisa who had married Garden Duff of Hatton, a descendant of a Duff lineage with its roots in the North-East and Fife. Garden Duff senior was the eighth laird of Hatton, lands to the south-east of Turriff in Aberdeenshire. The big house there was once known as Balquholly after the burn that ran through the valley to the south of the Wood of Hatton but Garden Duff had the house rebuilt and renamed Hatton Castle. After Sir George Dunbar's death, his title of Lord Duffus fell to Garden Duff's son Benjamin, a captain in the 92nd Highlanders. Benjamin did not assume the Duffus title. The Caithness estate, however, was bequeathed by Sir George to the grandson who took on the surname Duff-Dunbar (Fig. 10).

Garden Duff-Dunbar, as he now became, was born in 1837. He received a commission in the 79th Regiment, the Cameron Highlanders, and at some point joined the regiment in India, where it had been stationed since the conflict in 1857 known in Britain as the Indian Mutiny. The 79th saw action on the North-West

Fig. 10   The family of Captain Benjamin Duff, de jure 5th Bt.

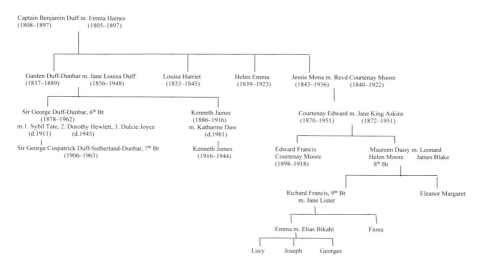

Frontier and at the Khyber Pass in 1863–64 before it was recalled to Britain in 1871. Garden resigned his commission but stayed on in India to work in the forestry service. He held the post of deputy conservator in the Beas Division, a district south-east of Amritsar in the Punjab, when the vital telegram reached him to tell him he now owned broad acres in Caithness. Perhaps it was on the strength of this inheritance that he married on 26 September 1876 his first cousin Jane Louisa, the eldest daughter of Lieutenant Colonel James Duff of Knockleith.

Two days later the *John o'Groat Journal* carried a long report on the preparations for the Duff-Dunbars' homecoming to Ackergill, with the curious proviso that the nearly completed arrangements were 'if not as effective as possible' it was 'not for want of the hearty good wishes entertained towards himself and his bride by his numerous tenantry.' Mr Duff-Dunbar, opined the *Groat*, 'has come here making at once a name for himself by a love of justice, charity, and a desire to take his place at once in the interests of the community.' Was this a thinly disguised hint to the incoming laird on how he was expected to behave? The newspaper advised that the couple were expected to reach Wick on the 5.20pm train on the coming Tuesday 3 October. The tenants had already held a dinner in the New Hotel, the staff at Ackergill had already had a celebratory supper and ball, and the servants on the farms of Reiss, Ackergill and Gillfield had come together for a ball in the loft at Upper Ackergill. Flags and bunting were sprouting on the steadings, and material for bonfires was being collected on the hills of Tannach, Newton and Harland and at the North Head. The *Groat* anticipated 'a grand display.'[14]

The dinner in the New Hotel had brought together all the local notables – the provost, the sheriff, the big farmers, ministers, merchants, solicitors (but no women, judging from the reported guest list) – for a boozy celebration. Numerous toasts were called and drunk, first for the royal family, in anticipation of a visit from the Prince and Princess of Wales, also due to cross the Ord in the following week. William Mackay, Quoys of Reiss, as chairman praised the late Sir George Dunbar for his attention to the progress of agriculture and looked forward to his successor, noting that Garden's experiences in India and in business would have made him 'very well fitted to surmount the many difficulties attending the management of men and land in this county.' The tenants were glad to welcome him 'more particularly as he would be a notable exception to the absentee landlords of Caithness' and, continued Mackay, he was sure the new laird realised he had duties as well as rights and would be willing to leave his tenants a margin of profit.[15]

The railway had been completed only two years before the arrival of the Duff-Dunbars.[16] On 9 July 1874 the spanking new station at Wick had welcomed the first train to make it over the new line from Helmsdale, a train driven by the Duke of Sutherland, an enthusiast for the latest mode of transport, in his locomotive called *Dunrobin*. Building the track over the county boundary and across the bogs of the Flow Country before it could be laid over the flat arable land of Caithness had been a considerable achievement. Sir George Dunbar had been peripherally involved in the project, as the last three or so miles of track threaded through Dunbar land along the south bank of the Wick River. A few pieces of correspondence with the railway company exist in the Dunbar Papers (chiefly 129.1 and 131.6).

In the event, the train with the Duff-Dunbars arrived late, by one and a half hours, and it was not until nearly seven o'clock in the evening that the couple stepped from their carriage to a hearty cheer and to greet the assembled worthies. Admission to the station, decorated for the hour with garlands, flags, flowers and coloured streamers, to hear the town clerk read the burghal address 'in a distinct voice' was restricted to ticket holders. The *Groat* reported that the welcome speech had been 'beautifully written' by the provost William Rae. Garden Duff-Dunbar delivered his reply, shook hands with all the members of the town council and, preceeded by the artillery band, he and his wife rode in a carriage on a roundabout procession route from the station via Union Street to Williamson Street and then back up the High Street. Here 'rain began to fall most piteously' but Garden gave a thank you speech before the carriage hood had to be closed. Despite the weather, the horses were taken from the shafts and the carriage was pulled all the way to Ackergill by 'willing hands' while back in the town another celebratory dinner took place in the Caledonian Hotel. The whole business had been nearly as grand as the celebration of the visit to Thurso at the same time by the Prince and Princess of Wales.

The Duff-Dunbars' first son, George, was born in 1878, another occasion for 'further manifestations of good feeling on the part of the tenantry', according to the *Northern Ensign*.[17] The health of the young heir was 'cordially pledged' at a cake and wine banquet in Wick. These were typical customs in the world of estates, lairds and tenants as it unrolled during the latter decades of the Victorian period.

At Whitsunday 1880 Sinclair Miller took over the tenancy of Clayquoys, land now part of the airport, and an additional four fields from Westerseat, for fourteen years at an annual rent of £212 along with road money and all other public burdens for which tenants were liable [112.4.]. Garden Duff-Dunbar reserved for his own use the mineral rights over any quarries and the rights to hunt game, including hares and rabbits. Apart from these general and customary rights, a few clauses of the lease related to specific items: the dung and fallowbreak left by the outgoing tenants of the Westerseat fields were to be paid for jointly by Miller and by the laird, and the laird agreed to enclose with wire fencing the four Westerseat fields in so far as they were not already fenced. Garden Duff-Dunbar also agreed to erect a dwelling house and four 'offices' – steading buildings – with Miller carrying the materials at his own expense. If a threshing mill should be built in the new steading, Miller was to receive the value of it at the end of his tenancy. Miller also agreed to give the use of his horses and men to harvest and transport crops from the Westerseat fields, to cart the grain to Wick or Pulteney, and to provide accommodation for harvest hands near Gallowhill. The mention of wire fencing is a reminder that agricultural was now well advanced from the old systems current at the beginning of the nineteenth century.

By the late 1800s, the Royal National Lifeboat Institution had become an established body, much respected for the service it provided and for the way the boats were crewed by volunteers from local communities. Wick had a lifeboat from 1848. Then, in a fierce storm on 23 December 1876, after a schooner *Emelie* was driven ashore near Ackergill Tower and wrecked with the loss of nine men – five of the *Emelie*'s crew, and four local men who had joined volunteers in a rescue attempt in a coble – a move was made to have a lifeboat permanently stationed at Ackergill. Garden Duff-Dunbar provided the site and the materials for the boathouse and eventually, on 14 March 1878, the new boat arrived by train and was led in procession to Ackergill where she was named *George and Isabella* by Mrs Duff-Dunbar. Launching the lifeboat by running it down the beach into the sea proved difficult and in 1909–10 a properly designed slipway was built, the first of its type in ferro-concrete in Britain. Ackergill lifeboat station was to be closed in April 1932.[18]

The 'public burdens' that landowners had to pay at this time came in several guises [112.4.]. For the Hempriggs estate in 1883–84, they amounted to £1,379 16s 2d, and comprised the land tax (£39 9s 9d), the parochial rates for Wick and

Halkirk (£928 7s 7d and £3 9s 3d respectively), a share of the Church of Scotland ministers' stipends for both parishes, a road assessment for the burgh of Wick, and county assessments totalling £517 3s, of which a half was recoverable from tenants. The county assessments and the land tax were payable to the so-called Commissioners of Supply, the main body concerned with local administration until the introduction of county councils in 1889. The estate also gave support to retired former employees. One such list of pensioners, dated May 1887, and what they received is given in Appendix 13.

Garden Duff-Dunbar died on 1 June 1889 in Devon after having been ill for some time. He was 50 years old. The report of his passing in the *Groat*, on Thursday 6 June 1889, stated that he had 'the closest attention to the welfare of his tenantry, and the improvement of his estate', and had spent large sums on draining, fencing and the building of steadings, had served as a member of the Wick Harbour Trust, and had encouraged local sport, including curling on the Bilbster pond.[19] The rival paper, the *Northern Ensign*, was slightly less adulatory in its appraisal of the man: '... though of a quick and impulsive temperament [he] showed in many ways that he was also considerate and kind-hearted.'[20]

His widow Jane Louisa Duff, known to all her friends and family as 'dear Louie' continued to live at Hempriggs. Their two sons, George (1878–1962) and Kenneth (1886–1916), followed careers in the army and the navy respectively, as we shall see in later chapters.

9 | 'the use of a keeper and a dog can be arranged'

References to hunting in its various forms crop up several times in the Dunbar Papers, but as part of the lifestyle of the country gentry the pursuit of game becomes increasingly significant as we approach the more recent past. One early reference is in a letter from William Horne at Stirkoke to George Dunbar on 8 August 1823: '... From the lateness of the breeding season and from the unfavourable state of the weather throughout I am desirous that no shooting shd take place on my grounds before the 20th ...' [16.2.1]. On 11 September that year, James Traill wrote from Castlehill: '... I am very much obliged to you for your kind offer of accommodating me with your days for the Moor. I have a very good bitch and two promising young dogs, who are at present quite sufficient for my wants – I am also very much obliged by the trouble you took respecting my brother's house – If you can I hope you will let us see you here before the conclusion of next week, as I think it very probable by that time we shall set forth again for the moor – we were out for two days this week but miserably disappointed – very few birds & horrid bad shooting. Lady Isabella desires me to thank you for your black Gun ...' [26.2.23].

James Sinclair in Thurso wrote to George Dunbar in October 1824 saying 'I have had such an attack of rheumatism that I regret exceedingly I cannot be with you today or at the Pigeon Shooting tomorrow. I could hardly hold the gun up ... Wishing you good sport ...' [11.4.5]. Then again, on 10 August 1833, there is a letter from a James Sinclair at Forss (possibly the same man) with an early reference to the Glorious Twelfth, the day in August that has long been the traditional start of the grouse shooting season. 'My dear George,' writes Sinclair, '... If you are not going out on the 12 will you send me up one of your pointers for a few days as I intend to take the field this season ...' [3.4.4].

One country sport that is now illegal was hare coursing. Sir George Dunbar became patron of the Caithness Coursing Club. The president was F. Bentley-Innes of Thrumster and the vice-president Major Horne of Stirkoke in 1873 when the autumn meeting took place at Stirkoke on 13 November [31.4.20]. There were various trophies for the greyhound owners: one was the Puppy Stake, limited to young dogs born in 1872. The entry fee of 10s must have excluded many poor dog owners and the first prize was advertised as £5 sterling 'to be expended in Plate or Jewellery' – hare coursing was not the sport of the working class, at least as practised in Caithness.

Another sport that became exceedingly popular among the emerging groups of professional townspeople was golf. In 1872, Sir George had offered Wick Golf Club, formed two years before in September 1870, access to play on the Links at Reiss on one day a week and hold competitions there. The club retained the use of two parks on South Head for informal sport, where they earned the nickname of 'mad gowfers' among the fishermen and farmers, but playing on the natural turf of the sandy links was a great boost. The founder members, some twenty in number, included Dr George Banks, medical officer of health in Pulteneytown, banker James Gilchrist and his sons, and John Mackie, editor of *The Northern Ensign*, who wrote: '…in the event of a suitable ground being assured – an object of some difficulty – there is no doubt that a numerous club will be established.' By that time there were some fifty golf clubs in Britain but Wick boasts the distinction of being the oldest club north of the Grampians and was in at the beginning of the great expansion in the sport that resulted in there being almost three thousand clubs on the eve of the First World War. The Duff-Dunbars gave the club a favourable lease on Reiss Links in 1892, allowing play every day except Sunday, and, with tenure secured, the club was able to invest in a small clubhouse and improve the access road. In 1906, Lady Duff-Dunbar offered to pay for the extension of the course from nine to eighteen holes, if the club would take over responsibility for maintenance. She was honoured to preside over the formal opening. Two scratch players from the Royal Dornoch Club, John Sutherland and Thomas Grant, put on an exhibition match. In 1908 a three-day bazaar in Pulteney Academy raised funds to help pay for the newly built clubhouse, which was also formally opened by Lady Duff-Dunbar. She also donated a nominal sum for ten years. The club could now employ a professional player and greenkeeper in the person of Tom Jameson from Carnoustie who lived on the clubhouse premises with his family. These developments made Wick Golf Club the best in its class in the region until Andrew Carnegie, who had a home at Skibo, gave financial backing to the Royal Dornoch. From that time until the 1960s Sir George Duff-Dunbar was listed as either vice-president or honorary president of the Club, and was followed in this role by his son Patrick.[21]

By the end of the Victorian period hunting and fishing had become important leisure pursuits not only of the landed gentry but of wealthy people with any pretension to a position in society. Where once the laird had shot, trapped and fished game for his own larder, he now derived considerable income from letting parts of his estate for short periods of time. Hempriggs and Ackergill estates were no exception, and the attractions of the shootings in Halkirk were laid out in advertisements such as one from 1887 (Appendix 14).

Another description of what was on offer to the sportsman on Dunbar land survives in a document that seems to be the draft of an advertisement placed with Messrs Dalgleish Gray & Dobbie, 21 Hill Street, Edinburgh, a legal firm that acted as letting agents for estates, in 1895 [53.1.51]. 'Grouse and mixed Season and Winter Shooting, Trout and Salmon fishing in river and loch, and Golfing. Splendid family residence,' it reads with regard to Ackergill Tower. 'The mansion house of Ackergill Tower is romantically situated,' it continues, 'handsomely furnished and contains 6 public rooms, 11 bed chambers and [?] tenants (4 of which can be used as bedrooms or dressing rooms) 2 (combined bath and dress rooms and rooms for ....[?] ... to 8 servants besides other usual accommodation, stabling for up to 8 horses, 2 coachhouses and rooms for coachman and groom, kennels. The shootings – 12,738 acres of which 1,120 are grouse with 8,618 arable and 300 sea links including about 20 acres near the house enclosed as a Rabbit warren. The place has by arrangement been lightly shot for some years past and for this season ... The average bag shot on Ackergill including Hempriggs now offered separately for the three previous years up to 1892 was 2786 brace grouse, ... [?] partridge, 5½ brace woodcock, 39 duck, 192½ brace snipe, 44 hares, 118 rabbits as well as a large number of golden plover, rock pigeon and wild fowl. Only a small proportion of the above average bag was shot on Hempriggs. There is a good trout and salmon fishing in the River Wick and trout fishing on Wester Water and Loch Wester and on Hempriggs Loch all on the estates. There are two first class sea boats, with a jetty close to the Tower and capital sea fishing is got: There is also one boat on each loch. Supplies of fruit vegetables flowers from the garden at market prices. The tenant will have the privilege of golf on a private course of 9 holes, close to the [house?] kept in good order by a local club. Views of the house and scenery will be sent on application to the agents. Rent £400 including rates and taxes and services of one keeper. Railway station, supplies, boat and telegraph office within 2½ miles. The winter shooting with accommodation ... the use of a keeper and dog can be arranged.'

On 4 March 1895, Alex Dunnet wrote from the Hempriggs estate office in Sutherland Villa in Wick to Dalgleish Gray & Dobbie, to tell them that a Colonel Ilderton had let him know the outcome of the latter's tenancy of the winter shooting [112.1.1]. 'The Colonel says he likes the Wick district and the people,' said Dunnet, who was the land steward, 'and would like to come back again if there is a good wild shooting – duck and snipe to let.' Ilderton included his bag list: hares 5, rabbits 5, partridge 1, woodcock 5, wild duck 40, snipe 51, golden plover 22, making a total of 129 wildfowl and mammals.

This was quite a modest list. Another headed 'Game shot on Ackergill 12th Aug to 20th Oct 1894' records a much larger impact on local wildlife numbers.

Grouse	117½ brace	235 head
Partridge	81	162
Snipe	96 cpls	192
Duck		24
Golden plover		15
Rock pigeons		91
Curlew		2
Landrail		2
Hares		37
Rabbits		450
		1210
Salmon		9
Trout		14
		1233

Colonel Ilderton enjoyed his sojourn around Wick blasting birds from the sky but not all the visitors were so well pleased. Such was a certain W.J. Laidlaw who rented Hempriggs House for the summer of 1893. He first appears in a letter on 10 May from the law firm of Paton & Son to Dalgleish Gray & Dobbie that advises them Laidlaw had agreed to take Ackergill estate without seeing it first for one year from the beginning of June but with agreement to sublet should it turn out to be unsuitable. Paton & Son described their client as 'not much of a sportsman but is an artist. He resides just now in France.' [112.4.3]. Dalgleish Gray & Dobbie wrote back to say the House would need cleaning and would not be ready on 1 June. A second letter a few days later reminded Paton & Son that the intention had been to allow the present tenant to give possession of the House to Laidlaw for the season, 'a more profitable arrangement than to let for the whole year' but this had been changed to give the artist a year. They were also informed that Calder the head gamekeeper at Ackergill would act as keeper-gardener at Hempriggs and that Laidlaw would pay ordinary gardener's wages. In mid-May Laidlaw sent a postcard with the first of many complaints – he would be unlikely to occupy the House before 10 June 'unless the cholera gets worse' (there was an epidemic in the region of Boulogne), and queried why he was being asked to pay a gardener's wage when the rent already included the cost of a keeper. And, he added ominously, he had heard from a former tenant that the head keeper was 'entirely past his work from age'.

Dalgliesh Gray & Dobbie tried to mollify the client. 'There is not sufficient work for a keeper on the Hempriggs portion of the shootings and we intended … to make the keeper attend in whole or in part to the garden. A tenant for a year has to keep the garden himself and we simply propose that Mr Laidlaw should employ our keeper as gardener … Mr Laidlaw will get value for his garden work and pay Calder instead of another gardener.'

Paton & Son conveyed Mr Laidlaw's objection to having to pay an extra £40 for a gardener but accepted the arrangements on two conditions – that there should be no further gardening expense and that there should be no more than £2 spent on seeds and up to two loads of manure. He was now asking if any sporting rights were allowed to the farming tenants. He was assured that these conditions were fine and that the tenants had no sporting rights and a lease was sent for his signature.

While this exchange was taking place through the lawyers, Mr Laidlaw wrote directly to the estate from Equiten near Boulogne, addressing himself to the 'Gamekeeper at Hempriggs, nr Wick, North Britain'. After complaining that he had sought the keeper's name and address in vain several times, he asked for an inventory of the contents of Hempriggs House, whether or not he needed a servant such as a cook 'But what I chiefly wish to know is whether there is anyone in the house just now who could do for myself and wife for a few days until we get servants.' He also wanted a good supply of peas, French beans and salad ready in the garden and offered to send late pea seeds in advance. 'As regards the shooting and fishing I have no doubt you have done what you can to protect both the grouse and the Loch but what I wish to know is have you any dogs?' He thought two 'really strong setters' would do very well; he could easily get them and he had a 'very good retriever' already. He wanted the kennel clean and lined all over, as in the last place he had rented his dogs had been ruined by mangey quarters. He had a few other points, hoped the grouse shooting would not prove a disappointment and ended with what could be read as a threat, 'We are but two (my wife and myself) … while I hope and believe you will not find us either exacting or troublesome you will find it in your interest to make things as easy for us as possible.'

A man called Mowat who had lived in Hempriggs House for some years moved out at the end of May. Dalgliesh very politely let Mr Laidlaw know that the house needed a good deal of papering and doing up, and would two public rooms and two bedrooms with servants' rooms be enough for them? No, wrote back Laidlaw, he needed three bedrooms and it was an 'absolute condition' they were well done up. The inventory showed a lack of essentials such as plates, pots, pans and a bath. There was no need to ask the head keeper at Ackergill to flit to Hempriggs on his behalf, said Laidlaw, 'all I ask is a quiet sober man with if possible a willing disposition and moderate opinion of himself.'

The Laidlaws came, and stayed, and suffered. There was a mix-up over the purchase of a bed from Wick that forced Alex Dunnet to write with an apology and a hip bath. At the end of July Laidlaw grudgingly sent a cheque for £240 (£200 for the House and shootings, and £40 for the gardener) to Dalgliesh, Gray & Dobbie. He enclosed a complaint. 'I confess I fail to understand not only how the enclosure (called by courtesy a garden) could be described as a good garden but also how any charge no matter however small could be made for so worthless and neglected a piece of ground. There are no vegetables in it and the greater part of the ground is covered by a dense neglected jungle which it would take a good day to penetrate.' What was more, the House was 'really exceedingly poorly furnished'.

A full list of grievances followed from Laidlaw to the lawyers a week or so later. 'I see my kindly consideration has been mistaken for mere weakness,' he protested. He found the Wick River 'simply a public river' and the heather excessively burnt 'to the probable destruction of the grouse shooting.'

The correspondence between Alex Dunnet and Dalgleish increased in volume in early August. In one week, Dunnet took pen in hand almost every day over the grumbling occupant of Hempriggs. On the 7th, he told the lawyers that he had not had time to deal with Laidlaw's problems as he had just returned from Edinburgh and had other matters to attend to, including an inventory of furniture in Ackergill Tower, but gave his version of the affair over the bed. On the 8th Dalgleish replied to say they had arranged a meeting with Laidlaw's law agents. On the 9th Dalgleish confirmed this meeting had occurred and said 'We … trust to get matters smoothed over', but now plumbing work had to be done at times to suit Laidlaw and 'as far as possible to meet his views'. On the 10th Dunnet told Dalgliesh: 'I learnt from the plumbers who were out there yesterday that his [Laidlaw's] chief cause of complaint is the state of the garden & because he finds that he has not the sole right to fish in the River. I have come to think that Mr Laidlaw is an extremely childish individual …'. Clearly fed up with his guest, Dunnet expanded on this theme on the 11th and protested that 'very few people would have acted as Mr Laidlaw has done after getting a reasonable explanation. He just took the pet …'.

Dunnet and a Mr Sinclair went out to Hempriggs to make an inventory and valuation of the furniture. They found only Mrs Laidlaw at home – 'she was very pleasant' – but Mr Laidlaw returned before they left, disappointed that he had bagged only six and a half brace of grouse. 'He was quite civil to me,' wrote Dunnet to Dalgleish, '[but] I heard Mr Laidlaw – while I was talking with Mrs Laidlaw – tell Mr Sinclair all his grievances about the place.' These concerned mainly 'misrepresentations regarding the house furnishings and the garden' and the probability that the overall bag was unattainable. 'I hope the whole question may be amicably settled,' wrote Dunnet. The correspondence ends with the letter of 16 August.

Letting for field sports remained an important part of the estate economy. In 1904, the estate was using the agent Walker, Fraser & Steele, 74 Bath Street, Glasgow; this firm published 'The Scottish Register' of estates, fishings, grouse moors, deer forests, 'low country shootings', and 'coast, country and West Highland houses', a reminder that in the last decades of the reign of Victoria and in the years leading up to the First World War much of Scotland was seen as a playground and game park for the rich and fashionable in pursuit of wildlife. The income and expenditure associated with running the estate as a sporting concern are detailed in various documents, for example in the accounts for the twelve months between 1 July 1903 and 30 June 1904 [simplified from 17.1.8] (Appendix 15).

The Dunbars were related to the Sinclair Wemyss family at Southdun. Sir Benjamin's second daughter, Henrietta, who had died in 1820, had married William Sinclair Wemyss. Their son David Sinclair Wemyss married Elizabeth Sackville Sutherland of Aberarder in Inverness-shire, hence the name of Sackville House for the Sinclair Wemyss home near Hastigrow, a mansion that has been partially restored after a disastrous fire in 1930. The Sinclair Wemyss family also let shootings on the Southdun lands, as is recounted in a letter to Mrs Duff Dunbar on 31 December 1907 [2.4.2]. The tenant had been elderly, unable to walk for more than four hours, a handicap that had not prevented him and one other 'gun' from accounting in the space of three hours on 12 August that year for 40 grouse. The bag for the season was 371 grouse, 102 partridges, one woodcock, 14 duck, 197 snipe, 13 hares, 24 rabbits, 43 plovers and three of a species not decipherable from the handwriting. 'I do not think this at all bad seeing it was so wet in August & September,' commented Mrs Sinclair Wemyss cheerfully.

When sporting tenants had the occupancy of Hempriggs House, Louise Duff-Dunbar normally went south to live in various places. She kept in touch with affairs at home and the management of the estate through correspondence with various friends and employees. In the autumn of 1912 there was some difficulty with a tenant Mr W. Hambro, probably a member of the Hambro banking family, over a gamekeeper (the details are unclear at present but Hambro had hired his own man while the Dunbars preferred to let Ackergill under their own keeper) [2.4.28; 2.4.23]. In the course of this bother, Mrs Duff-Dunbar herself – she was staying in Bournemouth at the time – wrote to Mr Hambro: 'Dear Mr Hambro, I am much obliged to you for the old lease sent me in your letter of yesterday. The tuning of the piano has always been done by tenants who had the use of it, but that is a trifle and I am willing to meet you about it [the cost]. The other point is difficult and I am sorry not to be able to alter the terms of the lease as regards it. The keeper's work has not been done as it should be and the moor ought to yield a larger bag than the present limit. I hope to achieve that and McNicol must start fair as the responsible man. If he does as well for Ackergill as his brother has done at Thrumster I shall be fortunate. If strange keepers were allowed to shoot over the ground except under special circumstances and about these you will not find me unreasonable, there would be no check on the game they killed and selling might go on undetected. Besides quarrels and friction would be pretty sure to occur. It is not always what is done but how it is done that counts in these things!' [2.4.23].

10 | *'the dullest people in the Punjab'*

Garden and Louise Duff-Dunbar had two sons, George born in 1878 and
Kenneth James born in 1886. After completing his education at Harrow,
George went to the Royal Military College, Sandhurst, and was commissioned as an
officer in the Queen's Own Cameron Highlanders in 1898. In 1902 he transferred
to the Indian Army and in July 1903 married Sybil Tate, a colonel's daughter. In
January 1904 the couple went by steamer, the SS *Persia*, through the Suez Canal
and the Red Sea to India, and George revealed a talent for descriptive writing in
the full accounts he sent his mother of their journey and the sights – the pyramids,
the Sphinx – they saw en route [118.1.5]. When they stopped at Aden, Sibyl was
slightly shocked by the scores of Arab labourers and traders who beset the ship
[118.1.3]. In April, George wrote from Government House in Lahore in great
excitement about the flourishing vegetation: 'the brilliant rowan red of the coral
tree, which is perfectly leafless and glows, covered all over with vermilionish spikes
of flowers' [118.1.2]. The House, he told his mother, was built around the tomb of
an old patron of wrestling who had lived nearly three centuries before; the tomb
was used now as the dining room 'not quite so big as the dining hall at home but
wonderfully high' and the arabesques and painted designs on the walls had been
done by Lockwood Kipling 'the father of the celebrated poet'. The dinner parties, he
admitted, were 'attended by the dullest people in the Punjab' and couples such as he
and Sibyl, 'just out' as the parlance had it, had not a single topic in common with
the Anglo-Indians. At this time George felt awkward in colonial society 'chiefly
of the Hon'ble Colonel type', but enthused about the red sandstone of the fort,
the tilework and the other sights, while not forgetting his roots: 'from some little
distance the highest building of the Fort looks like the keep of a northern castle

… & there are, to add to the effect, carved projections that give the appearance of gargoyles.' Sibyl was not coping with the heat and would have to go to the cooler Murree Hills to the north on 1 June.

At the end of April, they were settling into a new house at 229 Peshawar Road, Rawalpindi. Thieves had stolen a silver salver, a watch chain, a locket with Sibyl's miniature and a lock of her mother's hair, money and other items from a despatch box in their tent when the orderly had been asleep – or else in league with the thieves, thought George – and he was depressed by his financial situation, although that ought to improve over the summer after he passed exams [118.1.29]. They saved money by sharing the house with a Mr Styan and having to pay only a proportion of the wages for the servants – the cook, mali, dhobi, bhisti and sweeper, without whom no colonial household could function properly. 'The heat was 103° in the shade the day before yesterday,' wrote George on 3 May [118.1.7].

As time passed, George adapted to colonial India. On 11 July 1905 he wrote to his mother from a houseboat called Langley Castle, during a stay in Srinagar in Kashmir, to elaborate on his (still) disappointing financial circumstances but also enthuse about the 'delightful country' he was in [118.1.15]. Sybil also kept in touch with Mrs Duff Dunbar, often filling in the gaps that her husband left in his letters. For example, on 14 November, when the couple were once more at 229 Peshawar Road, she told how George had just got back that day from Kohat – 'He looked very well and had been having a little shooting on the march' and Kohat, a town and cantonment around 100 miles west of Rawalpindi on the edge of the North-West Frontier, had been 'very jolly' [119.1.14]. The Dunbars were considering leave – service on the Frontier earned three months and if George came to Britain on P&O he would get nearly two months at home and 'miss all the most hot weather at Bannu', another town in the border country. Sybil also enthused about a camp being built nearby, an elaborate luxurious establishment with tents with satin drapery and electric lights.

The North-West Frontier, the broad strip of mountainous territory between the fertile plains of Punjab and Sind and the desert plateau of Afghanistan, was home to the Pashtun or Pathan people, divided into various tribes, not unlike the Highland clans in their propensity for fighting and loyalty to their homelands. The British Raj had a grudging respect for them and often resorted to paying different clans to keep the peace. Occasionally, however, conflict broke out. For George it would have been by no means an easy posting and in March 1908 he wrote to his mother from Bannu to tell her some of this: 'We are not likely to have a show here now. Apart from the present policy it appears unlikely. Only – & this is confidential – Government are proposing to build a new road behind the Mahsud-Waziri [names of tribes] country. The Waziris are quite agreeable as it means money in their pockets; the Mahsuds only see an ingenious method of cutting off their line of retreat from the Afghan hills, & are therefore inclined to resent this outward sign of encroaching British Rule … When I tell you anthing confidentially it means I have gleaned it from some L.G. or Commissioner or some military big gun or other – when the great man has been, so to speak, *déboutonné* [unbuttoned] after dinner …' [119.1.2]. Someone had advised George to go for the Frontier Militia where pay would start at 800–900 rupees per month, and he had applied for the North Waziristan area. A week later, George wrote again to say that Sybil had gone off that day, that he could not stand staying in the 'lonely' house by himself and that he had transferred to quarters in the fort until he followed her in a fortnight. 'The Mohmands [a Pashtun tribe] raided a village near Peshawar on Sunday night,' he continued, 'It is difficult to see what they are playing at particularly as they were as good as the gold they get in subsidies … Perhaps the tribes are not being as well behaved and amenable in the negociations now being conducted at Touk as it was supposed they would be.'

The North-East Frontier of India adjoining Assam was also fraught with unrest at this time. In 1911 George found himself on the Brahmaputra River on a steamer called *Waziri* at the city of Dibrugarh where he reported on 16 June that 'affairs on the Abor frontier slumber' and went on to tell his mother how the military forces had a strong post now in the heart of the Abor community [4.4.2]. He was referring to the people in the Abor Hills in the state of Arunachal Pradesh near the Indian frontier with China who occasionally rose against their colonial masters. One such rebellion took place in 1911 when a British political officer and his colleagues were murdered, precipitating the advance into the area in October that year of a punitive expedition of Indian troops. By that time, though, George had had to face a family tragedy. Sybil fell ill in June with severe gastric pains and very bad malaria; George wrote that the strain was frightful [4.4.7]. In her delirium, he wrote, she said the most painful things [4.4.6]. She grew a little better and was making plans to return to England when George wrote on 26 June but two days later she died. The couple had one son – referred to in the letters as little George – who had been born on 3 August 1906 and, at the time of his mother's death, was in Whitchurch, Hampshire. George soon became known in the family as Patrick from his middle name Cospatrick.

While George pursued a career in India, Kenneth Dunbar found his niche in the Royal Navy. As a midshipman he served aboard the cruiser HMS *Good Hope*. On 27 February 1903 – he was 16 years old – he wrote to tell his mother, then living in Ventnor on the Isle of Wight, about his adventures crossing the Bay of Biscay: asked to measure the wave length as the ship encountered rough seas after leaving Arosa Bay on the Galician coast, he wrote 'They were 195 feet from crest to crest' [119.1.36]. A very heavy sea hit the ship at dinner time: '… nearly all the gear went over to starboard & the state of affairs was awful. After that for the rest of the dinner it was getting worse & worse & you had to hang on like grim death to anything you wanted … At about 9 o'clock heavy gear began to take charge & it was a case of run for your life when a sofa or armchair charged at you … We were rolling 24° each way during the first watch + 30° each way during the middle … I have been feeling most happy the whole time, I am very glad to say.' He continued the letter later: 'We were off the Start [Start Point on the Devon coast] at 2.30 this morning & found no less than 17 lights there.' December that year found the *Good Hope* in Lisbon, where Kenneth wrote home two days after Christmas: '… I can hardly realize that George & Sibyl [sic] have left for India & that the family is scattered about as far apart as they can be on the face of the earth,' he said before telling about the football and cricket at Las Palmas, Christmas Day on the ship, commenting on items he had read in the *Northern Ensign* through which he kept up with events in Caithness, and imparting the news that they were now at sea en route to Barbados [118.1.2]. Three weeks later he was sending postcards from Grenada and Dominica [118.1.17; 118.1.18].

Kenneth opted to serve in submarines and was ordered to join HMS *Mercury*, the depot ship for the Portsmouth Submarine Flotilla, on 25 April 1907 [4.4.20]. He married Katharine Bennett from Ealing in February 1915 but the couple had met some years before; in October 1911 he had written to his mother from HMS *Arrogant*, another submarine depot ship at Portsmouth, to say that Katharine [sic] was leaving school at Christmas and he was very glad [4.3.45]. His mother worried dreadfully about him, especially after a disaster befell the submarine HMS *C 11* in July 1909. The sub collided with a steamer off the Norfolk coast and thirteen men out of the sixteen aboard were lost. Mrs Duff-Dunbar wrote to a friend to say 'Ken is not with the "Bonaventure" just now but the "Thames", both East Coast Flotilla ships. They are never safe, <u>never</u>. A fog in these crowded seas & all may be over in a moment without hope of succoar [sic]. Surely some safety apparatus will be perfected soon to give air & the chance of escape from those horrible things … I cannot get the thought of that last struggle shut up in that boat out of my mind …' [1.5.31].

11 | *'our gallant sailors & soldiers'*

Then the First World War broke out in August 1914, Mrs Duff-Dunbar may have been much relieved that Kenneth was then serving aboard a battlecruiser HMS *Princess Royal*. An almost-new ship (she had been commissioned in 1913), the *Princess Royal* was the second of the so-called Lion class of battlecruisers, with a main armament of eight 13.5 inch guns and a top speed of 28 knots. There was great excitement at Ackergill in September 1914, as someone called Jessie conveyed to Mrs Duff-Dunbar in a letter begun on the 20th [4.3.18]. 'My own dearest Madam,' begins Jessie. She describes the weather in detail – northerly gales and rain 'in buckets' the day before – before going on to the main news: 'some ships passed yesterday, and one warship stayed in Wick bay & one of the men bought one hundred newspapers from Arthur Bruce! [Arthur Bruce was one of several newsagents in Wick.] No one has heard the name of the ship – some people are so "dull", to never think of asking names! We saw several ships yesterday, far out tho', except two which were nearer Noss, the ships passed southwards – Search lights were going Friday night from Scapa [Scapa Flow, the naval base in Orkney, only some fifteen miles north of Ackergill] ...'. One of the passing ships had three funnels – as had the *Princess Royal* - '... we wondered if it was our PR if it had been coming here we had a dinner ready & how we would have loved to give it to our Sailor – I don't think the PR goes by herself does she?' Jessie also wrote what the rumour mill was bringing her way: '... Oh dear I do trust and pray that the war will be over before next year, the cold weather on sea & land will be so hard for our gallant sailors & soldiers – The Zeppelins are being made, but we heard a report that they have used all their petrol, and they used to get it all from Russia. Our Navy will be ready when they do attack, and tho' there will be many dear fellows killed, it may not be so bad as some people think, if Germany wished not to fight at sea, would the Allies consent to that? One longs to hear if the sea battle may <u>not</u> come off … Are the Russians in France, I mean <u>did</u> they land in Scotland – the papers say no, or rather they make fun of the rumours.'

The rumour that Russian troops had passed via Scapa Flow to the south became notorious – there were jokes that they had been seen in Inverness with snow on their boots – but it was only a rumour. Jessie carried on recording what they could see from the Tower (she would have been horrified to learn that she may have been committing an offence under the defence regulations): '<u>6.30 17 ships are passing now</u>, first a destroyer, then a 3 funnel – then destroyers (6) then a 3 funnel wonder if PR <u>8 more – 25 in all</u> <u>30 passed this morning</u> about 6 the servants saw them, but I did not, then the <u>22 passed Scapa </u>way about 10'.

In the autumn of 1914, George came back to England. On 12 August he was in Bombay. 'War was declared after I sent off my last mail,' he wrote to his mother, '… The hand of the censor is rightly drastic' [4.3.42]. Perhaps his letter had reached its destination with sections deleted but this did not prevent him from speculating on the conflict. He spoke about the Royal Navy inflicting a crushing blow on the German fleet: 'Yesterday we heard by wire that 19 German ships were sunk. If true it is the Nelson touch once more.' It was not true; the first major encounter between the enemy fleets took place on 28 August in the Helgoland Bight. 'Indian opinion is interesting,' George continued, 'it would appear that a natural dislike of England is completely overshadowed by something deeper than a suspicion of German methods. From us the Indian hopes for an eventual government on South African lines: a thing never to be dreamt of from either Russia or Germany.' He also mentioned China causing trouble on the Burma frontier and there was a report that 50,000 Indian troops would be embarked in a few days for Egypt, another eventuality that did not materialise. In London George was given a post in the War Office.

During wartime Kenneth's letters to his mother were of course subject to censorship and he often says very little beyond reporting he is well. He had in fact been present at the first clash between the British and German navies off Heligoland on the morning of 28 August. In a confused action beset by fog, a strong Royal Navy force ambushed a patrol and sank three German cruisers before the remaining ships turned back to port. On 12 November, the *Princess Royal* set sail from Invergordon to Halifax in Nova Scotia and on 1 December moved south to Jamaica and the West Indies before returning to Halifax as Christmas approached and then steaming home to Scapa Flow, where she arrived on 2 January 1915. Two days before departure, on 10 November, Kenneth had written in a most understated fashion to his mother: 'So many odd things have been cropping up lately that I have had awfully little time for writing & I am afraid you have been badly neglected. The trawler stockings are simply splendid, you have no idea what a comfort they have been to me as the nights are turning colder …' [he had also received gifts of food] 'I am not quite like the fat boy in Pickwick yet, so don't be too much alarmed.' He had been glad that George had made 'such good progress' and hoped to see him before he was sent to the Front [4.2.2]. On 26 November, when the battlecruiser was in Canada, he wrote to say that the refit had been postponed until the new year, adding 'I suppose George will soon be off to France' [4.3.41].

HMS *Princess Royal* was made the flagship of the 1st Battlecruiser Squadron in January 1915. On the 6th Kenneth wrote again to regret that his time for answering the many letters he had received had become very limited by his duties [4.4.14]. 'By now of course you know all of our recent doings & such meagre scraps as I am allowed to write Katharine can tell you.' He mentioned with some pride that on their recent 'errand' they had steamed 12,820 miles. His ship was in action again towards the end of January in the battle of Dogger Bank when the Royal Navy, alerted by their ability to intercept and read German signals, dashed across the North Sea to catch the German fleet off guard. As at Helgoland, British losses were slight in comparison to the German. These reverses convinced the German high command to remain close to home and devote more effort to the U-boat war. In July 1915 Kenneth was given command of his own ship, the submarine HMS *E 16* [4.3.25]. The *E 16*, launched in September 1914, was one of a large class of vessels with varying characteristics but in her case with a length of 181 feet, two Vickers diesel engines capable of pushing her along at 15 knots on the surface and just over 10 knots when submerged. She was armed with four torpedo tubes. On 27 July 1915, Kenneth and his crew sank an enemy destroyer, *V 188*, off the Dutch island of Terschelling and, on 15 September, near Stavanger, became the first British submarine to sink a U-boat, *U 6*. On 22 December, Kenneth and his men pressed home an attack on a German auxiliary vessel, penetrating the target's protective screen to torpedo it, an action for which he was awarded the Distinguished Service Order (DSO). His career as a submariner came to an abrupt and tragic end, however, in the minefields off Helgoland on 16 August 1916 when his boat struck a mine and was lost with all 31 of her complement. At first the *E 16* was reported missing but by early September any hope for her or her crew had been exhausted.[22] Katharine was left to give birth to their son, named Kenneth James after his father, on 21 November that year; the birth notice appeared in *The Scotsman* on the 27th and gave the widow's address as the Grange, Ealing. In July, exactly a month before the fateful encounter off Helgoland, Kenneth had written to his mother to ask her to stay with Katharine in Ealing as he had to go back to sea on the 26th [4.3.44].

On 3 August 1916, George was promoted and gazetted as a major in the 31st Punjabi regiment in the Indian Army [23] and early in the following year was back in India. In May 1917, presumably on the basis of his previous experience, he was appointed to the School of Mountain Warfare, an organisation founded a year before to train men in how to combat the tribes on the North-West Frontier. On 11 June, George wrote home from Fort Sandiman in Baluchistan; the paper bears the letterhead of the XIX Punjabis [4.2.3]. 'The year has been a strange one indeed,' he began, ' – & full of sorrow – but still with its promise of a certain happiness in this world. And I know that I – with you – have now a sure & certain hope for the next. This time last year I was on the brink of France. It is probable of course that my possibly premature unleashing of myself, from the absorbing & difficult work that I had – as an embusqué – at the War Office is now handicapping my energetic health. In other words I'm not absolutely fit or full of go – but I am quite <u>well</u> of course. I've lost everything professionally but I did the right thing; I'm sure of that. Had no one at all been about me; I mean were it not for you and Patrick I had rather been dead at the head of the London Scottish than anything else of value that the world can offer. But these things are not in our hands. The regiment, the Bde, the Div & the Corps would have welcomed my appointment to command. And now this. Still, I know I did the right thing. Nothing can take <u>that</u> away.'

George had been through some kind of crisis but at present its nature remains obscure. His letter continues with a more positively written account of a recent action. 'On Corpus Christi [7 June] I went out, at 10 pm, at 1½ hours notice, with 150 men to try & catch 300 Mahsuds. Some cavalry went out ahead of us. We marched all night & came up soon after sunrise to the position the Mahsuds had left some hours before. The cavalry got some ineffectively long range shooting at the flying enemy: got one or two – but the crowd got off. It was tantalizing to hear distant firing & not get to it. I had such a charming letter of appreciation from the Political Agent … I night marched home again … Some of my people did nearly 35 miles.'

Several days late George was writing that he was to have treatment in Quetta for a slight recrudescence of pyorrhoea which had affected his health [4.2.4]. 'Have the English mails been persistently dumped on the sea floor week after week or what?' he asked, clearly depressed by the absence of news from home. He was looking forward to seeing friends in Quetta, 'getting to Mass' and 'being once more in comfort & civilization,' although he had an 'amicable fight' with the CO about his 'exodus'.

On 20 July 1919 George wrote from the military hospital at Ras el Tin near Alexandria to say he hoped to sail on or after the 23rd on a ship called *Valdivia*, which was something to be regretted, and expected to be in Marseilles on the 28th, Le Havre on the 31st and finally Southampton and London on the 1st [4.2.20]. He hoped to take Patrick to a farmhouse at Lydford for his holidays – 'It's my one chance of getting to know him', a poignant reminder that the father and his son had been separated for a long time and were in effect strangers to each other. George also gloomily warned his mother: 'If I have another relapse I shall get him (I believe I can) to Osborne – where I would go.'

In May 1921 George married again. His second wife was Dorothy Hewlett, a colonel's daughter living on the Isle of Wight, where presumably the couple met. In April 1922 they were in Egypt. George wrote a stern admonition to Patrick back in England on the 15th: 'I cannot believe that you are deliberately throwing away a happy & brilliant career …' – what folly Patrick had committed is unknown but he had been given a second chance and his scholarship at Harrow was still in place – '…you are in honour bound to do your best & justify the benefaction that enabled me to send you to Harrow.' If Patrick did not improve, his father threatened, he would have to attend St Paul's or some grammar school: 'Another such report & the disaster to your life is final and complete.' The letter has a postscript: 'You quite realize I hope that this sort of thing developed into manhood unchecked would make it quite uncertain whether you could survive your COs reports on your first two years in the Army…' [4.2.9].

The school report that had provoked George's anger is preserved in the Papers [4.2.9]. It states that Patrick, aged 15 years and eight months, Form V Classical Division 1 for 2nd half term 1922, had done as follows: 'Divinity, English – Good, especially in History, but he has been known to scan work in which he was not interested; Latin – Good, shows particular ability in translating & some of his compositions reach a high standard; Greek – Good, has a wide a range of vocabulary & writes with taste – Always gets good marks in Greek History; Maths – Quite satisfactory. Geometry fairly good. Has done better.' This would appear to have been enough to please any father but the succeeding comments by the housemaster did the damage: 'He is idle … otherwise his real ability would put him much ahead of the others … he may jeopardize his Scholarship if he does not mend his ways …'.

Patrick's response to this paternal chastisement is unknown but he went on to study at New College, Oxford, and was admitted as a barrister to Middle Temple in 1931; he was appointed an honorary colonel in the Second World War and died unmarried on 4 February 1963.

While the son was presumably reflecting on his conduct in Harrow, his father and stepmother toured in the Middle East. George wrote a long letter to his mother on 23 January with a description of the sights in Jerusalem [4.2.11] and Dorothy sent her own opinions a few days later [4.2.12] with the extra information that her husband was in 'splendid health … I have never seen him so well not even in Cyprus.'

The couple were back on the Isle of Wight in the late summer of 1923. Patrick had been to visit them. George confessed to his mother that 'After a slightly sticky beginning' the boy's 'visit has we gather gone off very well …' [4.2.19]. He was planning to go north to Caithness in the following month. 'I think that if Dorothy sees Caithness before mid October she may get to like it & be happy there. And my happiness is hers …' [4.2.15].

The visit to Ackergill did not get off to a good start. George poured out ill feeling to his mother in a letter written on 14 November, a letter that began uncompromisingly with the statement: 'The state of affairs which Dorothy foresaw & warned me against when she advised me against our move north has arisen' [4.2.21; 4.3.27]. A gale had taken some slates off the roof of the Tower. George asked someone called Jemmina, presumably the housekeeper, to look out the keys to the attic while he took Dorothy to visit Dr Leask in Wick. (She was much run down by worry, wrote her husband, and had strained her side – Dr Leask thought it could possibly be a case of appendicitis.) On returning to the Tower, George was told in the front hall by Jemmina, in front of Dorothy, thus making the offence worse, that 'Mrs Duff-Dunbar put me in charge on Aug 1st. She said that you would only want two rooms until she came up.' 'I cannot take my place in the country' under one of the servants, protested George, 'In spite of all, I am the head of the family…'. There were two solutions, in George's view: either we stay under the conditions Dorothy was led to believe would pertain, that she is in charge; or we go at once.

This letter must have reached Mrs Duff-Dunbar in Folkestone like a bombshell. She replied to her son to ask if he were 'really serious', that when she had left Ackergill in July she had had no idea he would be up in October [4.2.22]. On the same day she appealed to Dorothy's mother in confidence: 'I want your help. There has been trouble at Ackergill to my bitter disappointment!' [4.2.23]. Her doctor would not agree to her travelling north at that time so she was unable to locate keys. When she had left in the summer, parts of the Tower had been locked up before tenants had taken possession for the shooting season, and she had had no idea that her son would want to access the attic. There had been no intention of insulting George. 'Do you know of anything else to account for the trouble,' asked Mrs Duff-Dunbar, 'You may know that I do not & my fear is that some mischief has been made.' George had also refused to admit his mother's maid to the Tower because she had a small breast tumour removed some five years before. 'She is examined every six months & is as sound as I am,' protested Mrs Duff-Dunbar.

Mother and son were soon only partly reconciled. George wrote from Ackergill on 23 January 1924 to thank his mother for sending cheques and a parcel of knives, and included in his letter what he intended to do: 'After all that has happened – & I say this not wishing to cause pain but to prevent it – we shall not return [to Ackergill]. Dorothy & I both feel strongly that if there is to be any return to the feelings that existed prior to our return from Egypt it can only be by the complete obliteration of what has occurred since. We have made a mistake – too costly a mistake for me to dare risk its continuance. And now, my dear mother, I do hope that on the receipt of this letter you will join with us in wiping out these unpleasant months. We shall live abroad. Jemima [sic] has been given reasons of health for our departure.' [4.3.34]

Mrs Duff-Dunbar replied at once from Folkestone: 'My darling George … I understand what you feel much better perhaps than you think … You did your best & so did I as far as I knew & we failed. I know that if we had been face to face together at Ackergill there wd have been none of the sore part of all this. I love you dearly my Geordie … I hope that Bruges may set you & Dorothy up, & do all you can wish … Write & tell me your plans & especially whether I can see you before you go abroad …' [4.3.33].

The *London Gazette* noted George's retirement from the Indian Army with effect from 3 January 1925.[24]

12 | *'what I want is a middle-sized farm'*

The number of documents in the Dunbar Papers falls off during the 1920s and 30s. Most of them deal with day-to-day administrative matters on the estate or in the household or personal family business as related in the previous section (Appendix 16). Thus, in a letter dated 8 April 1905, we learn that the Works Committee of the Road Board (presumably of Caithness County Council) dealing with the Staxigoe road will meet in about ten days and will need a letter of consent from the trustees of the estate for work to be done [1.1.3]. Mr Harrison the road surveyor wanted a stone wall to be put up at one point where the road went near the cliff, and this would cost £8. The prices of work seem comically small now until the effects of a century of change in the value of the pound are taken into account; £8 in 1905 is equivalent to a price of around £865 in 2020.

Alex McEwen & Sons, Wick, charged 18s 6d in November 1907 for cleaning, repolishing and sending south a sideboard [1.1.4]. Alex Dunnet, the factor who had to deal with the troublesome Mr Laidlaw in 1893, was still presiding over the estate office in Sutherland Villa in 1911. On 16 February he wrote to Mrs Duff-Dunbar about several issues: regarding preparing a barrel of eggs for someone called Kyler on Friday morning, he sought confirmation that it would be like the herring barrel got once before; and he discussed gravel to be carted to Ackergill at 3s per load plus 3s per load for collecting, riddling [seiving] and carrying it in bags up the brae [1.5.29]. Mr Dunnet said gravel cost the townspeople 5s, and asked if Mrs Duff-Dunbar still wanted four loads.

It has already been mentioned that the main railway line to Wick completed in 1874 passed through Dunbar land on its last few miles. Several batches of correspondence deal with the construction of the light railway between Wick and

Lybster at the end of the nineteenth century (24.1.8-25; 41.2; 118.1.55; 1182.1-7; 119.2; 132.2). Iain Sutherland has summarised the story of the Lybster line and describes how the Dunbar trustees negotiated for compensation for loss of land, and the inconvenience for some of their tenants in having their properties divided so that they had to use level crossings to access the different parts. The railway opened for service on 1 July 1903, and closed on 1 April 1944.[25]

Among the letters from the 1920s, a number deal with repairs to buildings, farms and steadings on the estate. For example, the Wick building contractor, Donald Harper, wrote to Mrs Duff-Dunbar on 29 September 1927: 'I believe the principal work at Hempriggs would take about two months but if you intend to do the work I would recommend it to be started as early as possible. I intend to draw the front elevation as it would look if the new work is proceeded with and I shall go and take the measurements for this purpose as early as possible … This sort of work [the design] does not cost me anything and I am delighted to do it for my friends' [47.2.19]. Mrs Duff-Dunbar approved the following list of repairs on 13 March 1928 [47.2.21]:

Mr Gray's Barn, Byre and Stable Roofs at Myrelandhorn. Facing boards and about a roll of felt to catch the facing board.   Cost about £5.

John Dunnet's Byre Roof, Kilminster [sic]. Sarking and felt put on, Ventilator and felt on Byre facing road.   Cost £10.

Mrs Harper's House, Wester. Take lining down and pierce couples as suggested.
                                    Cost about £5.

James Sutherland's Byre Roof. Repair this roof as suggested with a roll of felt.
                                    Cost 25s to 30s.

In December 1927, one of the tenants, Mrs Bremner in Hempriggs Row in Wick, apologised for troubling Mrs Duff-Dunbar 'at this season of the year' but protested that she had informed the estate office frequently about the 'smokey-ness' of her house to no effect [47.2.25]. 'I feel it my duty,' wrote Mrs Bremner, 'that you should know as I don't think if you knew of it that you would like any tenant to suffer so much as I have done through smoke …'. She pointed out that she was paying her rent but was hardly able to sit in her house for the smoke blowing back down the chimney. A note penned at the top of the letter reads 'Sent Masons'.

Several letters are about keeping or obtaining tenancies of the farms on the estate. John Bremner, Northfield, Hempriggs, wrote on 10 January 1928 to offer for the tenancy of Upper Humster 'as advertised' and presently occupied by J. Sutherland [47.2.23]. Mr Bremner offered to pay a rent of £27 per year. 'As you are aware,' he told Mrs Duff-Dunbar, 'our farm at Northfield is the dearest on the Estate and as we are working together we could afford to give a rent which would help us to pay the Large rent of Northfield viz £90 for 92 acres. Hoping you will favourably consider this to a son of one of your oldest tenants.' As the Caithness Valuation Roll for 1929–30 shows a Mr Albert Hood as the tenant of Upper Humster, it would appear that John Bremner's request was unsuccessful; in the same Roll, however, Northfield is occupied by the representatives of the late John Bremner, so perhaps he died before the matter could be concluded.

Some of the tenants of long standing affected a respectful familiarity with Mrs Duff-Dunbar. Such a one was Jessie Coghill at Hillhead, Wick, who thanked her landlady on 9 January 1928 'for your goodness to Robert in allowing him the privilege of farming Killimster Mains. I hope that he prove worthy of your good opinion. In my early youth it was held by Mr William Grant and was considered a very good farm. I trust that you are keeping well and you will be able and willing to come to see me before you leave the North again' [47.2.24].

Agitation over land reform in the Highlands and islands came to a head in 1911. Large areas of the Highlands had been made into deer farms, privately owned and run as hunting reserves. Crofting communities faced a dearth of land for traditional farming and for many families and individuals emigration seemed the only answer. The Congested Districts Board, modelled on a predecessor in Ireland, had been established in 1897 to try to ameliorate the problems but had only partial success. A large meeting to debate land reform took place in Canisbay in March 1911.[26] In September that year, the Crown Office of Woods and Forests began to break the recently purchased estate of Scotscalder into smallholdings; the large farms of West Calder and Calder Mains became holdings of 30 to 50 acres in extent to give opportunity to new tenant farmers.[27] Amid great controversy, a land reform bill was passed by the House of Commons just before Christmas. This new Small Landholders (Scotland) Act extended to all tenants the rights formerly associated with crofting tenure, and the Scottish Land Court began its work to implement the new legislation. Much of this dealt with the setting of fair rents. During the following years, including when the First World War was being fought, the Land Court conducted its business across the north. Applications for rent review came in from tenants in several Caithness parishes and Dunbar tenants naturally took the opportunity to have their rents examined. The Land Court, under Lord Kennedy, sat in Wick in May 1912 to hear applications from various tenants on several estates relating to compensation for improvements. Alex Dunnet wrote to Mrs Duff-Dunbar from Upper Gillock on 28 August 1912 to say that he was sending 'per bearer' a list of nineteen applications by tenants to the Land Court [17.7.7]. Another sitting of the Court took place in Wick in October.

The year 1912 also saw negotiations with the Board of Agriculture, which had newly taken the place of the Congested Districts Board, over the formation of smallholdings on Sibster. Garden Duff, Mrs Duff-Dunbar's cousin, joined the negotiations from his home in Hatton Castle near Turriff, for example writing to Mr Georgeson, the Dunbars' solicitor in Wick, with his objections to the terms suggested by the Board of Agriculture and particularly to the inadequate compensation offered to the estate for the Sibster holdings [17.7.11].

Peter Bain wrote from Murza, Bower, on 26 August 1912 about taking on Sibster; he thanked Mrs Duff-Dunbar for her letter and said that the farm would suit him better at the size of 414 acres than at 200. 'What I want is a middle-sized farm near the town & railway & Sibster as reduced would suit me fine. My son shall stay on our present farm. Would you kindly send me the conditions of let & any other information you consider fit. You might say when I could examine the farm' [17.7.9]. In the event, Bain did not move to Sibster; in the 1914–15 Valuation Roll he is still tenant of Murza with his son John.

In September 1912, John Gunn wrote from North Killimster: 'Dear Mrs Duff Dunbar [I] have been thinking of writing you since some time to see if you could give me the chance of another farm on your estate as I am thinking of leaving this one. My boys are speaking of going to Canada as this farm will not afford any wages for them. I used to work very hard on this farm myself trying to make ends meet but I am not able to do that now. I would not like to leave your estate if I can get another farm on it. Kindly let me know if there is any opening this year, With Kind regards to you, I am your truly' [17.7.8]. According to the Valuation Roll for 1914–15, Gunn remained as tenant of Upper Killimster.

The Land Court published its decisions, for example, for Latheronwheel and Forse in July 1915. In August it sat in Wick to hear cases, and in September, sitting in the Canisbay parish kirk, considered rent review applications from the Freswick and Mey estates.

The Wick solicitor D.W. Georgeson acted on behalf of Mrs Duff-Dunbar in the dealings with the Land Court. He took pains to make clear to the press that sometimes the application to the Court for a rent revaluation came from the proprietor rather than from the tenant. This was the case with some tenants in Clyth in November 1915 [8.7.18]. Mr Georgeson was also exercised over the practice of the Land Court of accepting as sufficient legal proof the uncorroborated testimony of a single witness, as happened with regard to alleged permanent improvements to a croft carried out by the tenant or his predecessors. Mr Georgeson had referred one case to the Court of Session and was frustrated not to receive a reply after two and a half years [8.7.17]. It is possible that in 1915 Mr Georgeson's concern that a 'very grave and widespread injustice' was being committed on landowners may not have been widely shared. The solicitor complained after the morning hearings of the Land Court in Wick on 24 November 1915 that Alexander Dewar, the presiding officer, was 'in no very friendly frame of mind from the landlord's point of view' and 'I had to speak to him rather sharply' regarding the situation of a tenant in Papigoe [8.7.16]. The *Groat*, which carried a long verbatim report on the exchanges during the hearings, was of the view that Mr Dewar had done his work 'with rare geniality and a patient indulgence in many trying situations'.[28] Mrs Duff-Dunbar upheld her solicitor's opinion of the Court in a letter to Garden Duff on 25 November [8.7.19]: 'In Mr Dewar we have the worst member of the Court, except perhaps Lord Kennedy – now in retirement again I understand,' she wrote, 'Mr Dewar has not all Lord Kennedy's Judge-Jeffreys-like Bench-manners but I am not sure that he is not quite as dangerous.'

Judging from the accounts of the Land Court hearings in the *Groat*, the evidence presented became at times a battle of wits between crofter and solicitor, as statement followed statement to unroll complex patterns of inheritance, repairs made or not made, irregular acquisitions of bits of land, and so on. In the weeks following the November hearings, the Court published its decisions on matters raised by Hempriggs' tenants. For example, with regard to a claim from George Rae, Elzy, that the estate had failed to provide buildings required for the cultivation of his holding, the Court found in his favour and asked the proprietor to make good the remedy.[29] Although it seemed at times that the Land Court tended to favour the tenant, the outcomes were not always what tenants desired. Angus Macdonald, Papigoe, was paying £4 10s rent for the place he occupied, a house and garden and area of grass amounting to 0.4 acres, but the Court found it to be too small to be considered a holding in the meaning of the Act.[30] and William Fairweather, Myrelandhorn, had his rent raised by the Court from £10 10s to £11.[31]

One of the last letters in the Dunbar Papers is one from Mr Georgeson the solicitor on 6 April 1933 to tell Mrs Duff-Dunbar that '…I have just handed Colonel Robertson a cheque for £100 for shares in the new Highland Airway [sic] Ltd. Apparently only £500 had been allotted for Wick. Colonel Robertson was sending his own cheque for £300 but he mentioned that if you wished to invest £100 in the Company he would make over to you shares to that amount. I think the Company should do all right' [43.3.28]. With hindsight, Mr Georgeson's guarded optimism provokes some amusement. Highland Airways Ltd, to give the company its correct title, was founded by Captain Ernest Edmund 'Ted' Fresson and on 29 May 1934 began the first airmail service in the north, linking Inverness to Wick and Kirkwall. Highland Airways flourished and was finally nationalised, by being incorporated into British European Airways in 1946. Today Captain Fresson's memory is honoured. His first flights into Wick landed on Dunbar-owned land, on the grass airfield that had been at one time the contested Hill o' Wick, from 1933 until 1939, when it was requisitioned by the Air Ministry and became an important RAF base.

Mrs Duff-Dunbar died in 1948. Meanwhile, George had gone on to serve his country during the Second World War, in the War Office as a lecturer in the Army Education service and in the India Office; his second wife Dorothy had died in November 1945 but in 1956 he married Dulcie Wescombe Joyce. He used his knowledge of India to write several books about the sub-continent, including *India and the Passing of Empire* (1951) and a biography of Robert Clive (*Clive*, 1936), and to make over fifty broadcasts on the BBC. [31] He died in April 1962, bequeathing to his son Patrick the baronetcy of Hempriggs. Patrick – or Sir George Cospatrick Duff-Sutherland Dunbar, 7th Baronet, to give him his full title died without a direct heir in February 1963. Kenneth, the son of George's brother Kenneth who had been killed in the submarine HMS *E 16* in the First World War, was himself killed in action in Normandy in August 1944. A captain in the Seaforth Highlanders, he had fought with the 5th Battalion through North Africa and was in the 7th Battalion, part of the 15th (Scottish) Division in France. [33]

Once again the inheritance of the Dunbar lands in Caithness shifted to another line of descent within the family. Captain Benjamin Duff, who had become the 5th Baronet by inheriting the title from his uncle in 1875, on his death in 1897 bequeathed the lands to his son, Garden Duff-Dunbar (Fig. 10). Benjamin and his wife, Emma Haines, also had three daughters. The eldest, Louisa Harriet, died as a child of 12. The second, Helen Emma, never married and died in 1923. The youngest daughter, Jessie Mona, born in 1843, married a vicar of the Church of Ireland, the Revd Courtenay Moore. Born at Ballymoney in County Antrim in 1840, Courtenay studied at Trinity College in Dublin and was ordained as a deacon in June 1865 in the parish of Brigown, centred on the small town of Mitchelstown on the northern fringe of County Cork. [34]

Jessie and Courtenay had four children. The eldest, Courtenay Edward, became an engineer, working for the Irish railway network, and married Jane King Askins in 1898. The couple later separated but not before they had two children – a son, Edward Francis Courtenay, who became known in the family as Paddy, and a daughter, Maureen Daisy Helen. Paddy was studying at Oxford in 1917 when he was commissioned as a 2nd Lieutenant in the Rifle Brigade; on 24 March 1918 he was killed during a German advance in the Somme valley, in a defensive action for which he was posthumously awarded the Military Cross, and lies buried in the British military cemetery at Pargny. [35] Maureen became an accomplished violinist. When she went as a teacher to Twyford, a private school near Winchester in Hampshire, in 1935, she met Leonard James Blake, who was himself a music teacher and distinguished organist. The couple married on 27 August 1940 in Oxford. After the war, Leonard became director of music at Malvern College.

As noted above, in February 1963 Patrick Dunbar died without a direct heir. His death had been preceded by that of his father only a year before in 1962. A trust, the Sir George Cospatrick Duff Sutherland Dunbar Trust, had been formed in 1951 with two trustees, Ronnie Watson, a solicitor in Edinburgh who was a lifelong personal friend of Patrick, and Katharine Duff-Dunbar, who had been born Katharine Isabel Daw and whose father had made his fortune building many properties in Kensington, Ealing and Notting Hill as those areas of London had grown in the latter decades of the nineteenth century.

Neither Patrick nor his father had paid much attention to the day-to-day management of the estate in Caithness, which was now faced with double death duties after their passing. To meet these taxes, the two trustees had to sell many of the farms, while maintaining Ackergill Tower, the family home that Mrs Duff-Dunbar was insistent would never be sold during her lifetime. Almost all the estate's income came from the agricultural land and was needed to maintain the Tower, and it was unfortunate that Mrs Duff-Dunbar, a very wealthy woman in her own right, did not give some of her fortune to help with its upkeep.

In Malvern Leonard and Maureen Blake now received a surprise. The story is best told in Leonard's own words: 'Maureen had been busy teaching … when the morning post was delivered, and I had not more than glanced at the foolscap envelope, with an Edinburgh postmark, which came along with some correspondence for me … It was not until late afternoon that I handed it to her. We were dumbfounded when it turned out to be from a leading firm of Scottish solicitors – Brodies – acting as agents for the executors of a recently deceased baronet of whom we had never heard.' After much difficulty, the solicitors had identified and tracked Maureen down as the nearest legal heir to the baronetcy and the estate in Caithness. The Blakes were astonished and excited. '[Maureen] could remember being told by her mother that there was a title somewhere in the family, which might come her way in the event of two particular people dying prematurely,' wrote Leonard, 'but she had never been told their names.'[36] Lengthy investigation followed until, in 1965, the solicitors had the full story to lay before the Court of the Lord Lyon. Maureen thus became a baronetess, the first woman in Scotland to be so designated for three hundred years, an unusual occurrence hailed by a long piece in *The Scotsman*.[37] Maureen and Leonard now divided their lives between Ackergill Tower and their home in Malvern, in the former finding themselves in, what Leonard called, the circle of Caithness 'upper crust' and continuing in the latter their careers in music.

Katharine Duff-Dunbar, who had lost her husband in the First World War and her son in the Second, had continued all this time to live at Hempriggs House. Leonard wrote that her devotion to Ackergill was absolute. 'Her jealous guardianship of its possessions and traditions was not, indeed, to be wondered at, and she kept a very careful if not actually suspicious watch over us to begin with. There came a softening of her attitude … due not merely to advancing age but also to a genuinely warm if shyly expressed acceptance of our own place among her family connections.' She resigned from being a trustee and died two years later on 25 February 1981, aged 88. She is buried in Wick Cemetery.

On assuming the baronetcy, Maureen became Lady Dunbar of Hempriggs and took on an active interest in Caithness life. Her obituary in the *Groat* on 7 March 1997 (she had died on 15 February) described her as 'kind, charming and forthright' and spoke of her 'small, upright figure and infectious laugh'.[39] She and Leonard had two children, Richard Francis and Eleanor Margaret. Richard inherited and is now Sir Richard Francis Dunbar, the ninth baronet. He was born of course as a Blake but changed his name to assume that of Dunbar of Hempriggs, as James Sutherland of Duffus had done back in 1706, in an echo of history that brings our story in full circle again to its beginnings.

'The Tower was a white elephant, saddled with massive death duties, and with very little income as well as having been neglected for decades, and I was never encouraged to participate in much of the family history nor any decision the trustees were making', recalls Sir Richard, 'My mother, in her late 50s, was overawed by the unbelievable reality of it all, as indeed were all four of our family – my father and sister included. Neither parent had business acumen and it was some years until my mother was invited to become a trustee, in about 1968, I think. Alister Clyne, who farmed Field of Noss, at Staxigoe, became a trustee about 1964 and his local knowledge of farming was invaluable.'

Sir Richard feels that it was most unfortunate that he and Patrick had never met, as apparently he would have much enjoyed having a young man around the estate shooting and fishing with him on those occasions when he came to Caithness. Others in Caithness said how sad it was that Katharine did not encourage Sir Richard to visit regularly and to be involved in the running of the estate. 'Perhaps she thought or her friends and advisers recommended against that because of the uncertainty of the estate's future and our being unknown,' said Sir Richard.

Sir Richard now takes up the story: 'I had been told by anyone I asked and by my parents "It's a white elephant. You cannot expect to keep it going. You'll have to make your own future". Also, in part because there was no chance of any farm becoming available during my lifetime, as all tenants had likely inheritors, except possibly for John Angus at Quoys of Reiss, and he was not much older than me. Looking for sage advice I asked numerous people their opinions about possibly going to agricultural college, training to be a surveyor or other similar ideas but all gave me the same answer. I asked Ronnie Watson, trustee and legal advisor, about going to agricultural college and his reply was "you could do worse". That was not very reassuring, let alone encouraging!

'In 1983 aged 37 (by which time I had emigrated to California, married Jane Lister and had two daughters, Emma and Fiona) I became a trustee, and was encouraged, as opposed to being discouraged, to take an interest in the estate, as it continued to disintegrate physically and financially. In 1986 Alister and I decided to sell Ackergill Tower. It was simply that or continue limping along putting all the income into the already seriously neglected building. Only after it was sold was the extreme burden of financial survival of the estate avoided and we were able to stem the flow of red ink. Patrick Stirling-Aird replaced Ronnie Watson as solicitor and trustee, and he together with Alister Clyne and me made many repairs and improvements over the next decade. These included building large steadings to meet the needs of modern farming, as well as completely renovating two abandoned Georgian farmhouses, while enlarging and improving other dwellings and arranging for drainage work to recover unusable fields for arable use again.

'It is essential nowadays to keep abreast of ever-changing legislation for farmers and landowners, and I work with expert advisers who can provide me with the best available advice on the way forward to comply with the regulations and benefit the estate and the tenants. Though my home is in the United States I have a great love for Scotland and in particular for Caithness and will continue to make regular visits to manage estate matters, meet tenants and discuss any concerns they may have and arrange for improvement work to be done where it is needed on land and buildings. The sale of Ackergill Tower in 1986 was a difficult decision to make but it proved that, with careful planning, financial and otherwise, Hempriggs Estate could become the viable entity it is today and it is to be hoped that this will be the case for many years in the future.'

Notes

1. For a full biography see Rosalind Mitchison, *Agricultural Sir John: The Life of Sir John Sinclair of Ulbster 1754–1835*, 1962.
2. John Henderson, *General View of the Agriculture of the County of Caithness*, 1812.
3. *New Statistical Account of Scotland*, Wick, 1841, v. 15, pp. 147–8.
4. Sir John Sinclair, *General View of the Agriculture of the Northern Counties and Islands of Scotland*, 1795, p. 169.
5. James Miller, 'Modern Times', in: Donald Omand (ed) *The New Caithness Book*, 1989, p. 106.
6. M. Glendinning & S.W. Martins, *Buildings of the Land: Scotland's Farms 1750–2000*, RCAHMS, 2008.
7. Major William Innes inherited Sandside in 1787 and was to die without a direct heir in 1842, when Sandside passed to his nephew Captain Donald Macdonald.
8. Harry Gray, Wick, tells with regard to this incident that the Davidsons and their followers boarded themselves into Wester House. The court officers took tools from the smithy to break in to deliver the eviction notice. The smith later sued the officials for theft of his tools, won his case and built a house on the proceeds.
9. James Miller, *Salt in the Blood: The Story of Scotland's Fishing Communities*, 1999.
10. Joseph Mitchell, *Reminiscences of My Life in the Highlands*, 1883. David & Charles, 1971, vol. 2, p. 130.
11. Bishop Robert Forbes, quoted in J.B.Craven, *A History of the Episcopal Church in the Diocese of Caithness*, Kirkwall, 1908, p. 271.
12. A facsimile edition of this work was published by Birlinn in 2006. *Daniell's Scotland: a voyage round the coast of Scotland and the adjacent isles, 1815–1822: a series of views, illustrative of the character and prominent features of the coast*, by William Daniell.
13. Charles Thomson, 'Parish of Wick', *New Statistical Account of Scotland*, Edinburgh, 1845, vol. 15, p. 141.

14. *John o' Groat Journal*, 28 Sept 1876.

15. *John o' Groat Journal*, 5 Oct 1876.

16. Much has been written about railways. A full history can be found, for example, in *The Highland Railway*, by David Ross, 2005.

17. *Northern Ensign*, 4 June 1889.

18. For a full account of the lifeboat service around Wick and Ackergill, see Jeff Morris, *The Story of the Wick and Ackergill Lifeboats*, 1984.

19. *John o' Groat Journal*, 6 June 1889.

20. *Northern Ensign*, 4 June 1889.

21. The history of Wick Golf Club has been thoroughly researched by Roy Mackenzie, and we are grateful to him for much of the detail about the club's early years.

22. German divers located the wrecked hull of *E 16* in July 2001 lying in 30 fathoms north-west of Helgoland. Several letters about the loss are in 13.3 in the Dunbar Papers.

23. *London Gazette*, 1 Dec 1916.

24. *London Gazette*, 18 Mar 1925.

25. Iain Sutherland, *The Wick and Lybster Light Railway*, 1987.

26. *People's Journal*, 11 March 1911.

27. *People's Journal*, 30 Sept 1911.

28. *John o' Groat Journal*, 26 Nov 1915.

29. *People's Journal*, 5 Feb 1916.

30. *People's Journal*, 18 March 1916.

31. *People's Journal*, 25 March 1916.

32. *Who Was Who,* accessed on http://www.ukwhoswho.com (accessed 19 Nov 2014).

33. The 7th Seaforths landed in Normandy on 16 June 1944. Early on the morning of 6 August the battalion advanced to attack Lassy, a village in the Calvados region south of Caen. The enemy was far stronger than initially reported and the leading companies were pinned down by heavy machine gun fire and Mk IV tanks. Kenneth was killed in this encounter.

34. Information about Courtenay Moore is available through the website http://www.corkpastandpresent. ie/ history/coleschurchandparishrecords/ colesrecordsdioceseofcloyne *(last accessed 8 July 2015)*.

35. *Richard Dunbar, The Blake-Dunbar Family Histories, private typescript, p. 11.*

36. *Leonard Blake 'Retrospect: An Attempt at an Autobiography', in: Richard Dunbar, The Blake-Dunbar Family Histories, private typescript, p. 143.*

37. *The Scotsman*, 6 August 1965.

38. *John o' Groat Journal*, 7 March 1997.

APPENDIX 1

Ane accompt of what sommes of money have bein raised be the Earle of Breadalbane for such of his lands in Caithnes as have bein sold off since the year 1687, How
much of the Earles debt the same hath payed and how other ways disposed upon,
Whereof Coline Campbell writer to the Signett had the vinst & management
(Source: National Archives of Scotland, NRS 02024 GD112/58/90/2)

Charge

	Lib s d
Imprimis Ther was payed & advanced be William Dunbarr of Hemprigs in the year 1687 for and upon the bargaine of Oldwick & pendicles thereof Viz: Charitie & mylnelands thereof Humster Quoisdale Harrow Newtoune and Bankhead The lands of Kirkfield Milntoune & Telstane with ther parts and pertinents Over and above his paying of 10000 lib of Wadsett which was upon the lands Of Oldweik for the prequisitione whereof the Earle was bound to Telstane And of the Somme of 4000 merks Which was of Wadsett upon the Lands of Milntowne includeing the debt that was found by a fitted accompt to be due by Telstane to the Earle 19000 marks Which with some arrents payed by Hemprigs makes up in all	012790: 06: 10
Item by John Gunn of Braemore upon the lands of Braemore Of Wadsett more than he had upon it before	003333:06:08
Item by Baillie Mansone for the lands of Wattin Strath of Wattin Wester Wattin Strath of Wester Bylbster Achahoy Achalibster Scorrclett Hallisary and Scouthille and Rocome and Kinsary Over and above the payment of 8192 lib of Wadsett qch was upon the lands formerly And for qch the Earle was bound	015666:13:04
Item more payed by the Baillie of arents for the pryce Confirme to the aggrement	000300:00:00
Item by William Sutherland for the lands of Geisemeikle	004000:00:00
Item more payed by him for arent for the pryce	000150:00:00

Item by Donald Williamsone for the lands of Half Bannaskirk Geise Little & the Feuduetie And two bolls of Teynd duetie of Achorlie	004157:08:00
Item more payed by him for arent of the pryce	000187:01:00
Item by Langwall & Ausdale for the pryce Davachs of Berriedale Viz: Ausdale Langwall Breanaheglish Dallnagavich except the Nether Borg and Millary except the Forresters croft The Salmond fishing of Berridale Reisgill and pendicles Monosarie and Golliclay over and above – 840 lib which they are yitt posting for the pryce of Acoldibae pendicle of Breanaheglish and 216 lib which they are yitt posting for the pryce of Golliclay for both wch they gave Bonds – payable when they attend to the possessione And also over and above the payt of 11666 lib 13s 4d of wadsett which was formerly upon the lands for the recognitione of most part whereof My Lord was bound by the Contracts 12240 lib and 303 lib 13s 4d which they payed for the clamper that My Lord had from Toftingall upon the old Wadsett of Ausdale Inde payed	012543:13:04
Item more by them of arent for a part of the pryce	000038:03:00
Item by Sir George Sinclare for the lands of Breadwall Gairstane and milne thereof Halkirk and milntowne thereof Substerbrawll Sordell Hoy Skinand and Sixpennyland Over and above 2035 lib 4s which he is yitt posting for the pryce of Hoy and 666 lib 13s 4d which he is yitt posting for the pryce of the Reversion of the Milne of Garistane for both whch he granted bonds payable when he attains to the possessione And also over and above the payt of 1733 lib 6s 8d of Wadsetts which was upon the lands formerly for the Requisitione whereof My Lord was Lyable	025858:05:00
Item payed by him of arent for a part of the pryce	001023:12:06
Item more by Hemprigs which he advanced upon accompt of some new addition to his former bargains viz for the Salmond fishing of the Water of Weik the pennyland called the Lairds Pennyland and the Fardine & Octo of Cooksqueis and the Halfpennyland of Reinsbarnes All parts of the lands of Weik & Papigo and the two Tenements of Bankhead upon the South Syde of the Water of Weik At qch tyme the pappers of his former bargain were renewed Including the foresd additione After the forme of thes made with the other bargainers Qrupon the first rights he gott were retained	001440:00:00
28th July 1692 Approb Breadalbane	

APPENDIX 2

B81F2.4

Notes: 1. Uncertain or obscure points in the original are marked ?; 2. Grain is measured in Bolls, Firlots, Pecks and Lippies

Accompt betwixt Sir James Dunbar of Hempriggs and William Miller Tacksman of Ackergill etc

William Miller

	Oats	Bear	Money
To Fearms and Money: rent of cropt 1721 and rentall		1057B 1F 1P 2.5L	£1090 12s 4d
To seed sown ... several Labourings in 1718	155B 1F	54B 2F	
To Meall as 1 peck to the boll out of one third of Willm Miller last sowing		4B 2F ?	
To oats received by him from the seald(?) Growers of cropt 1721	60B 1F		
To Inbreak of Oats betwixt the proof and the growers delivery	12B 3F		
To cattle and the several Labourings in 1718			£329 13s
To the ploughing Grath(?) in Do sd years			£29 16s
To his tickets to the several tennents			£39
	228B 1F	114B - 2P	
		1230B 1F 3P 2.5L	£1489 2s
Ballance due to William Miller		299B 3F 1P 2L	£1069 1s 1d

	Victuall		Money
Contra			
By the tennents rentall & victuall and Money for crops and Morts debt		833B - - 2.5L	£907 13s 10d
1721 as per parlar(?) accompt			

	Oats	Bear		Money
By 73 bolls 2 firlot 1 peck bear sown in the Labourings according to Sir James Dunbars redding is at the 5th[?] Grain for Crops 1721		367B 3F 1P		
By 178 bolls 1 F 1 peck Oats sown Do according to the reddings as above is in meall at 3d Gram	267B 1F 3P 2L			
By 109 bolls 1 firlot 3 pecks 2 Lippies of difference betwixt the accompt of sowing given in by the Grieves and the redding as above of which the arbitrators decerns William Miller to loss 6 bolls 1 F 3 P 2 Lippies & Sir James	48B			
By 6 bolls oats sown in Jas Harper's labouring	3B			
By cost to the Servants (?) Marts last asp acct	11B			
By 65 oxen and cows in the several labourings delivered in Feb 1722 at 20 Mk each				£866 13s 4d
By the prices of the horses Mares and sheep as appreciated				£194 6s
By the labouring materials as per acct				£35 6s
By the ballance of (?) of the fishing materials etc				£31 8s 6d
By the Tenants Bests by the accepted bills & stated accompts as pr acct				£522 16s 2d
		1530B 1F 1P 0.5L		£2558 3s 10d

Att Wick the twentie fourth day of February [1722] the above accompt of debt and credit is perused and approved by the above designated Sir James Dunbar and William Miller and the ballance due to the said William Miller being Two hundred and ninty nine bolls Three firlots one peck and two lippies of victuall which victuall consists of two third parts Bear in the Boll measure of Staxigoe and the other third in oatmeal at eight stone and a half per boll and the above ballance of money being One thousand and sixty nine pound one shilling and ten pennies Scots money. The said money and balance is to be made good by me the said Sir James Dunbar in the termes of the deed arbitrall which balances and in full [?] of all contained in the said (?) except the sum of four thousand and two hundred merks Scots in witness whereof we have subscribed thir presents written by Robert McNale servitor to the sd William Miller day month place and year of God (?) in presence of Sir Robert Dunbar of Northfield, John Sinclair of Barrock, George Manson of Bridgend and James Campbell sheriff clerk of Caithness.

APPENDIX 3

Servants' wages in 1737 [88.3.10]

Regulations made by the Justices of the Peace of the Shyre of Caithness as to servants ffees Viz

Att Nether Bilbster the Tenth day of Nover [1737] years, the Committee of the Justices of the Peace of the County of Caithness after named Viz Charles Sinclair of Bilbster, George Manson of Bridgend, George Sinclair of Stircock, Donald Sinclair of Olrick, and David Sinclair of Southdun, Who were appointed at the last Quarter Sessions held at Week upon the 25th Oct last, To regulate Servants ffees & other points recommended to them.

Having mett this day in obedience to the last adjournment

The said Committee having fully considered the points recommended to them with respect to the Regulation of Servants fees, They have unanimously agreed & come to the ffollowing resolutions thereanent Viz.

1mo   That every Sufficient Ploughman that can semble his own Plough or keep it in good order after it is sembled to his hand Shall have of ffee for the winter half year Eight pounds Scots, an pair of shoes or ten shillings Scots therefore, a Quarter of a Rochhide & Three bolls of Cost, Whereof half in oatmeall at Eight Ston pr Boll, And half in Bear Meall at Nine Stone pr Boll, the said ffee & cost to be in full of all demands.

2do   That a drover shall have Six pounds Scots of ffees, a pair of shoes or ten shillings therefore, A quarter of a Rochhide, & Two bolls & a half of Cost, half oatmeall, half bearmeall at the above Weights for the winter half year.

3tis   That a Barnman that takes charge of the Barn & Compts for the whole Victuall shall have the same fee & Cost with a Ploughman, a pair of shoes only without any Rochhide, And the Barnman that does not take charge of the Barn shall have the same Cost & ffee as a Drover, a pair of shoes only, & no part of a Rochhide.

4to   That the Sparter & Harrower, if Boys, shall have Three Merks of ffee, a pair of shoes, or sevenpence therefore, a Quarter of a Rochhide, & six firlots of Cost, half oatmeall half bear meall at the above Weights; But if the Sparter & Harrower be men they shall have the same cost & ffee with a Drover, And a Carter shall have the same cost & ffee with a Ploughman.

5to   That a woman servant for out service shall have three merks of ffee, a pair of shoes or seven shillings Scots therefore for Summer half year, And Three pounds Scots for winter, for castings

& all five firlots two pecks of Cost for Summer half year, and Six firlots for Winter half year, half oatmeall, half bear meall at the above Weights.

6to   That a man servant shall have in Summertime ffour pounds Scots of ffee, a pair of Shoes or ten pence therefore, and ten firlots of Cost, half oatmeall & half bear meall at the forsaid weights.

7mo   A man servant that engaged to thrash by the Boll shall have for Cost & ffee the sixteenth part of what he thrashes humiles & winnows clean of bear or oats.

8vo   That any servant that removes from his Master, do take leave of him six weeks before the Term, and if he faill that he be bound to stay the next half year; And the Master likewayes to premonish the servant that does not encline to keep him six weeks before the term, And if the Master fail to such premonition That he be obliged to keep the servant the next half year; And in case the servant take his leave in the time above limited That he ffee himself with another Master before the term, or be lyable to be taken up by a constable for the first man's use that wants him, And pay a Merk to the constable, And in case he cannot get a Master that he apply before the term to a Constable to get him one, And then he is to be free of a fyne, and if no Master be inclined to keep his servant two half years, Upon acquainting the servant six weeks before the first half year run, He may do it for the ordinary ffee & Cost & no longer, And no servant shall stay out of his service betwixt terms above three days under the pain of being taken up by a constable.

9oo   That every master be obliged to pay his servants ffees & within six weeks after the term, in Money or Sufficient Commodity & At the Country price in the Master's Option, And if payment be not made in that time That the Master be thereafter bound to pay in money, And upon Complaint to two next Justices of Peace that they give summar warrand to poind for it.

10mo   That if a servant does not take leave of his Master as above and ffee with another master, or ffee with two Masters, That the servant shall belong to the first Master, & the other Master shall have the ffee.

11mo   That every servant that engaged for the above ffees & undertakes the said work & shall not be found to perform their said service or shall absent themselves for a time or run away & desert their service, Shall upon complaint by the Master to any two or more Justices of the Peace, Upon proof that they did not truly & faithfully perform the service they engaged for, or did absent or run away as above, That the servant shall lose his half years ffee & be punished otherways in his goods, And failling thereof in his person at the Justices discretion.

12mo   In case any master maltreat or use his servant worse then Rochhide & three bolls of Cost, where half in oatmeall at eight ston pr boll, and half in bear meall at nine stone pr boll, the said ffee & cost to be in full of all demands.

Of the other Justices Mett at the said Quarters Sessions, Appoint the above resolutions to be published at the severall paroch kirk doors of this shyre with all convenient speed, to the End no person may pretend ignorance thereof for the future, And that the same shall be a standing rule betwixt Masters & Servants untill the Justices upon due consideration shall find it necessary to make any alterations or additions sic subscribitur G. Sinclair Don: Sinclair D. Sinclair Cha Sinclair Geo Mansone

[Added in a different hand] And the Justices mett at Wick at their Quarter Sessions the second day of May 1738, did approve of the said regulations and finding that the sd regulations were not duly published at all the Kirk Doors, They appointed the same to be done at all the Churches where they were not formerly published, with this addition, That if any bargains be made for this current half year betwixt any Masters & Servants contrary to or inconsistent with the said regulations That parties passing from the said bargains and conforming themselves to the rules herin prescribed shall be exempted from the penalties enacted.

APPENDIX 4

Voters' roll for Caithness in 1754
(Source: National Archives of Scotland: Extracted from NRS 02024 SC14-63-1-100122)

1. Sir Patrick Dunbar of Northfield Baronet
2. William Sinclair of Freswick
3. The Honourable my Lord Murkle [John Sinclair was a judge who assumed the title Lord Murkle when he joined the bench. He died in June 1755.]
4. George Sinclair of Ulbster
5. James Budge of Toftingall
6. Donald Sinclair of Olrig
7. Captain John Sutherland of Forss
8. George Sinclair of Brabster
9. Sir James Sinclair of Mey Baronet
10. James Sinclair of Dioun [Dunn]
11. John Sinclair of Dunnet
12. David Sinclair of Southdun
13. James Sinclair of Harpsdale
14. The Honourable Captain George McKay of Skibo
15. Sir William Sinclair of Dunbeath Baronet
16. Hary Innes of Sandside
17. Sir Robert Gordon of Gordonstown Baronet
18. Captain John Scott of the Royall Scots regiment
19. Peter Hay of Leyes [The Hays of Leys are a branch of the House of Erroll. Their central lands lie in Perthshire.]
20. Sir William Dunbar of Hempriggs Baronet
21. James Sutherland of Langwell
22. Robert Manson Sinclair of Bridgend
23. Ensign Alex Sinclair Son to Sir William Sinclair of Dunbeath Baronet
24. John Gun of Braemore
25. David Scott of Scottstarvit Liferenter bnd & Claim David Scott of Scotstarvit younger Esq: his fiar if the Liferenter does not attend claim his Vote [David Scott of Scotstarvit was MP for the Aberdeen burghs in 1754. Previously, between 1741 and 1752, he was MP for Fife.]
26. William Taylor Writer in Edinburgh
27. John Gordon of Craigiehead Writer in Elgin
28. Maurice Trent of Pitcullo
29. John Dalziel son to Thos Dalziel of Craigfurdale
30. George Cowan factor to David Scott of Scottstarvit Esqr
31. James Sutherland of Swinzie
32. Lieutenant Alex Sinclair of the Royall Scotts Regiment
33. Ensign Alex Joass of the Royall Scotts Regiment [A family called Joass was prominent in Banffshire in the eighteenth century.]
34. Alexander Orem junior Writer in Edinburgh
35. David Cowan son to George Cowan factor to David Scott of Scottsstarvit Esq

APPENDIX 5

The list of freeholders in Caithness, as recorded at Wick on 30 September 1766. This list also represents the electorate for the General Election held that year [88.3.].

1. William Sinclair of Freswick
2. George Sinclair of Ulbster
3. James Sinclair of Durren
4. John Sinclair of Dunnet
5. James Sinclair of Harpsdale
6. The Hon George Mackay of Skibo
7. Sir William Sinclair of Dunbeath
8. Sir Robert Gordon of Gordonstoun
9. Capt John Scott of the Royal Scots Regt
10. Sir William Dunbar of Hempriggs
11. James Sutherland of Langwall
12. Robert Manson Sinclair of Bridgend
13. John Gun of Breamore
14. David Scott of Scotstarvet liferenter & David Scot of Scotstarvet Fiar if the liferenter does not attend & Claim his vote
15. Maurice Trent of Pitcullo
16. John Dalyiel son of Thos Dalyell of Craigperdale
17. George Cowan factor to David Scot of Scotstarvet
18. James Sutherland of Swinzie
19. Capt George Sutherland of Forss
20. Robert Sutherland of Brabster
21. Sir John Sinclair of Mey
22. Charles Sinclair of Olrig
23. The Hon Colonel Alexander Mackay of the 65th Regt

Sandside & Capt Dunbar added at Michaelmas 1765
But struck off by the Court of Session.

Mr Colquhoun younger of Luss also added.

APPENDIX 6

Inventory of Household Furniter, 1793 May 6 [83.4.3]

Sundrys in the Little Drawing Room

4 Chairs covered with Cloth of Chintz
1 Window curtain Chintz
1 Truema (?) Dame Table and apparatuses
1 Sofa compleat with a Chintz Cover
1 Looking Glass Gilt
1 Carron Grate, Tongs, poker, Shovel and fender
2 half round Mahogany Tables wt gran Covers
2 fixed Brass Candlesticks
1 Mahogany Tea Tray wt brass handles
2 Japaned Coffee Pots wt plated Colnes Compleat
1 pair Ballases [bellows]
8 Volumes Humes England in quarto
7 Volumes Smollets England in quarto
3 Volumes Elegant Extracts in pros, Verse & Epistle
1 English Grammatical Introduction
1 Book of Sermons by Mr Enfield
1 Book on paistry and Cookery
1 Case in 2 parts wt apparatuses Hoyles Games
1 Small Mahogany box
3 fixed Brass knobs
1 small Water pan
1 figured Carpet

Sundrys in the Large Drawing Room

23 large framed prints Glassed over
17 small framed prints Glassed over
4 Gilt Mirror Glasses
1 Large Chimney Mirror
1 Cabinet wt Glass Doors and 1 Desk Drawers
1 Mahogany wine Cooler with brass bars & handles
3 China punch bowls
1 Mahogany side Board wt Aperatases & brass mounting
3 parts of a Mogany [sic] Dineing Table

246

2 Mahogany Tea Tables
1 small writing Desk
1 Tea Chest & Sugar Cannister
1 Childs Chiar & Standerd Mahogany
9 Leather Mounted Chiars
1 Laether Mounted Plleau Chiar
1 Framed Grate finished wt Glass cover
1 Polished Grate Tongs, Poker, Shovel & fender
1 Harth Brush
1 Carpet
Silver Plate in the Beauro [sic]
1 Sett of Casters Compleat
1 Silver Bread Basket
2 Silver Porter Muggs
4 Pair Salts Compleat wt 4 Spoons
2 Pair Salts pinchback Gilt within
2 Pair Castors or bottle Casses
1 Pair Mustard pott
1 pair Silver Candles Sticks wt a branch Silver
Snuff dish and Silver Snuffers
1 doz Silver table Spoons
1 half doz divers Silver Spoons
1 Silver dealing Spoon
1 Turkey leather Bottle Stand
1 doz Black handled Knives and forks
1 doz white handled Breakfast knives and forks
1 doz Tea Spoons Sugar (Spe) say Tongs & Sugar Spoon
2 large Tea Cannasters

Sundrys in the Dineing Room

13 painted pictures
10 printed pictures
1 Eight Day Clock
3 parts of a Dineing Table
1 Bath Chair
1 painted fire screen
2 small wainscoat Tables wt Drawers
1 Childs Chiar
1 Cave Case wt   Bottles of   Gallons of   Geneva &   Galons of Brandy
1 Mahogany server
1 Mahogany Corner Cupboard
1 Chrystal Lamp
1 Chrystal Glob [sic]
I Leather bottomed Chair
1 Toance Bass
in a corner cupboard: 1 doz China Cups and Saucers Blue Gilt; ½ doz Coffee cups and saucers; 1 Teapot, 1
    milkpot, 1 Tea Cannester & 2 Bread plates 1 red & white [?] Tea China [added in a very small hand] 9 [?]
    & 15 Cups; 6 Coffee Cups with pat [?] sugar box & 2 bread plates

Sundrys in the Nursery	£	s	d
1 box bed and press above	2	15	
1 box bed and press above	1		
1 dressing table		8	
1 Chist		5	
1 foot Stool		1	

	£	s	d
1 wood Chair		1	
3 Spinning wheels @ 7/ - 7/ - & 4/ -		18	
1 pair Tongs and Oil Lamp & 2 buffet Stools		3	6
1 screen 4 dressing irons 1 small press		9	

Sundrys in the Chist Room

	£	s	d
1 Bed wt a press and fore Caurtains	1	10	
1 Table & Chiar		11	
1 Roped Bed Stead		1	6

Sundrys in the Green Room

	£	s	d
1 Mahogany bedstead and Goun Container		9	
1 Green window Courtain			
2 Chairs Covered wt Cloth & Chintz Covers			
1 Bassen Stand wt 2 Bassens & water bottle			
1 Feather Bed Bolster & pellaias wt a matrass			
1 Shaving glass 1 glass print & 1 Room brush			
2 Japaned Candlesticks 1 Tongs & fender			
1 Taylor Table Covered wt Green Cloth			
2 Extinguishers & 1 Snuffer 1 Small Carpet			

Coledge Room

1 Beach Tent Bed Slaunted(?) 1 Mahogany Tent Bed Maunted 1 Chest Mahogany Drawers
2 Mahogany foot Stools printed covers 2 Elbow Chairs covered wt printed Cloth
1 Trunk 1 Taylor Table 1 plated dressing box 1 looking glass 1 cloth brush
2 Feather beds Matrasses Bolsters & Pillows Compt
1 Tongs Poker & Shovel wt fender & Room brush
1 figured Carpet 1 water bassen

Liberary

1 folding up bed wt Stript Courtains Matrass
feather Bed Bolster & pillows
1 Box bed 25/ - 1 Small Elbow Chair 1 Mahogany Bassan Stand 1 bassan & 1 water bottle
1 Green window Courtain 1 Shaving glass
1 Room brush 1 Shovel 1 Poker & fender 2 Japaned Candlesticks
1 Taylor table Covered wt Green Cloth
1 figured Carpet

Lettermate Room

	£	s	d
1 iron Bound chest(?) 10/6 5 Ale casks 2 Ankers & 1 bag 10/6	1	1	
1 trough 1/6 1 yetling Stove 2 ankers 1 Teel(?) 2/6			
2 boxes & 1 Ashes bucket 1/3			
1 Brewing Kettle 100/ - 1 brewing Vatt 10/6 2 .....(?) 6/ -5	16	6	
1 Washing machine 70/ - 1 Stand 1 funnel /8 1 hand barrow 1/ -	3	11	8
1 washing tub 1/ - 1 yetling poll 1/ -	2		
1 large yetling poll 7/ - 1 Cloth mangle 10/6	17	6	
1 Washing tub		3	
1 Cask		1	6
1 wine chest(?)		8	

James Huttons loft

	£	s	d
6 ware barrows 12/ - 2 pitch forks /6 1 Corn Chist 4/ -		16	6
2 hay rakes 2/ - 1 Mill Trundles wt iron Spindle 4/ -	6		
1 old Box bed 1/ - 2 black bags 3/6 1 bed J. Huttons		4	6

	£	s	d
East Garret			
18 Chesses partly wt glass 36/ - Mahogany Cradle 35/ -	3	11	

	£	s	d
Old Nursery			
7 (?) & 1 Chist of leather 3/6 1 old box bed 1/6		5	

Sundry China & Plates etc

	£	s	d
1 Complete Sett blue and white English China; 12 doz Stone plates or English China; 2 Large Turreens wt Spoons; 4 deep dishes wt covers; 21 Ashets; 4 Butter Turreens wt pletts and Spoons; 4 Sauce potts; 1 doz puckel dishes		7	
1 Blue edged sett Common Stone 4½ doz plates; 16 ashets; 8 deep dishes wt 2 covers; 3 butter dishes; 5 blue and white milk bowls		3	
5 old white Stone dishes 6 Earthen Milk bowls			
18 Tairt pans; 2 pudding dishes; 1 drainer; 1 bread Toaster;			
2 flamers[?]; 1 white iron Stum[?] kettle wt drainer and cover (in the Tower Hall)			

Tower Hall

	£	s	d
2 meal Chists 20/ - 9 dry Casks wt meal etc 12/ -			
2 butter Kitts & 1 Norway Kitt 3/ - 1 Ale stand iron hoped 3/ -	1	18	
2 Candle Kitts 1/8 1 meal pock & 1 cog 2/ - 1 meal Sive 1/6		5	2
1 plate & Basket lined with place eron(?) 15/ - 1 Table 3/ -		18	
1 Visrel Board 10/6 1 old pron Chist 2/ - 2 boxes 1/ -		13	6
1 pair Scaefles(?) and 1 Rul (?) 6/ - Mahogany Tea Tray 1/ -		7	
1 weather glass 1 Coffee mill 1 leather shot bag			
1 powder horn mounted wt brass 3 old Gunns & 2 Swords			
1 Sword harness 2/ - 3 Old oil lane (?) 1/6		3	6
1 Baking Trough /6 1 Marble Morter & pestal 2/6		3	
3 Butter Ankers 3/ - 1 Beef Stand 5/ - 1 half anker 1 kitt 1/4		9	4
1 Double Barreled Gunn 63/- 1 Japaned bread Basket 1/6	3	4	6
1 Basket wt 2 doz Bobens 5/- 1 lanthorn 1/-		6	
1 milk siver /2 4 lead Candle Moulds@ 1/6		1	8

Kitchen

	£	s	d
1 Kitchen dresser 10/- 1 Baking Table wt a Trough 7/6		17	6
1 old Table 2/6 1 Vessel Board 3/- 2 water casks iron bound & iron handles 20/- 2 water Stoups 2/-	1	17	6
2 Sauce pans 1 frying pan 12/- 2 yetling pots & covers			
2 Branders 3/- 1 yetling Stove 6 yetling pots 5/-			
1 Taik(?) Compleat 60/- 1 Crook 4/- 1 Goau(?) & 3 Coans 10/6	3	14	6
1 Salt Cask 3/- 1 Tongs 2/- 3 Boxes 2/-2 Spits 2/6		9	6
2 pot Bouls /9 2 pot hooks & 5 Sawers(?) /5		1	2
1 flesh fork and Ladle 1/6 1 flour box 2/- 1 drop pan 4/-		7	6
1 pair Shoe brushes /4 1 form 8d 2 Tea Kists yetling 10/-		11	
1 fire Screen & 2 brass Candle Sticks			

Compting House

	£	s	d
1 writing desk and Drawers 10/6 1 Table 8/-		18	6
1 press & Standard 8/- 2 Leather bottomed Chairs			
1 Elm Chair 2/- 1 Rush bottomed Chair /6 1 old prospect(?) 2/-		4	6
10 Golf Clubs 15/- 1 dogs Chain /8 1 Cross bow quiver & arrow 16/-	1	11	8

	£	s	d
1 Glass linthorn 1/- 2 baskets wt papers 3/- 1 Elbow Chair 10/-		14	

*1 Coil Small rope@   1 pair Skitchers   1 small basket
1 Speaking Trumpet 1/6
[* marginal note: rope to enter among Labouring utensils]

West Landry

	£	s	d
2 old bed steads 3/6 1 old Table 1/- 2 old Sadles 14/-		18	6
11 pieces Coach harness 11/- 2 dry Casks 1/6 & 1 box /3		12	9

John Basses loft

[+ items are marked thus]

	£	s	d
1 oven stove 21/- a parul+ Coach harness 30/- 7 dry Casks 7/-	2	18	
1 Coach+ box 2/- 1 Turnip+ planter 10/6 1 iron+ shovel 8/-		15	6
2 hay+ knife 2/- a parul horse+ graith & old ropes 2/-			
2 Coal+ -[?]			
1 hay+ scythe & 2 [?]+ knives 2/- 5 herring+ nets 50/-	2	15	

The Dinning [sic] Room Pantry

1 Bud[?] with Table China 6 doz & 3 plates 20 ashets
1 doz large blue morning Cups and Saucers (only 10 Saucers)
12 Cups & 12 Saucers Different kinds 2 Slab Bowls
1 punch bowel 1 punch Spoon 2 pitchers 1 white Ston jugg
2 Small glas cruits 1 Mustard pot & 1 paper [pepper] box
2 black Tea Potts 3 Milk potts 2 sugar boxes
half doz egg Cups wt blue edges 4 doz & 8 wine glasses
12 Rummers 6 Barrel glasses 4 punch glasses 9 floured glasses
2 Strong ale glasses 1 large Tumbler
6 wine decanters 2 pint Decanters 1 Compleat Salver Stand and glasses
1 Chrystal Cream bowl & spoon
butter boul glass 6 glass puckle dishes 3 Watter Crafts
1 glass flour pot 5 China Muggs 2 China Tea potts 1 China Tea Cannester
1 yellow Tea pott 1 doz wood punch Spoons 1 Japaned Tea Tray
1 Copper Tea Kettle & Chaffer 1 white iron Tea kettle
2 Brass Candle Sticks Snuffers and Stone dish 4 whitening brushes
1 Table and drawer 2 bottle Stands paper 4 Mustard pigs

In the Inner Cellar and Box

18½ doz port wine 10 doz white wine 4 doz Claret
14½ doz Empty Bottles 2 large and 1 Small Watter Bottles
10 Gray hard Bottles

Table Linnin and Bed linnin

36 pairs of Sheets 23 pairs pillow Slips
3 Bolster Slips 64 Table Cloths 16½ doz Towels
18 bairn half sheets 3 doz Course Towels 6 Chas[?] beds and Bolsters
6 bed quilts

Blancats

32 Scots Blancots 12 English Blankots 6 Binders

Sundrys Omitted in Dining Room

8 Saucers & 7 Cups Black and white China
gilt 8 Coffee Cups 1 Milk pot 2 bread plates

APPENDIX 7

The officers of the Caithness Legion when the regiment was established were listed in *The London Gazette* on 24 October 1795, pp. 1104–5 (See also www.thegazette. co.uk)

Colonel	Sir Benjamin Dunbar Bart
Lieut-Colonel	Major William Munro, 42nd Foot
Major	William Innes
Captains	Hugh Innes (from the Marines), Robert Sinclair, John Taylor, Alexander Leitch, John Burton, David Skene
Capt-Lieutenant/ Adjutant	Alexander Strange, late of the 55th Foot
Lieutenants	Robert Kennedy (from the Scotch Brigade) (served as Quartermaster), John Saber, John Yardley, Daniel Miller, William McKenzie, Andrew McDonald, George McBeath, Daniel Banks, William Ross, John Watson, [?] Tod, G.G. Munro, W.H. Terrence (served as surgeon), Alexander Manson, Joseph Nield, Alexander Murray, John Stuart, Daniel M'Kay, William Murray
Ensigns	Patrick Innes, William M'Pherson, Robert M'Kay, John Parmenter, Alexander M'Pherson, Donald M'Donald, [?] Degulier, John M'Kenzie
Chaplain	John Taylor, clerk
Adjutant	Alexander Strange
Quarter-Master	Robert Kennedy, gent.
Surgeon	W.H.Terrance, Gent.

APPENDIX 8

Roll of Sir Benjamin Dunbar's company, 2nd Battalion, Caithness Legion, on 17 November 1798.

Andrew Dougall, Finlay M'Crae, Alex McKay – ensigns.
John Smith – corporal.
Privates

William Bell
Bryce Gordon
William Sutherland
George Fotheringham
John Douglas
Andrew McKay
Rob McKay
Alex Campbell
James Stewart
David Kelly
James Boyd
James Arthur
John McKay
John Burke
Wm Macdonald
John McBeath
Alex Stewart
David Martin
John Dick
Wm Darlin
Thomas Tunpothy
David Millar

Hugh Arthur
Samuel Doun
John McKay
Wm McBean
Arch^d Brown
Alex Campbell
John Hutton
James Kennedy
Alex Sutherland
Richard Dale
Alex Munroe
David Sutherland
Arch^d McDonald
John Gunn
Rod^k Morrison
Alex Sutherland
James Ross
Donald Munroe
Wm Shippard
Peter Crumb
John Mahonny

Signed: John McLean, lieutenant, 2nd Battalion.

APPENDIX 9

Roll of Captain James MacBeath's company, 2nd Battalion, Caithness Legion, on 17 November 1798.

Whiteside Godfrey, John McDonald, Alex Ross – sergeants
George Emesley – corporal

Privates

Edward Couper	Robert News
Andrew Darling	James Wright
David Gilchrist	Joseph Carless
Robert Martin	John Lousie
John McCulloch	John Law
James Malcolm	George Edwards
Alex McKay	Daniel Gorman
Timothy Obrian	Philip Innes
Alex McLeod	James Kerr
Joseph Probert	William Biffin
James Rainy	Joseph Patt
James Barry	Alex Bogg
James McRae	John Watt
Timothy Butley	John Gillan
Richard Williamson	James Douns
Thomas Willis	William Cock
Thomas Grady	Angus Barkley
James Gun	John Ainsley
William McDonald	Donald McKay Junr
James Fleming	John McKay
Daniel Sulivan	John Cormack
Samuel Beight	Barry McLean
Donald McKay Senr	Thomas Swenny

APPENDIX 10

Men listed by Sir Benjamin Dunbar as lately belonging to the Stircoke Company of Volunteers in 1806 [63.2.2].

James Malcam	Tenant	Blingery
Alex Mowat	Tenant	Bilbster
John Davidson	Taylor	Stircoke
James Whier	Tenant	Heshwall
James Jack	Joiner	Howe
Alex McGregor	Mason	Wick
William Cormack	Cooper	Wick
Alex Mulliken	Shoemaker	Bilbster
Alex Whier	Joiner	Wick
Donald Sutherland	Shoemaker	Blingery
John Whier	Tenant	Thuster
William Bremner		Husquoy
John Whier	Day Labourer	Wick
Andrew Forbes	Servant	Berridale
Donald Thomson	Joiner	In Ulbster
Peter Sutherland	Servant	Milnton Wick
George Alsherson	Tenant	Bilbster
James Doull	Tenant	Bilbster
Alex Bain	Tenant	Thuster
George Whier	Mason	Stircoke
William Sutherland	Shoemaker there	
Alex Don	Tenant there	
Donald Alsherson	Servant	Bilbster
William Finlayson	Servant	Bilbster
George Reach	Servant	Thuster
John Thomson	Joiner	Ulbster
Alex Finlayson	Servant	Stircoke
Capt John Sutherland	Tenant	East Watten

APPENDIX 11

Population change in Caithness parishes between 1801 and 1831 (*see table overleaf*).

Parish	Population in 1801	Persons employed in agriculture	Population in 1811	Families in agriculture	Population in 1821	Families in agriculture	Population in 1831	Families in agriculture
Bower	1572	880	1478	220	1486	208	1615	161
Canisbay	1985	366	1936	313	2128	333	2364	405
Dunnet	1366	1355	1393	171	1636*	181	1906	195
Halkirk	2545	1227	2532	408	2646*	419	2847	420
Latheron	3672	3435	3926	629	6575	386	7020	1068
Olrick	1117	332	1042	140	1093	180	1146	128
Reay	2541	1051	1456	296	2758*	354	1868	247
Thurso	3628	2044	3462	306	4045*	268	4679	279
Watten	3246	694	1109	160	1158	150	1234	189
Wick	3986	2879	5080	627	6713	573	9850	488
	22,609	13,263	23,419	3,270	30,238	3,052	34,529	3,580

*1821 increases attributed wholly or partly to immigration from Sutherland. The growth of the herring fishing is held to be responsible for the large increases in Wick and Latheron, but in the latter case immigration from Sutherland and the growth of the herring fishing probably happened together with a postive feedback effect.

Data source http://www.histpop.org

APPENDIX 12

A list of the Ackergill cows under Donald Campbell Charge [sic] [24 October 1825].

Cows to be kiped [kept].
1. Nosek
2. Spotag
3. Betsy
4. Fleaky
5. Gessy [probably meant to be Jessie]
6. yong Bell Dull [young Belle Doull?]
7. Matag
8. Daisy
9. Marry
10. Goldag

3 Cows Doutful but all the 3 is in Calf
11. Boney Haks ["to be kept" added in pencil]
12. Sordal   Do
13. Longlegs   to be kept

Cows to be Cast
Marchag ["not in calf" added in pencil]
Cow Boney not in calf to be fed
Dan Corley in calf Reiss
Old Bell Dull not in calf to Shorelands
Sincler   late in calf to Reiss
Topence in calf to Reiss
Fifeag   in calf best not kept to Reiss
Wifeag   Do to Reiss

A list of Donald Campbell's cows at Shorelands [25 October 1825].

To be kept Hogstown
  Grigor
  Noseag (Nansey horned)
  Pold [polled] nanesy
  Pinkag
  Fotom
  Betsy
  Pinkag akuy
  Boney
  Bronnag
  Hogg
  Niseag
  Drover
  Brokag
  Maggi

4 cows doutfull but they are in calf
  Thrumster
  Lady
  Hoppag
  Lithag

2 cows to be cast
  Goldag not in calf
  Jess not in calf

APPENDIX 13

Hempriggs estate – List of pensioners showing the amounts they each receive yearly – May 1887 [53.1.58] [This is one of several such lists in this period.]

Name	House	Meal	Coal	Money & other allowances
Pensioners				
Donald Calder	Yes	Yes	No	£2 per mnth & 6 bolls meal p. an.
Alex Finlayson	Yes	Yes	Peats	10 guineas & 6 bolls meal p. an.
William Cormack	Yes	No	No	1/- p working day
Magnus Cormack	Croft	Yes	Peats	10/- p mensam & 8 bolls of meal
				[This line is scored through – had Magnus recently died?]
Mrs McLean	House	No	5 tons	30/- p mensam & 8 bolls of meal
Mrs Sutherland	House	No	No	1/- p working day
Annutants				
John Cormack	Gardener			£14 p. as in will of late Sir George Dunbar
Gamekeepers				
David Calder	Yes	Yes	5 tons	20/ p week & 6 bolls of meal. Also 2d p diem in lieu of milk formerly received from the farm, & 15/4 for a ton of Scotch coal to cook dogs food.
				[Added in red ink] 2 Bolls meal for dog food & 2d of work p day
Alex Sutherland	Yes	No	5 tons	£46 p annum
Gardener & Assistant				
John Cormack (same man as above)	Yes	No	5 tons	£25 & 8 bolls meal p an
John McLeod	Yes	No	1 & Peats	40 chains potatoes ½ pint milk & 3d p hour when working
Dyker				
William Duncan	Yes	No	No	4d p hour when working
Quarryman				
William Calder	Yes	No	No	Paid for work only

Money is now paid in lieu of the above allowances at the following rates:
Meal = 19/ per boll; Milk = 4d per pint (Scotch); Potatoes = 9d per chain; Coals = (2 tons of Scotch & 3 of English) 18/ per ton; Peats = About £3 for a year's supply including cartage.

APPENDIX 14

Shootings in Halkirk, May 1887.

PARTICULARS
AND

CONDITIONS OF LET OF SHOOTINGS
IN THE PARISH OF HALKIRK AND COUNTY OF CAITHNESS
BELONGING TO THE
TRUSTEES OF GARDEN DUFF DUNBAR OF HEMPRIGGS

1. THE SHOOTINGS to be let extend over the Property of the Trustees in the parish of Halkirk, consisting of the Farms of Balavreed and Thulachan, and there will also be let the right of fishing on the Lochs on the Property. House accommodation for a Shooting Tenant will be provided – a suitable Boat will be provided for fishing on the Loch.

   The extent of the Shooting is about 2390 acres, but the measurement is not guaranteed. The ground slopes gently, and is covered with grass and heather, except the arable ground extending to about thirty or forty acres. The ground is easily walked over.

   The Agricultural tenant is obliged by his Lease to preserve the Game to the utmost of his power, for which he is remunerated by the Proprietor.

2. The House accommodation consists of two Bedrooms, Dining-Room, with roomy Pantry attached, Kitchen with large Pantry, Servants' Bedroom and Scullery. A Game Larder and Kennels for four dogs will also be provided.

3. The period of Let will be from 1st August 1887 to 1st February 1888, or for a term of years if desired.

4. The Rent, which includes Rates and Taxes, will be £170, and will be payable before 1st August in each year.

5. The Proprietor will keep the buildings in repair.

6. The Tenant to maintain and leave the Household Furnishings in as good order as they are at his entry, due allowance being made for tear and wear.

7. Annexed is a note of last season's bag. The Tenant will be required to exercise his right of shooting in a fair and sportsmanlike manner, and to leave a fair stock of game on the ground.

8. No keeper is provided, but should the shooting tenant so desire, it is understood that the son of the agricultural tenant can be arranged with to act as keeper or gillie.

9. Supplies of mutton, fowls, eggs, butter, milk and potatoes could be obtained from the tenant of Balavreed. The tenant would also do any carting required. Peat fuel for the season will be given.

10. Halkirk, on the Sutherland and Caithness Railway, fourteen miles distant, is the nearest railway station. It is about 145 miles north of Inverness and traps can be hired, and stores and hotel accommodation procured there. Letters and papers are taken daily (except the Sundays) to within three miles of Balavreed.

11. It is understood that a boat and Salmon fishing can be got on Loch More (three miles from Thulachan House) from 1st August to 14th September for £10, or for a day at a time for 15s, no gillie being provided at these prices, but a good gillie can be had from Westerdale when wanted for 3s 6d a day.

12. No subletting or reletting will be allowed.

> 66 Queen Street,
> Edinburgh, May 1887.

NOTE OF BAG FOR SEASON 1886

Grouse	263 brace
Snipe	1½ "
Ducks	3 head
Hares	49 "

APPENDIX 15

Income and expenditure for letting Hempriggs House for sport, 1903.

		Income	£	S	d	£	S	d
		Rent of Hempriggs House and Shootings for season 1903				£200		
		Expenditure						
		Upkeep of Hempriggs House						
Aug	4	To paid Alex Robertson & Son, for sundries		10	2			
Nov	10	Paid Alex McEwen & Sons, for coals	6	10				
Mar	11	Paid Wm Johnston & Son, for general repairs	1	13	8			
June	17	Paid D Cormack, West Bank, for cartage of furniture to Hempriggs		4				
		Game expenses						
Aug	4	To paid Alex Robertson & Son, for ammunition for keeper	1	4	6			
		Paid David Calder Jn, Asst Gamekeeper, wages for year	39					
	28	Paid gun licence for –do-		10				
Nov	10	Paid Alex McEwen & Sons for wood for repairs to Hempriggs boat		12	1			
Dec	31	To paid Alex Robertson & Son for rowlocks for Hempriggs boat		2	8			
		Paid –do- for ammunition for keeper		5	9			
Feb	29	Paid licence on male servant		15				
Mar	7	Paid Walker, Fraser & Steele, shooting agents, Glasgow, commission on renewal of let of Shootings	2					
May	28	Paid David Calder Jn allowance on grouse and partridges for season 1903	1	6	2			
		Paid David Calder wages for year to date	10					
		Rates and Taxes on House and Shootings						
		To paid County Rates	4	10	6			
		Paid Poor Rates	4	8	4			
		Paid duty on use of furniture by Shooting Tenant	1	7	6			
		Paid for patrolling Wick River during season	7	7				
		Total	82	7	4			

APPENDIX 16

The extent of Dunbar holdings in Caithness as listed in the Valuation Roll for the county of Caithness for 1905–06.

In the parish of Wick.

Properties of Mrs G. Duff-Dunbar of Hempriggs, G.A. Duff of Hatton and T.D. Gordon Duff of Drummuir, Trustees of the late G. Duff-Dunbar of Hempriggs, per W. Paterson Smith, factor, Wick.

Farms: Toftcarl, Northfield, Barnyards, Upper Milton, Stemster, Waterloo, Inkerman, Hillhead, Noss, Clayquoys, Westerseat, Upper Ackergill, Lower Reiss, Shorelands, Gillfield, Lower Gillock, Harland, Quoys of Reiss, Wester Loch, South Killimster, Winless, Sibster, Ackergill Mains, Mains of Tannach.

Hempriggs House, with various houses and lands.

Ackergill Tower and policies.

Lands and houses: Brough, Rockhill, Lower Barnyards, Lower and Upper Humster, Charity, Dhulochs, Muirfield, Hill of Newton, Row of Newton, Whitebridge, Gaultiquoy, Cruives, Newfield, Drumdry, Milton, Aquavitae Meadow, Mosspalm, Papigoe, Millrock, Elzy, Staxigoe, Lochshell, Upper Gillock and Kettleburn, Laysmith, Tayfield, Whitefield, Reiss, Plover Inn, Nordwall, Hillhead of Reiss, Killimster, Wester, Skitten, Crofts of Sibster, Markethill (including joiner's shop and smiddy), Herringlass, Tannach, Swarthouse, Grudgehouse, Cairniquoy, Kinlochy, Tannach, Myrelandhorn, Redhouses.

Rights of water: Janetstown.

Salmon fishing: Ackergill.

Shootings: Hempriggs.

In the burgh of Wick

Miscellaneous properties, e.g. ground in Louisburgh, Robert Street, Henrietta Street, Green Road, all on the north side of the river.

In the parish of Halkirk

Farms and shootings: Thulachan, Balavreed.